D0956046

PRIMER OF PUBLIC RELATIONS RESEARCH

Primer
of Public Relations
Research

DON W. STACKS

THE GUILFORD PRESS
New York   London

© 2002 The Guilford Press
A Division of Guilford Publications, Inc.
72 Spring Street, New York, NY 10012
www.guilford.com

Printed in the United States of America

This book is printed on acid-free paper.

Last digit is print number: 9 8 7 6 5 4

Library of Congress Cataloging-in-Publication Data is available from
the publisher

ISBN 1-57230-726-9

Microsoft Windows, Microsoft Word, and Microsoft Excel are registered trademarks of the
Microsoft Corporation. Lotus 1-2-3 is a registered trademark of the International Business
Machines (IBM) Corporation. SPSS for Windows is a registered trademark of SPSS, Inc.

Preface

This book is the product of many years spent attempting to prove that research really does matter in public relations. Most books—both text and trade— talk about research as being important, as in the ROPE or RACE models, but very little is said regarding its application in day-to-day practice. Over a decade ago in Montreal, Donald K. Wright (University of South Alabama) and I packed a room at the Association for Education in Journalism and Mass Communication's annual meeting discussing the need for research. At that meeting we made an argument for a book that would present research (and statistics) in a simple, "primer" way. Although the academics demonstrated their desire, no publisher at that time (or for the next 10 years, for that matter) was willing to take a chance on public relations research. Instead, the argument was that mass communication or speech communication or sociology research methods books sufficed for the area.

Over these years this book languished. Although it was clear that today's practitioner needed to understand and interpret research, little was being done to provide both the student and the practitioner with a quick and simple approach to research. Further, academic books took rather aesthetic approaches, focusing on science and theory (as appropriate for their interests—to extend the knowledge base of the humanities and social sciences) instead of the bottom line, or establishing how research added to an organization's or client's ROI (return on investment).

In 1997 Jack Felton of the Institute for Public Relations suggested that what public relations practitioners and students really needed was a "research for dummies" book. While this is not a research for dummies book, it is a primer for research. It presents in what I hope is simple and direct language what research is, why it is conducted, and what strategies (methods) are appropriate to answer the questions being discussed. Further, it provides understanding into what statistics are, how they are interpreted, and what they actually tell the practitioner. Finally, the book offers advice on how to present research findings in direct and simple ways, avoiding what some call the "chi-square approach."

I am indebted to several people in getting this project off the ground. First, to Jack Felton, Donald K. Wright, Bill Adams (Florida International University), and Dean Kruckeberg (University of Northern Iowa) for their support, encouragement, and continual prodding to provide something usable for both public relations students and practitioners. I am further indebted to Don Wright and Melvin Sharpe for help in selecting and analyzing the various cases used to make the research speak to the reader. I would also like to thank Shara Pavlow, who argued for a more student friendly book and carefully went over the chapter review questions and practice problems. Second, to Peter Wissoker and Kristal Hawkins of The Guilford Press for having a belief in the importance of the project and the direction that would entail.

Finally, it should be noted that there are many good research methods books available to the reader who wants a more in-depth understanding of the relationship between theory, method, and analytical tool. The reader can find them in sociology, psychology, and business, as well as both speech/human and mass communication. My treatment is based on the belief that public relations practitioners need to understand the research process—not that they will conduct research daily (some will), but they will have to make important and informed decisions about hiring research firms, evaluating their proposals and end products, as well as helping to determine how that research benefits the "bottom line."

DON W. STACKS
Coral Gables, Florida

Contents

An Introduction to Research in Public Relations

What is research? How do public relations practitioners approach research? What are the major research methodologies employed by public relations researchers? How does theory relate to practice? What are the ethics of conducting research? These are some of the questions examined in Part I.

Chapter 1 begins our exploration of public relations research by asking the more general question "What is research?" and discusses the two major research methodologies (informal and formal) used in conducting research. The difference between theoretical research, as typified in academic research, and applied research, as typified in business practice, is examined and the relationship between the four approaches to public relations is briefly examined. Finally the four major research questions asked in any research are explored.

Chapter 2 focuses on public relations and answers two major questions. First, "What is public relations?" Here we grapple with the problem of definition and establish how we perceive public relations and its place in the business world. Part and parcel of this discussion is what constitutes a "public" and how it relates to research. Second, we examine the assumptions of how public relations research should be approached and how we go about setting up a program of research complete with objectives, outputs, and measurable outcomes.

Chapter 3 rounds out our brief introduction to general research and public relations by looking at the ethical conduct of research. It will be noted that nowhere in the official documents of the three major public relations organizations—the Public Relations Society of America (PRSA), the International Association of Business Communicators (IABC), and the International Public Relations Association (IPRA)[1]—are the ethics of research formally spelled out. Further, most research texts either ignore the topic altogether or they limit its treatment to such a generalization as "[Public relations] researchers are bound by ethics to be honest with their subjects [sic] and to provide full disclosure about how and why the research . . . is being done."[2] Chapter 3 explores not only why research participants or respondents should be treated ethically, but also how that can be accomplished.

Part I sets the course for an examination of both formal and informal research methodologies and the analysis of data gathered according to these methods. It establishes the whys of research and assesses the basic assumptions that the public relations researcher must make in daily practice.

NOTES

1. Public Relations Society of America, New York, NY; International Association of Business Communicators, San Francisco, CA; International Public Relations Association, Ester, Surrey, U.K.
2. E. W. Brody and Gerald C. Stone, *Public Relations Research* (New York: Praeger, 1989), p. 163.

Chapter 1

Research

AN INTRODUCTION
WITH PUBLIC RELATIONS IMPLICATIONS

One of the more pragmatic or practical areas of public relations concerns something that most public relations practitioners seem to fear most: research. Why? The reason offered by many academic writers is that the field's history—arising from journalism and being applied in a written, creative format—produced an "informal" approach to research.

This may be true to a certain degree. Public relations practitioners have always relied on research in one form or another to demonstrate to clients that what they have produced has impacted on some public or audience (we use "public" to indicate that we are looking at a group of people or specific segment of that group with *human characteristics*, in contrast to "audience," in which we look at a group of people en masse as defined by demographic or psychographic *variables*—interest areas by sex, for example—and to differentiate advertising and marketing from public relations). The simple counting of press releases for the client is a rudimentary form of research. Examining media outlets to see which has carried those releases is another form of research. Both, however, are _informal_ research methods; they fail to provide much information beyond potential reach and effort.

Today's practitioner is in a business that demands more. Modern public relations research strives to deliver evidence that the bottom line has been enhanced by the practitioner's activities. In so doing, the way we approach research has moved from a primarily informal to formal, social scientific approach to understanding the impact of public relations across the many public relations specializations.

WHY CONDUCT PUBLIC RELATIONS RESEARCH?

Research is essential to any public relations activity or campaign. As evidenced in many public relations models, research is the beginning of a process that seeks to bring about a specific objective. Hendrix's ROPE (Research, Objectives, Program, Evaluation),[1] Marston's RACE (Research, Action, Communication, Evaluation),[2] and Cutlip, Center, and Broom's four-step process (Defining PR Problems, Planning and Programming, Taking Action and Communicating, Evaluating the Program)[3] models posit that any serious public relations activity must begin with the research step.

Why is research (and definition) so important to public relations? As Donald K. Wright has pointed out, research is important because public relations people are finding that research is part and parcel of their jobs when they offer communication strategy, counsel on communication problems, and educate clients as to the best public relations strategies or actions.[4] Without research, practitioners are left to "fly by the seats of their pants"; that is, they are reduced to taking, at best, educated guesses regarding the problem and potential intervention programs, and thus run a greater risk of being unable to predict outcomes accurately. Without research the practitioner cannot assess where a public relations program begins, how it evolves, or what the end product will be. Quite simply, without research you cannot demonstrate the efficacy of your program.

As public relations has transitioned from a technical to a management function, the role of research has become increasingly important. Management decisions cannot be made in a vacuum; decisions are influenced by a myriad of factors, of which both the acquisition and analysis of data have become basic to good public relations practice. Think of research (and data) as part of a continuous feedback/feedforward function: research planning and accurate data lead to valid assessments and analyses of public opinion, program effectiveness, and in the end may help to predict behavioral outcomes.

Public relations practitioners use research in many ways. In general, public relations research is used to monitor and track, measure and assess, and finally evaluate public relations actions. It is used to monitor and track trends and developments as they occur to help understand and examine current and future public relations positions. It is essential to the assessment and measurement of public relations messages and campaigns to ensure that planned actions are occurring as expected, and when not to implement correction strategies. Evaluation is conducted during all segments of a public relations campaign: at the precampaign research phase (i.e., how well was previous research conducted?; which strategies have produced the best results given the current or projected conditions?), during the actual campaign (i.e., how effective has the campaign been at meeting its objectives at phase one, phase two, phase three, and so forth?), and at the end (i.e., how well did the campaign do what it was supposed to do?; how did it affect the "bottom line")?

WHAT IS RESEARCH?

Just what then is research? Research encompasses two methodological approaches to *data*. Data are the observations we make of the world around us via some methodology. Data may be gathered formally or informally.

Data are gathered informally when gathered from the researcher's experiences. They are largely intuitive, the evaluation largely consisting in the researcher's "gut feelings." As such, data constitute informal (sometimes called "humanistic" or "qualitative") observations made even daily. Such data are observed, noted, and judged as being appropriate or inappropriate, good or bad, fitting or not fitting expectations and found in case study, interview, focus group, and participant-observation methodology.

When thinking of formal methodology we take an objective approach to the data—the data are simply points that when examined systematically lead us to some conclusion. This is the method of the social scientist, and our focus throughout this volume will be mainly along this method of inquiry—surveys and polls and to a lesser degree experiments.

It is wrong to believe, however, that one methodology is better than the other. Each methodology has advantages and disadvantages. As you may have already guessed, informal methodology is better for some types of research and formal methodology for others. We will explore this distinction shortly, but first we need to look at what differentiates formal from informal methods.

The Differences between Formal and Informal Research Methods

The major differences in method are found in Table 1.1. Note that major differences are found in all three categories: data collection, data assessment, and outcome.

Formal research is the controlled, objective, and systematic gathering of data. It is objective in that the researcher carefully defines the "things" under study, carefully defining what it is that will be studied. It is systematic in that we carefully follow prescribed rules in gathering and assessing the data. It is controlled in that we carefully define, gather, and evaluate the data according to prescribed rules that can be reviewed for error. *Informal research* is less controlled and subjective; it is not systematic in either gathering or interpreting the data. Informal research relies on the subjective evaluations of the researcher.

While informal research provides us with in-depth description and understanding of a particular subject or event, its lack of control and lack of objectivity do not allow us to predict and generalize outcomes beyond what was observed. Both methods describe, but the formal method provides a description based upon agreed upon or carefully defined units that can be measured and assessed for reliability (consistency) and validity (do all see and act toward the activity or concept of interest similarly?), whereas the informal method describes the data based on the intuition of the researcher.

TABLE 1.1. Major Differences between Formal and Informal Research Methods

Formal research methods	Informal research methods
Data collection	
Controlled	Uncontrolled
Objective	Subjective
Systematic observation	Random observation
Data assessment	
Can be measured reliably	Cannot be measured reliably
Validity can be measured	Validity is assumed
Is deductively interpreted	Is inductively interpreted
Outcome(s)	
Description	Description
Understanding	Understanding
Prediction	
Control	

Finally, the formal method provides a way of predicting and generalizing outcomes to groups or individuals that were not necessarily part of the research. The informal method enables us to look at the outcome only as it occurred with the particular group or event; whereas formal research allows us to extend our findings to similar groups ("populations") who, if researched in the same way, would within certain degrees of confidence respond or react similarly to those researched (i.e., we are $X\%$ certain of the responses). With the formal method we can depend on accurate data (within certain degrees of confidence) to drive management decisions (whether these decisions are good or bad also can be addressed by research, but only if the basic, underlying questions have been addressed first). Further, the formal method provides us a way to generalize from a smaller (and thus less costly) sampling of people to the larger population.

This is not to say that informal research is bad or that formal research is good. In most instances they are different ways of looking at the same problem. Each has advantages and each has disadvantages. With formal research, we are not interested in one person or event or object; rather, we are interested in *groups* of people. Thus, we lose an ability to understand in great detail how something occurred. Informal research provides us the opportunity to look in great detail at how an individual, group, or company acted or reacted to some public relations problem. It does not, however, allow us to predict or generalize—with any confidence, at least—about how similar individuals, groups, or companies would react. Obviously, each method complements the other and when used together allow us to both predict *how* groups acted or reacted as they did and provide richer detail and understanding as to *why* they did. This process is called *triangulation*, where both formal and informal methods provide data that lead to a better understanding of the problems under study.

Research Questions

Now that we have distinguished between the two main types of research, we turn to how research is actually conducted. In so doing, we must differentiate between two basic types of research: *theoretical*, which seeks to provide the underlying framework for the study of public relations, and *applied*, which seeks to use theory-driven research in business world situations.

The best way to examine the two research approaches is via an analogy. The theory-driven researcher can be described as an architect. Just as the architect creates abstract plans composed initially of related concepts or ideas about what a structure should look like, the theoretical researcher creates a conceptual framework for how different communication concepts and ideas work together toward some end. The architect specifies how different materials are to be used, in what number and commodity, and under what conditions. Similarly, the theoretical researcher specifies which concepts or ideas can be used, how they relate to each other and under what conditions we can expect results. The builder takes the architect's plans and uses them to construct an end product (e.g., a home or office). Similarly, the applied researcher uses theory to solve "real world" (i.e., applied) problems.

The theoretical research's abstractions are first put to the test in laboratory settings. *Laboratory research* is research that has been carefully controlled to exclude anything that might influence the relationships under study than the specific concepts under study. In other words, the theoretical researcher tries to test predicted relationships in as "pure" a condition as possible. This provides important evidence that one concept actually does influence another in a predictable way. The researcher's theory establishes which "variables" (concepts that have been carefully defined for measurement) cause changes in other variables and in which direction. Unfortunately, as John Pavlik has noted, there is very little laboratory research conducted in public relations;[5] public relations researchers have relied instead on research conducted mainly by researchers from the disciplines of communication studies (speech and mass communication), psychology, sociology, management, and marketing.

These findings are then used by the applied researcher. While public relations theory seeks to add to what we know about public relations (creates a "body of knowledge" about public relations—the concepts of interest and importance, the relationships between those concepts, the outcomes as they *might* be applied in actual practice), the applied researcher practices that theory as *strategic research*. Strategic research then is the development of a public relations campaign or program that uses particular theoretical elements (e.g., messages, sources, communication channels) in a practical way. *Evaluation research* is then used to provide assessments of how well the program or campaign is working. It provides *benchmarks* against which other research can determine if the campaign or program has worked and how well individual components of that campaign are working.

The theoretical relationship between applied and theoretical and formal and informal research is driven by the kind of research questions being asked. A research question is actually a statement made into a question. There are four research questions found in most research: questions of definition, fact, value, and policy.[6] As we will see, the importance of the research question is that it in turn determines which research methodology and assessment technique is most appropriate for its answer.

Questions of Definition

The most basic question asked by public relations researchers is the *question of definition*. This question defines what it is that we are attempting to observe. Theoretical researchers ask whether a particular concept or idea actually exists and how it can be potentially measured. For example, we might be interested in determining how people react to certain political parties; the question of definition would specify exactly what we mean by "political" and by "party." We have two recourses: (1) we could go to the dictionary and look up the definitions of each word (or the paired phrase, if it is included) or (2) we could create our own definition, but the resulting definition would have to not only define what a "political party" is but also do so in such a way as to be potentially measurable.

Definitional questions are judgmental in that they seek to define what we should be observing. Attitudes toward a particular product or person, for example, are concepts that public relations practitioners are often interested in. The problem is that attitudes cannot be seen. However, they can be measured. Before you can assess them, the existence of the "attitude" must be determined. This is the job of the theoretical researcher, who not only defines what is meant by "attitude" but also provides an understanding of how different message strategies (which also must be carefully defined) influence attitudes toward that product or person.

The applied researcher takes those conceptual definitions and develops a communication program around them. To create this program the researcher must carefully craft a practical, concrete definition (in other words, one that can be used and understood by the population under study) upon which to build the program. Knowing, for instance, that certain messages have been found to change attitudes in an experimental setting, the practitioner will establish a message strategy that hopefully will maximize communication outcomes in a predictable way.

Questions of definition may be answered by either formal or informal methodology. Formal methodology requires that the concept be defined in an objective manner, one that can be used over and over again with similar results. The formal answer to a question of definition is much like a dictionary definition, providing a way to define the concept that all can agree upon. Informal methodology defines the concept as a point in time; that is, the definition is encased by the events or time in which it was defined. As such, the informal answer is extremely subjective and not amenable to reuse.

Questions of Fact

Questions of fact seek to compare across or between groups. They arise out of questions of definition and are tested quantitatively or "empirically." Questions of fact answer questions dealing with quantity—how much, how many—and are often referred to as *empirical questions*. As such, questions of fact are not amenable to informal methodology, which seeks to establish its perspective within the framework of a single event or individual or group. Further, questions of fact can be verified or refuted by observation. Public relations often uses questions of fact when they ask whether a particular communication strategy has produced a change in how a particular public views a product or whether a particular communication vehicle has made a difference in perceptions of an organization's communicated message. In each case, based on some measurement, we know whether the communication strategy in question has worked.

The theoretical researcher, guided by theory, predicts that the results of manipulating a variable will yield different outcomes for a particular public. In the laboratory the researcher artificially splits the variables of interest and sees if the theory has predicted the outcome on some measured variable. For instance, the researcher might argue that highly involved and personalized messages are received better by active than passive publics, who, in turn, respond better to noninvolved and depersonalized messages. By testing this in the laboratory (often on students who have been carefully screened and placed in "active" and "passive" conditions based on their knowledge of and expressed position toward the object of the message—say, giving blood—and then randomly exposed to one message or the other), the theoretical researcher can verify if the highly involved message actually did produce more change toward blood giving intentions in the active public and the noninvolved message in the passive public by giving message respondents a chance to volunteer for a blood drive. The behavioral outcome is thus changed by the condition, whereby participants responded to messages in the *predicted* way.

Applied researchers use such findings to establish message strategies. Assuming that the actual campaign was to increase blood donations, messages advocating high personal involvement (expected to work on those already giving blood) and messages advocating low personal involvement (which work best on nongiving publics) would be created and transmitted to the targeted publics. Instead of looking for differences between the two groups (one is already giving), the applied researcher would look at baseline or benchmarked data to determine success. During the actual campaign surveys might be conducted to see if the messages were changing attitudes toward blood donation and the messages would likely be altered if they were found not to work. Actual outcome assessment would compare actual blood donation against benchmark data from both groups. If the campaign was successful, proportionately more blood would be donated.

Questions of Value

Whereas questions of fact can only be answered empirically, *questions of value* can be answered quantitatively *or* qualitatively. Questions of value ask "how well" or "how good" something is. Answering such questions quantitatively requires the researcher to rely only on attitude measures and thus tends to reduce understanding to an empirical benchmark. Questions of value are best answered qualitatively, by directly asking individuals what they think of the research object and why they think so. Empirically we can ask whether you thought something was done well—a particular type of advertisement, for example. We can then test across groups—say, by sex—and determine whether one group or another feels it was better done through the creation of such empirical indicators as "How well do to you think this advertisement depicted Generation X? Did it do it Very Well (5), Well (4), Neither Well nor Poorly (3), Poorly (2), or Very Poorly (1)?" Such statements can then be treated as questions of fact, but they do not really tell us *why* the respondents felt as they did. For this determination, qualitative methodologies are superior. They provide the "richness" needed to truly understand what was meant by "well" or "poorly." Such questions require in-depth understanding, something not amenable to quantitative methodology.

Theoretical researchers treat questions of value the same as they would questions of fact. They create a measurement system and then in the confines of the laboratory seek to determine how various groups of people differ on their perceptions or attitudes. The qualitative researcher will often use a quasi-laboratory approach—bringing respondents into a specially prepared room to ask questions either individually or in small groups about the research object while in a still fairly controlled environment. Respondents' answers to carefully prepared questions are then recorded for later analysis.

Applied researchers would basically conduct the same study. Instead of a quasi-laboratory, however, applied researchers may use meeting rooms to conduct the research or actually do the research *on-site*. Thus, if we were interested in understanding how employees felt about the quality of a company's communications, we could conduct a survey to establish benchmark data and then conduct in-depth interviews and focus groups on-site to seek better understanding of why they felt as they did. This obviously is a triangulated approach.

Note that both theoretical and applied researchers address the same problem with slightly different approaches. Both provide important information for the public relations practitioner—one sets the underlying rationale and the other sees if it can be applied to what is often labeled the "real world." A second difference might be defined in relation to what each purports to research, the theoretical researcher most often dealing with opinions and attitudes while the applied researcher tries to take that research approach one step further by directly observing behavior.

Questions of Policy

Questions of policy are almost always strategic and often ask what should be done. Questions of policy lie outside of theoretical research and are almost always categorized as applied research. A question of policy is answered by carefully looking at the findings of questions of definition, fact, and value. For example, a question of policy might be: Should we target X because of Y? Because they are strategic, questions of policy require agreement on not only the definition of the problem (i.e., what the central themes or ideas are) but also on findings of fact (are there differences and if so how large?) and value (how good or bad are the differences?). Such questions are very complicated and often carry legal overtones.

Researchers do not usually answer questions of policy. Instead, the latter are best answered by theorists in the academic world and by executives in the business world. As noted, when answering questions of policy, agreement must be found not only on definitions but also on what constitutes differences and value. In its application to research, the question of policy addressed most often is the actual development and execution of the communication campaign or program. In the often artificial world of academics, computer and group simulations can be run under controlled conditions to see how well the variables under study work. If something has changed or the variables do not operate as expected, the theory can be reexamined and the situation resimulated. In the real world of public relations practice, however, such options are rarely available due to cost and time constraints.

USE OF RESEARCH IN PUBLIC RELATIONS

As the practice of public relations has grown over the years, so too has the use of research. As we will see in Chapter 2, as public relations has moved from the technical to the managerial realms, it has had to develop ways of measuring successes and failures. As such, not only is research use on the rise, but also it is getting increasingly sophisticated. For instance, from 1980 to 1989 the percentage of PRSA "Silver Anvil" award winners using formal research in their campaigns rose from 25% in 1980, to 40% in 1989, to over 75% in 1998.[7] Not only are public relations firms and departments conducting more research, but also research is getting increasingly more complex, often employing both formal and informal methods and increasingly sophisticated statistical analyses of the formal data generated. In addition, more public relations theoretical research is being conducted by the industry, as evidenced in the Institute for Public Relations (IPR) and the Council of Public Relations Firms (CPRF) forming a joint venture inquiring into the impact of public relations[8] and the IPR's continuing measurement task force.[11]

Finally, as public relations becomes increasingly global in theory and practice, there is a need for better understanding of complex social and economic issues. Public relations practices should be proactive, that is, they should be brought in before problems arise rather than only afterward. A larger and more comprehensive body of knowledge is needed to address questions dealing with change in social and economic environments, change and change management, crisis communication, and so on. Only short- and long-term research aimed specifically at the public relations function will be capable of addressing such questions

SUMMARY

This chapter has answered the question "What is research?" Chapter 1 builds upon the insights of this Introduction, moving the focus from a general review of research with attention to public relations to *the practice of public relations research*. While in this introduction we have been necessarily vague on public relations applications, the next chapter prepares us for such applications. Further, Chapter 2 will examine the assumptions we make regarding public relations and public relations research in particular. In rounding out Part I, Chapter 3 will examine the ethics of conducting research in general and in public relations in particular.

To review, this introduction has differentiated between two classes of research, formal and informal, and two applications, theoretical and applied. It should be noted—and will be reinforced later—that formal research takes a distinctively social scientific orientation, one that is quantitative and involves large numbers of observations to reliably and validly describe and predict communication outcomes. Informal research, qualitative in nature, involves intense rather massive observation and focuses on a relatively small number of observations to better understand particular events or individuals. Throughout this volume we will continually refer to the type of question asked, noting again and again that the type of question often determines the *best* research method (formal or informal) and the *appropriate* evaluation or assessment techniques.

REVIEW QUESTIONS

1. Why do public relations practitioners require more knowledge about and skill in conducting research?
2. How does research strengthen public relations' position within a company or with a client?
3. What kinds of formal and informal methods are applied in today's public relations? Why?
4. Differentiate between the kinds of research that theoretical and applied researchers might do. Can you think of instances where one approach might provide insight for the other, and vice versa?
5. Think of five definition, fact, value, and policy questions that you think might be used in a public relations campaign. Can you begin with a policy question first? Why or why not?

PRACTICE PROBLEM

You have been hired by a public relations firm and assigned to your first account. In briefing you about the client and its needs, you find that not much initial research has been conducted and, further, many of the concepts and ideas the client has are murky and not well defined. You will meet with a team from the client in two weeks. How would you establish the need for a research program? What would you tell the client about the relationship between public relations and the need for research? What specific kinds of questions would you seek to answer? Which methods (formal, informal, or both) would you suggest that the client consider? Why?

NOTES

1. Jerry A. Hendrix, *Public Relations Cases,* 5th ed. (Belmont, CA: Wadsworth, 2000).
2. John E. Marston, *Modern Public Relations* (New York: McGraw-Hill, 1979).
3. Scott M. Cutlip, Allen H. Center, and Glen M. Broom, *Effective Public Relations,* 6th ed. (Englewood Cliffs, NJ: Prentice Hall, 1999), p. 5.
4. Donald K. Wright, *Research in Strategic Corporate Communications,* The Executive Forum, New York, NY, November 1998.
5. John V. Pavlik, *Public Relations: What Research Tells Us* (Beverly Hills, CA: Sage, 1987).
6. Don W. Stacks and John E. Hocking, *Communication Research,* 2nd ed. (New York: Longman, 1999), pp. 7–16.
7. Wright.
8. Steve Lilienthal, "Models for Measuring PR Impact Sought by CPR, IPR," *PR Week* (April 10, 2000), p. 2.
9. Institute for Public Relations Research and Education, *Guidelines and Standards for Measuring and Evaluating PR Effectiveness* (Gainesville, FL: Institute for Public Relations Research and Education, 1997); Institute for Public Relations, *International Symposium 4: Putting the Yardstick to PR: How Do We Measure Effectiveness Globally?* (Gainesville, FL: Institute for Public Relations, 2000).

Chapter 2

Management of Research in Public Relations

W hat is public relations? This question has been posed over and over again. An interesting perspective was offered some years ago when I invited a friend to discourse on public relations before my introduction to communication class. This individual had significant public relations and advertising experience (he may have been one of the first integrated communication practitioners—but he didn't know it at the time). As he began the discussion, he carefully spelled out that he practiced both public relations and advertising. He then turned to me and asked me a simple question: "What do your students think the difference between advertising and public relations is?" I gave him the typical textbook answer about saving money as compared to making money, free versus paid placement, and intended publics. "No," he replied, "let me give them a historical example."

"What," he asked the class, "is the world's oldest profession?" After some giggles, he announced, "Prostitution!" And he then asked the students, "What is the world's second-oldest profession?" "Advertising," he replied. "The prostitute, in order to market him- or herself, had to advertise." "And now, what is the world's third-oldest profession?" By now he had the class's rapt attention. "Public relations!" he shouted. "Once the prostitutes had 'made it' they no longer wanted the 'prostitute' label and hired a public relations practitioner to change their image."

I've told that story to generations of public relations students (and many faculty). Unfortunately, many students come back years later and tell me that of all they have learned about public relations—cases, research methods, ethics, campaigns, writing, graphics—this is the story that sticks most in their minds.

Admittedly, it has a familiar and truthful "ring" to it. Public relations may be defined in many ways, but ultimately it deals with what Mark Hickson calls the "management of credibility."[1] We will look at both concepts, "management" and "credibility," throughout this chapter.

This chapter addresses two significant questions. First, just what is it that we practice in public relations? Looking back at Chapter 1, it should be evident that we are addressing a question of definition—*What is it we are researching? How does it differ from other similarly related fields?*—that will focus discussion throughout the remaining chapters. This is an important step, one that is not only difficult (inasmuch as there are many definitions of public relations) but also problematic in that we must not limit what we study too much. Part of this discussion will include the *people* and topics we conduct research on. Second, what assumptions should public relations practitioners make when approaching research? Here we look at the establishment of a *program* of research that is both "doable" and "measurable."

WHAT IS PUBLIC RELATIONS?

The first step in any research process is to identify the problem or (as discussed in Chapter 1) to define precisely what it is that you are studying. The central concept of this book is "public relations." What is it? Broadly defined (as in the opening example), public relations is best seen as the "management of credibility." Such a definition, however, barely suffices to explain an area as large as public relations. It does provide us with a general area of concern, one that differentiates public relations from journalism (from which, according to many, public relations arose), advertising, marketing, and management (competitors, to most minds).

Parsing out the differences between public relations and its related fields is not the chief object of this volume. Indeed, many excellent texts provide whole chapters devoted to spelling out the differences and similarities among the four areas.[2] An excellent beginning point is offered by Cutlip, Center, and Broom:

> Public relations is the management function that identifies, establishes, and maintains mutually beneficial relationships between an organization and the various publics on whom its success or failure depends.[3]

Grunig and Hunt use an even simpler definition, "the management of communication between an organization and its publics."[4] Both definitions employ similar terms, "management" and "publics," that provide both an action term (one that may be manipulable through repeated practice) and a specific receiver group or groups. Further, the focus is the study of public relations as from a particular entity (organization, in both instances). The "beneficial relationships" that are identified, established, and maintained are what research is all about—that is, the effective uses of communication between an entity and its publics.

Entities and Publics

In answering the question "What is public relations?", we now know that public relations is (1) a management function that (2) conducts research about an organization *and* its publics to (3) establish mutually beneficial relationships through (4) communication.

The concept of entity is fairly simple. An entity is an organization—it may be a complex Fortune-500 conglomerate, as simple as a "mom and pop" store, one person (such as an entertainer or athlete), or even a public relations firm. Each organization has as its goals both survival and advancement in an environment in which fierce competition for scarce commodities such as assets or capital is the main objective. The public relations function, then, is to identify avenues for survival and advancement, establish communication programs or campaigns that enhance the organization's advancement (and thus survivability), and maintain those programs against all competitors.

At whom does the public relations function target its communication programs? Figure 2.1 shows a number of publics that public relations researchers often address or seek to analyze. Note that such publics may be both internal and external to the organization. Stacks has observed that there are at least three basic publics relevant to any entity: those *external* to the organization (e.g., they may invest in the organization or report to groups that may invest), those that are *internal* to the organization (e.g., the organization's employees, stockholders, stakeholders, directors), and those that *intervene* between an organization and its external publics (e.g., in the case of the tourism industry, taxi drivers and maids).[5] Thus, public relations researchers may continually take the pulse of many different publics. Defining the

	External	Internal	Intervening
Active			
Passive			
Ignorant			

FIGURE 2.1. Target Publics

publics—whether they are active, passive, or ignorant, for example—also constitutes a continuing research program for many public relations practitioners.

Publics are researched both informally and formally. Informal research may be anecdotal, stem from discussions with people who deal with particular publics on a daily basis, come from structured interviews with key members of that public, or derive from focus group discussions of key and/or "normal" members of that public. Formal research usually takes the form of survey or poll methodology, where small or large groups are "sampled" from the public's larger population. Both methods are applicable when trying to identify, establish, and maintain communication relationships.

What are these relationships and how do public relations practitioners maintain them? Although the pat answer is "trust" through appropriate "communications" to key decision makers or gatekeepers through communication channels, the messages communicated must do something. By adopting Mark Hickson's concept that public relations is the management of credibility,[6] we can provide a sweeping outcome variable that can be fairly easily operationalized and measured. We should note, however, that credibility is not something that an organization "has"; instead, credibility resides in the "eyes" of the publics it does business with. Thus, when researching credibility issues public relations practitioners are almost always looking at variables such as organizational trust, believability, competence, fairness, openness, power, reputation, and so on.

It is important to distinguish between a target population and a target public. Melvin Sharpe suggests that this distinction can be further refined. He notes that a *target population* might be identified as women between the ages of 18 and 24 in a certain economic group or geographical area. A *target public*, however, would be identified through shared self-interest and shared communication—thus, our target public might be those women, but more narrowly defined to specify what interest(s) they share in common and who they communicate with (who their gatekeepers are). Further, Sharpe notes, the even more narrowly defined *target audience* can be identified as the activists or trend setters within the target public who are capable of influencing them.[7] By further defining the target public to special target audiences, the public relations practitioner can target messages to those whose support might be crucial to getting acceptance from the target public.

One final note: identifying publics is not an easy task. As Broom and Dozier point out, there are a number of different ways to characterize a public.[8] Publics can be identified by geographic location, demographics, psychographics, power, position, reputation, organizational membership, role in decision making, and behavior (latent, aware, or active[9]). To confuse matters even more, these identifiers can be mixed and matched; thus, you may have a public that is composed of active male northeastern college graduate yuppies involved with environmental organizations. As will be noted shortly, identifying the appropriate public(s) for an organization is a key goal of any research program and is found in the first research question asked, "Who is it I am researching?"

PROGRAMMATIC RESEARCH IN PUBLIC RELATIONS

It should be clear by now that public relations research should be programmatic in nature; that is, the research should be a continuous process that continually assesses an organization's position among its publics on a variety of outcome measures. A good research program or campaign has at its base a continuing cycle of data gathering and analysis, both formal and informal in nature. While this is what we strive for, in reality most organizations focus their research agendas on pressing problems or concerns. Good public relations practitioners—those who have a finger on the pulse of their publics—try to anticipate problems before they arise. This is called "proactive" public relations research and should be conducted continuously, especially with internal publics.

Most research projects, however, tend to be either reactive or are planned for a specific period of time. Ideally, research should be a major component of any public relations program or campaign; in reality, research is generally conducted at the end of a program as a way to assess success or failure. As backward as this may sound, and for any number of reasons (typically due to financial considerations, since research is not cheap), organizations prefer to put their money in areas other than research. The problem with this approach was discussed briefly in Chapter 1, when the concept of a baseline (an initial data collection that defines where you are at the beginning) or benchmark (similar to a baseline but capable of "moving" as goals are attained during a campaign) was introduced. Quite simply, success is dependent on two things: (1) where you were when you began the public relations program and (2) what your expectations were. While we often "research" the latter, we seldom find research conducted on the former.

General Public Relations Research Assumptions

According to Donald K. Wright, there are four basic assumptions that public relations researchers make when approaching a program of research.[10] First, *the decision-making process is basically the same in all organizations*. The way in which a decision is made follows a set agenda, one that we will examine more closely in a moment but one that generally follows a management by objective (MBO) approach. Second, *all communication research should (1) set objectives, (2) determine a strategy that establishes those objectives, and (3) implement tactics that bring those strategies to life*. As we will see, the kinds of objectives we set will require different research methods to assess whether they have been met. Further, strategies must be researched as to their potential for achieving the objectives. This often requires that informal methods such as secondary research (research conducted on research already collected) be undertaken to identify the best strategy for the stated objectives. Finally, implementing a strategy requires that a set of research tools be in place to assess throughout the program the strategy's effectiveness. As noted in Chapter 1, it is best to triangulate both formal and informal methodologies to gain the most data possible in assessing progress toward meeting program objectives.

The third assumption is that *research can be divided into three general phases*. First, there is the actual *development* of the program. This requires considerable secondary research and helps to define achievable research goals and objectives—that is, the specification of both broad and detailed research objectives, which in turn helps in the creation of appropriate research instruments such as survey questionnaires or focus group or interview schedules. The second phase typically is program *refinement*. A subassumption here is that the program, once initiated, is systematically evaluated throughout its lifespan. The goal of

program refinement is to ensure that the communication strategies being employed are working as projected during the planning, or development, stage. Without assessment research it is almost impossible to
tell if a strategy is working, whether it needs to be changed or refined.
Third, the program must have an _evaluation_ component built into it at
program's end that assesses whether it succeeded or not. Success generally is measured by how well the program met the various objectives
and goals. The evaluation may be as simple as counting the number of
people who attended an "opening" or the number of "hits" or page
views on a webpage or as complex as assessing what people feel about
a new product or change in an organization's culture. The key here is
that research is a planned (and budgeted) part of the program or campaign from inception to conclusion.

Fourth, _communication research is behavior-driven and knowledge-
based_. This assumption logically follows the first three. As we will see,
objectives must be measurable. To be measurable they must be at least
reflect behavior; thus, an objective may be to assess attitudes toward a
particular event or concept, something formal research can do quite
well. Public relations research must attempt to identify those things
that are behavior-driven and that yield data that can be systematically
and reliably assessed as leading to a desired behavior. To do so, _public
relations research must be based on applied research and informed by public
relations theory_. That is, the research must follow the same decision-
making process that the practitioner uses and provide data regarding
specified outcomes that not only inform what is occurring in a campaign but also indicate why particular strategies or substrategies are
working or not. Thus, effective research design is integral to program
creation, refinement, and evaluation.

The outcome of most public relations research tends to be linear
in nature. As depicted in Figure 2.2, Research yields Action yields
Communication yields Evaluation (RACE). Perhaps a better acronym
would be ERASE: continued Evaluation leads to Research that leads to
Action (or Objectives) that leads to Strategy that leads to Evaluation
that leads to more Research, and so forth.

Establishing the Research Program

It should go without saying that in order to conduct any meaningful
research you need some plan of action. Although there are several different ways to approach public relations program management, the
most widely used plan is a process called _management by objective_, or
MBO.[11] An MBO model or approach is actually a _process_ that closely
matches the RACE or ROPE public relations models discussed earlier

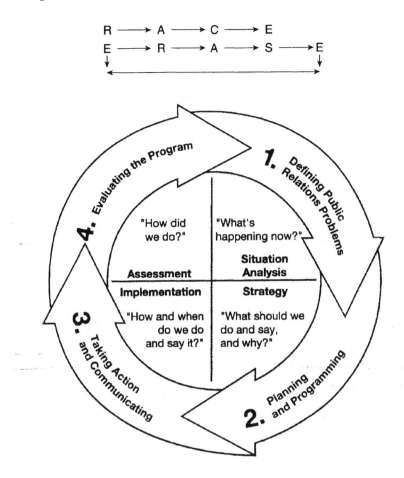

FIGURE 2.2. *Top:* the outcome of public relations research. *Bottom:* The four-step public relations process. The four-step public relations process. From S. M. Cutlip, A. H. Center, and G. M. Broom, Effective Public Relations, 8th ed. (Englewood Cliffs, NJ: Prentice Hall, 2000). Reprinted with permission from Pearson Education, Inc.

and consists of multiple steps, all of which are ultimately related to the question of definition (see Table 2.1). Other approaches can be employed, but all basically follow a four-step type public relations model: (1) define the problem, (2) state the program's objectives, (3) create a campaign or program that meets or surpasses the objectives, and (4) evaluate and provide feedback on the campaign. In internal corporate communication campaigns, one campaign often leads to subsequent

TABLE 2.1. Public Relations Management by Objectives[a]

General MBO approach	Specific to public relations

1. Define the problem
  a. Negative perception?
  b. One-time project?
  c. Continuing program/campaign?
	1. Define client/employer objectives
	  a. Informational
	  b. Motivational
	  c. Behavioral[b]

2. Set objectives
  a. Informational
  b. Motivational
  c. Behavioral (results)
  d. Set strategy and tactics
	2. Define audiences/publics[c]
	  a. Audience 1 (latent/inactive/
	    aware/active)
	  b. Audience 2 (self/internal/
	    external/intervening)

3. Define publics
  a. Entire public
  b. External publics
  c. Intervening publics
  d. Internal publics
  e. Establish relationships/links
    between publics
	3. Define audience objectives
	  a. Demographic analysis
	  b. Psychographic analysis
	
	4. Identify appropriate communication
	  channels
	  a. Which channels, for what?
	  b. Which are most appropriate for
	    problem and objectives?

4. Plan the program/campaign
  a. Written tactics
  b. Visual tactics
  c. Verbal/spoken tactics
	5. Establish media channel objectives
	  a. Identify gatekeepers
	  b. Identify story angles
	  c. Identify media attitudes toward
	    (5a) and (5b)

5. Execute program/campaign
  a. Establish timeframe/timetable
  b. Gather effectiveness data
    1. Prior to campaign
    2. During campaign
    3. After the campaign
	6. Identify source materials and
	  appropriate research questions
	  a. Questions of definition (what is
	    it?)
	  b. Questions of fact (what do
	    people know?)
	  c. Questions of value (how good/
	    how bad?)
	  d. Questions of policy (what should
	    be done?)

6. Evaluate objectives
  a. Entire program/campaign
  b. Informational objectives
  c. Motivational objectives
  d. Plan reevaluation
	7. Establish communication strategies
	  a. Publics factors
	  b. Client/employee factors
	  c. Media factors

	8. What is the message's(s') essence
	  a. To inform
	  b. To persuade

	9. Identify and define graphic support

[a] N. R. Nager and T. H. Allen, *Public Relations Management by Objective* (New York: Longman, 1983). Reprinted with permission from   .
[b] D. W. Stacks, "Crisis Management: Toward a Multidimensional Model of Public Relations," in D. P. Millar (ed.), *Crisis Management Communications* (Mahwah, NJ: Erlbaum, in press). Reprinted with permission from Lawrence Erlbaum Associates.
[c] Stacks.

campaigns; in the world of public relations firms, success in one campaign often leads to new contracts and business.

As suggested earlier, employing a programmatic research plan requires an additional first step, evaluation or preevaluation. In terms of program planning research, this first step is called *environmental monitoring* or *environmental scanning*.[12] As part of an ongoing process, research at this stage seeks to create a body of knowledge about an issue or client or organization that detects and explores potential concerns. Broom and Dozier suggest that environmental scanning is used primarily to detect and describe problems or potential problems.[13] In reality it has a larger function (although in the case of an ongoing program or campaign it truly does help detect problem areas)—namely, it provides the basic knowledge required to begin a campaign or, in the case of a public relations firm about to bid on an account, provides the information necessary to actually begin to state the problem.

Stating the Research Problem

Once the environmental scanning or monitoring phase has been started, the formal research process begins. This will entail answering questions of definition and fact, employing both informal and formal research methods. An MBO or similar programmatic plan will attempt to first state the problem as a cause-and-effect statement. For example, "people are not getting enough company information to do their jobs properly" (effect) and "company media are attracting readership" (cause). Note that the effect often precedes the cause here, but only because the effect is most noticeable. The question, however, is more complex and will require several revisions based on both informal and formal research to define specifically (1) the nature of the problem and (2) potential causes. Thus, informal research such as employee interviews and media analyses (e.g., readability, human interest, channels of distribution, design) may be employed first and then formal surveys of employees regarding both their reading habits and perceived attitudes toward company publications may be undertaken to define the problem properly.

The final problem then may be stated in such as way as to have a measurable outcome:

> Over the past three quarters company management decisions and strategic plans have not been adequately communicated to employees. Lack of employee knowledge of major management decisions and plans has hindered the company in the fulfillment of its goals for 2000, specifically in

regard to instilling the new corporate culture envisioned by senior management.

The actual problem statement might include specifics based on the research conducted, but is not needed. The problem statement has basically established the relationship between need (increased information flow resulting in better understanding of the new corporate culture) and the cause (lack of adequate communication). Research might find that the company newsletter is not being read for a variety of reasons or that the internal computer network is ineffective in establishing a credible relationship between senior management and employees (employees may not believe that anyone is listening to their concerns due to a prior lack of management feedback or perceived one-way, upward communication channels).

Goals and Objectives

Before we examine what an objective is, we need to distinguish between a campaign or program's goals and its objectives. According to Broom and Dozier, a _goal_ is a general outcome expected when a campaign or program is completed (or something to be reached at some point).[14] Thus, a goal is long-term and gives direction. An _objective_, on the other hand, is very specific (the more specific the better) and based on projected and actual program _outputs_. In _Guidelines and Standards for Measuring and Evaluating PR Effectiveness_, Walter K. Lindenmann argues that public relations should be evaluated according to specific outputs:

> In setting PR goals and objectives, it is usually important to recognize that measuring PR effectiveness per se—that is, the management of an organization's overall communications activities with its target audience groups or publics—can be quite difficult to do unless the _individual_ elements or components of the program are clearly defined. We suggest that instead of trying to measure PR as a total entity, steps be taken to measure the effectiveness of individual or particular PR activities.[15]

Thus, while goals may reflect the public relations campaign or program in general, the specific objectives to be met are defined in terms of both _outputs_ (specific tactics such as press releases, VNRs, speeches, media placement) and _outcomes_ (their effect).

A public relations program goal may be to "elect councilwoman Roberta Smith to a third term." The specific objectives to be met in meeting this goal must be carefully spelled out in terms of both outputs and outcomes. Thus, we turn to writing program objectives, objectives that are clearly defined in terms of both what they represent (output tactics) and their expected impact (behavioral or attitudinal outcomes).

Stating Objectives

While all the parts of the research plan are important, the writing of objectives follows only the statement of the problem in terms of importance. Consider the statement of the problem to be the general roadmap for getting from problem ("we need to be at a meeting at point Y by time X") to solution ("we will travel by car and airplane"). The goal statement(s) provide overall direction ("we will head north, then east, then south to get to our objective before time X") to overcoming the problem ("we need to get from point X to point Y"). The objectives tell us specifically how to attain that goal and solve the problem ("we will rent a car to get to the airport by 10:45 A.M. [objective 1]; take a plane leaving at 11:30 A.M. to the destination, arriving at 1:30 P.M. [objective 2]; rent a car at the airport [objective 3]; and drive to the destination, arriving at 3:30 P.M. in time for the meeting [objective 4]). Note that while the objectives are pretty specific, they are still "soft," that is, they do not tell us specifically what kinds of cars we will use, the distances we will travel, the airline taken, or what "in time" is. They are, however, measurable or at least potentially measurable—the car was rented (question of fact, yes it was), you got to the airport by 10:45 (question of fact; you did), and you flew at 11:30 to some destination (question of fact, you did), you rented a second car at the airport (question of fact, you did), you drove to the destination and arrived in time for the meeting (question of fact; you did).

This is obviously an oversimplified example. Most public relations goals and objectives are not quite as simple. In fact, when taking into consideration the goals of the client or organization, the public's needs, and the communication strategies available, stating objectives often becomes very complicated. Consider, for example, that there are at least three basic objectives of any public relations campaign: informational, motivational, and behavioral.

Of greatest importance to the client are the *behavioral objectives*—they are what are counted: your client won the campaign by X votes, X number of stockholders attended the annual meeting, revenue is up $X\%$, X number of articles were written about your client and appeared in X number of newspapers with $\$X$ placement value.

What if your publics have little or no knowledge about your client or organization? In that case you have to first provide the information necessary to alert them of the event, personality, goal, or the like. *Informational objectives* specify what the publics should know during and after the campaign or program. It is a common mistake to assume that publics have the necessary information to act in the way you want (even an active public may be ignorant about important things related to the campaign). Thus, the first objectives written should focus on what and how publics should know about the campaign's actual content.

Knowing something about the campaign does not mean that an actual behavioral act will occur. In many instances knowledge is not sufficient to move people to action (we all know that there are periodic blood shortages, but that knowledge does not necessarily produce more blood donations). Thus, we specify certain *motivational objectives*. To some, there is no difference between a motivational and a behavioral objective. It is assumed that motivated people act, but social science research does not support such a conclusion. Motivation is an *attitudinal* phenomenon. An attitude is most often defined *as a predisposition to act* but is much more complex; an attitude can be seen as possessing direction (like/dislike), salience (importance/unimportance), and understanding (ignorance/understanding). As such, motivation is more difficult to measure than either behavior or knowledge, and we will spend considerable time in Chapter 8 examining just what an attitude is and how it can be measured in both a reliable and valid way.

The key to motivational objectives is that once defined they can be tracked over the course of a campaign. When motivation toward the campaign goal is found to be lacking, it can be shored up via communication strategies aimed at providing more information (thus leading to more knowledge) or reasons for action (thus providing direction and salience). The key, however, is tracking and relating attitudes to strategic tactics.

Writing Objectives

Ask any teacher and she will tell you that the hardest thing about teaching is not the actual teaching but the specifying of objectives. The same is true in managing a public relations campaign or program. Good objectives are written with an output and an outcome in mind. Thus, good objectives almost always start with the word "to," followed by what will be done in behavioral terms—obviously a verbal phrase. Thus, our first attempt at an objective might be: "To increase the number of people attending event X." While this is good (we have "to" and "attending"), we have not really specified *whom* we want to attend. Thus, we need to change the objective: "To increase the number of employees attending event X." If the objective is still too "soft," providing neither the amount of behavior expected nor a specific completion date, then, finally: "To increase the number of employees attending event X through company media and supervisor interaction [outputs] from last year [existing research] by 22% [outcome]."

The preceding example was behavioral, and it assumed the target date was the event itself. However, prior to the event informational and motivational objectives are also necessary. Therefore you might propose objectives with target dates to lead up to the behavioral objective(s):

"To increase the percentage of employees who know about event X through stories in the company newsletter and intranet [outputs] from Y% [based on existing research or environmental scanning] to Z% [outcome] by 6 months prior to the event." (Informational)

"To increase the percentage of senior management who think that event X is important to the company's long-term goals through direct interaction at board and senior management meetings [outputs] from Y% [based on formal precampaign research] to Z% [outcome] by January 1 [target date]." (Motivational)

By now it should be apparent that there is a sequencing of public relations objectives:

Informational Objectives

Motivational Objectives

Behavioral Objectives

Informational objectives establish what knowledge should be known or is needed by the publics the campaign or program is intended for. Further, informational objectives specify the informational vehicles to be used and how. Motivational objectives test whether or not the information is having an effect and whether tactical strategies are having an impact on future behavior. Furthermore, the relationship between informational and motivational objectives is interactive; that is, if motivational objectives are not being met, informational objectives can be changed to overcome identified blockages. The behavioral objectives are often what "count," and they in the end define the success or failure of a campaign.

Creating Evaluation Strategies

What is a success and what is failure? In an election, success consists in your candidate or your issue winning at the polls. In establishing a new product or changing attitudes about a person or event, however, success becomes highly relative. While it should be understood by now that research is conducted continually during a public relations campaign or program, what constitutes "success" may at times be far short of "winning." If your goal is to "enter the marketplace and gain a 10% share of that market," an 8% gain may be acceptable. What is important is that you pretest the environment whenever possible (what *is* the average market share in this environment for a new company or product?) and implement systematic monitoring of that environment and the publics affected by the campaign. Thus, you have a research strategy in place that (1) has been pretested, (2) takes account of the relationships between tactical strategies and tactical outcomes, and (3) continually monitors progress toward the goal with an eye toward in-campaign tactical corrections.

SUMMARY

This chapter examined how public relations campaigns and programs are managed. Beginning with a discussion of what constitutes "public relations," the chapter examined what a public is and the publics that practitioners work with. The discussion then turned to a review of the assumptions of research in general and as applied to public relations in particular. The major underlying theme emerging is that without research the *management* of public relations is not possible. You have to first know where you are, then where you want to go, and then during the actual application of strategic communication strategies know how well you are progressing. The chapter then examined the systematic process of establishing a managed public relations program—defining the problem, stating the goals and objectives, and then using research to provide information before, during, and after the program or campaign. Special emphasis was placed on the writing of good—that is, measurable—informational, motivational, and behavioral objectives.

REVIEW QUESTIONS

1. Select a public relations concern or problem that you might face if you operated a public relations agency in your hometown in behalf of a particular client. What are your target populations, target publics, and target audiences?

2. State three informational, three motivational, and three behavioral objectives for the campaign that are addressable through research.

3. Walk through the four basic research assumptions that guide public relations practice and address each assumption and any subassumptions in the way that you would for the client.

4. What would your MBO look like? Are there any specific portions of the MBO that would require specific types of research? Why?

5. How would you evaluate campaign effectiveness or success? Which of your stated objectives would be the focus of your discussion of effectiveness or success? Why?

PRACTICE PROBLEM

A client has determined that it wants to make a major change in its product line, the addition of a new color to one of its candy products. Your research indicates that an earlier press "leak" warning of the change has already produced significant negative media coverage; the company has already received hundreds of communications (letters, calls, e-mails, faxes) from "traditionalists" who do not want change, and sales are already beginning to drop. Your client wants a plan to (1) counter any past or future disclosures and (2) to change the publics' perceptions from negative to positive. Prepare an MBO analysis with particular attention devoted to target populations, publics, and audiences.

NOTES

1. Mark Hickson, personal communication, November 1998.

2. See, for example, Scott M. Cutlip, Allen H. Center, and Glen M. Broom, *Effective Public Relations*, 8th ed. (Englewood Cliffs, NJ: Prentice Hall, 2000); James E. Grunig and Todd Hunt, *Managing Public Relations* (New York: Holt, Rinehart & Winston, 1984); Doug Newsom, Judy Vanslyke, and Dean Kruckeberg, *This Is PR: The Realities of Public Relations* (Belmont, CA: Wadsworth, 2000); Frazier P. Seitel, *The Practice of Public Relations*, 7th ed. (Upper Saddle River, NJ: Prentice Hall, 1998); Dennis L. Wilcox, Phillip H.

Ault, Warren K. Agee, and Glen T. Cameron, *Public Relations Strategies and Tactics*, 6th ed. (New York: Longman, 2000).

3. Cutlip, Center, and Broom, p. 4.

4 Grunig and Hunt, p. 6.

5. Don W. Stacks, "Travel Public Relations Models—Public Relations and Travel: A Programmed Approach to Communication in the 1990s," *Southern Public Relations, 1* (Winter 1995), 24–29.

6. Hickson.

7. Marvin L. Sharpe, personal communication, March, 2001.

8. Glen M. Broom and David M. Dozier, *Using Research in Public Relations: Applications to Program Management* (Englewood Cliffs, NJ: Prentice Hall, 1990), pp. 32–36.

9. Grunig and Hunt, pp. 144–160.

10. Donald K. Wright, *Research in Strategic Corporate Communications*, The Executive Forum, New York, NY, November 1998.

11. Norman R. Nager and T. Harrell Allen, *Public Relations Management by Objectives* (New York: University Press of America, 1991).

12. See E. W. Brody and Gerald C. Stone, *Public Relations Research* (New York: Praeger, 1989), pp. 39–68; Broom and Dozier, pp. 24-27.

13. Broom and Dozier, p. 24.

14. Broom and Dozier, p. 40.

15. Walter K. Lindenmann (Co-Chair), *Guidelines and Standards for Measuring and Evaluating PR Effectiveness* (Gainesville, FL: The Institute for Public Relations, 1997), p. 4.

Chapter 3

Ethical Concerns
in Public Relations Research

You've just sat down at the dinner table and the telephone rings. You think to yourself, "Oh, no. Another telemarketer," but you answer the phone anyway (after all, it could be a client or the boss calling about something left over from today's meeting). You're right, it is a telemarketer trying to sell you on a new long-distance telephone plan (you already use the service, but he or she's offering you something "new"). After a few seconds you say that you're not interested, but he or she continues the scripted spiel anyway. Finally, out of desperation (and hunger), you hang up. "A bad way to treat customers," you think to yourself.

Not possible in public relations? Think again. With the ever increasing need for research on publics and increasingly sophisticated tools to contact you (e.g., computer-scripted, punch "1" for yes, "2" for no; e-mail surveys popping up when you access the Internet, or even the company intranet at work—"damn HR people," you think), it is entirely possible that the conduct of research may border on unethical research practices. Have you ever promised a respondent a copy of something (such as the results) only to have senior management decide to "bury" the results due to the nature of the findings? Is that ethical?

Conducting ethical public relations research is difficult. The public relations researcher works for a client or for an organization who ultimately "owns" the research, the data, and the findings. If the goal of public relations research is to gather data that truly reflects the publics' knowledge, feelings, motivation, and behaviors toward the client, then treating research participants anything but ethically and honestly (there is a difference—you can be ethical and still be dishonest) runs counter to what public relations is all about.

The ethical conduct of public relations is a topic that rises to the top of most discussions about the industry sooner or later. It is interesting to note, however, that nowhere in the ethical guidelines of the three largest public relations associations is the word "research" to be found. Even in the three books on public relations research, ethics is minimally treated. In Broom and Dozier's *Using Research in Public Relations: Applications to Program Management* and Pavlik's *Public Relations: What the Research Tells Us* the term "ethics" is altogether absent from the index. Similarly, Brody and Stone's *Public Relations Research* offers statements about the "ethical researcher" only when discussing various research methodologies, such as survey or focus groups. In short, nowhere in the professional literature is ethics taken on as a serious matter for intensive study.[1]

To be candid, most public relations practitioners do not do their own research, preferring instead to outsource it to companies whose business is to quickly and efficiently conduct research studies for clients. With the exception of some very large corporations (e.g., AT&T, General Motors, IBM), you will rarely find research sections in corporate communication departments. You may find someone who interprets the findings of others' research, but typically you will not find someone whose main job is to conduct research (we are, after all, mostly creative types). Even if you do find a full-time researcher, that person will likely have very little research experience.

This chapter looks at the ethical dimensions of conducting research. It is divided into several sections. The first quickly examines the ethics of public relations in general. It then turns to the ethics of collecting and reporting of data collected in the process of research, and then looks at data ownership, an often sticky legal problem.

PUBLIC RELATIONS ETHICS

Ethics deals with how people see right and wrong in a particular society. What is ethical to Americans, for example, may not be ethical to other societies. But all societies have their own ethical codes and practices. The same is true of business and commerce. We have ethical codes and practices in many areas: medicine, law, accounting, and banking. An *ethical code* is something we live by in our daily interactions with others, setting forth acceptable standards of behavior by those who are subject to that code. Ethical codes, however, are only as good as their *enforcement*. In occupations where members are licensed to operate (e.g., medicine and law), unethical conduct can result in the removal of one's license and the banning from practice of those found guilty of unethical acts. Only regulated industries or occupations can truly enforce their ethical codes. Other organizations may publicly condemn unethical behavior but lack the legal right to remove or ban from practice those found practicing in an unethical manner (e.g., the Society of Professional Journalists).

Public Relations Ethical Codes

The field of public relations has several ethical codes of conduct. Perhaps the most cited and widely held code of ethics, and certainly the oldest one encompassing most of those who publicly identify with public relations, is that of the *Public Relations Society of America* (PRSA). PRSA's "Code of Professional Standards for the Practice of Public Relations" (see Table 3.1) was created in 1950 and has gone through several revisions, the latest in 2000. PRSA members pledge to act in accordance with the code, to conduct themselves fairly, truthfully, and responsibly when representing clients or themselves to the public and to help enforce the code when others are found to be in violation of it. The *International Association of Business Communicators* (IABC) has as its ethical charter the "Code of Ethics for Professional Communicators" (see Table 3.2). First established in 1995, this code was last updated in 1996. IABC members profess the following values: that professional communication is legal, ethical, and done in good taste according to cultural values and beliefs. *The International Public Relations Association* (IPRA) is the third association in this profession with an ethical code (see Table 3.3). IPRA's "Code of Athens" was adopted in May 1965 and modified in April 1968. When joining, members of each of these three associations pledge to follow code ethics and accept whatever enforcement is rendered (primarily shunning unethical practitioners and/or resigning from the association if so ordered). Most other public relations groups have either adopted or adapted the PRSA, IABC, or IPRA ethical codes as their own statement regarding responsible professional practice.

A fourth association, the *Arthur W. Page Society*, does not have a formal code per se but instead urges members to live "the Page principles" to (1) tell the truth, (2) prove it with action, (3) listen to the cus-

TABLE 3.1. 2000 Public Relations Society of America Code of Ethics

Pledge

I pledge:

To conduct myself professionally, with truth, accuracy,
fairness, and responsibility to the public;
to improve my individual competence and advance the
knowledge and proficiency of the profession through
continuing research and education;
and to adhere to the articles of the Member Code
of Ethics 2000 for the practice of public relations as adopted
by the governing Assembly of the
Public Relations Society of America.

I understand and accept that there is a consequence for
misconduct, up to and including membership revocation.

And, I understand that those who have been or are sanctioned by a
government agency or conflict in a court of law of an action that
is in violation of this Code may be barred from membership
or expelled from the Society.

Article XII of the Society's Bylaws

Section 1. *Powers of the Assembly, Obligation of Members.* The Assembly of the
Society shall have power to adopt a Code of Ethics, herein called the "Code,"
and amendments thereto, either at its annual meeting or at a special meeting
called for the purpose, after first receiving the report of the Board of Directors
thereon. All members of the Society shall, by virtue of their membership therein,
be bound by the Code as the same may be amended from time to time, and shall
be obligated to comply with the procedures.

Section 2. *Powers of the Board of Directors.* The Board of Directors shall have
power: (a) to propose to the Assembly a Code of Ethics; (b) to propose to the
Assembly from time to time amendments to the Code when they may appear to
be advisable; (c) to issue official interpretations of the Code and express its
opinion regarding proper professional conduct; (d) to adopt rules of procedure
regarding actions to bar from membership or expel from the society those who
have been, or are, sanctioned by a government agency or convicted in a court of
law of an action that is in violation of this code.

The affirmative vote of two-thirds of the entire Board of Directors shall be
requisite to take disciplinary action against a member

Section 3. *Conviction of a Felony or Misdemeanor.* The Board of Directors may, by a
vote of a majority of the entire Board, expel any member who shall have been
convicted of, or who shall have pleaded "No Contest" to a charge of, a felony or
misdemeanor related to the conduct of the public relations profession or
involving moral turpitude.

Section 4. *Board of Ethics and Professional Standards.* There shall be a Board of
Ethics and Professional Standards consisting of nine Members who are
Accredited, three appointed each year by the Chair and Chief Executive Officer

(cont.)

with the approval of the Board of Directors, each to serve for a term of three years. The chair of the Board of Ethics and Professional Standards shall be appointed each year by Chair and Chief Executive Officer, with the approval of the Board of Directors.

It shall be the primary duty of the Board of Ethics and Professional Standards to develop and implement educational programs regarding the Society's Code of Ethics for members and the public at large, The Board of Ethics and Professional Standards may also, at the discretion and direction of the PRSA Board of Directors, act as counsel to the Board regarding actions to bar from membership or expel from the society those who have been, or are, sanctioned by a government agency or convicted in a court of law of an action that is in violation of this code.

All proceedings of the Board of Ethics and Professional Standards acting in the capacity as Board counsel shall be confidential.

Section 5. *Miscellaneous.* Communications and proceedings among the Board of Ethics and Professional Standards and Board of Directors regarding actions to bar individuals from membership or expel members from the Society shall be confidential. However, final actions by the Board of Directors to bar individuals from membership or expel members from the Society may be made public.

Members of the Society shall respond to information requests of the Board of Ethics and Professional Standards or the PRSA Board of Directors within 30 days.

Section 6. *Agreement to the Code of Ethics.* Payment of annual dues to the Society shall constitute an agreement to abide by the Bylaws of the Society and its Code of Ethics and the procedures for its enforcement.

Note. Reprinted with permission from the Public Relations Society of America.

TABLE 3.2. International Association of Business Communicators Code of Ethics for Professional Communicators

Preface

Because hundreds of thousands of business communicators worldwide engage in activities that affect the lives of millions of people, and because this power carries with it significant social responsibilities, the International Association of Business Communicators developed the Code of Ethics for Professional Communicators. The Code is based on three different yet interrelated principles of professional communication that apply throughout the world.

These principles assume that just societies are governed by a profound respect for human rights and the rule of law; that the ethics—the criteria for determining what is right and wrong—can be agreed upon by members of an organization; and, that understanding matters of taste requires sensitivity to cultural norms.

These principles are essential:

- Professional communication is legal.
- Professional communication is ethical.
- Professional communication is in good taste.

(cont.)

TABLE 3.2. (continued)

Recognizing these principles, members of IABC will:
- Engage in communication that is not only legal but also ethical and sensitive to cultural values and beliefs;
- Engage in truthful, accurate and fair communication that facilitates respect and mutual understanding; and
- Adhere to the following articles of the IABC Code of Ethics for Professional Communicators.

Because conditions in the world are constantly changing, members of IABC will work to improve their individual competence and to increase the body of knowledge in the field with research and education.

Articles

1. Professional communicators uphold the credibility and dignity of their profession by practicing honest and timely communication and by fostering the free flow of essential information in accord with the public interest.

2. Professional communicators disseminate accurate information and promptly correct any erroneous communication for which they may be responsible.

3. Professional communicators understand and support the principles of free speech, freedom of assembly, and access to an open marketplace of ideas; and, act accordingly.

4. Professional communicators are sensitive to cultural values and beliefs and engage in fair and balanced communication activities that foster and encourage mutual understanding.

5. Professional communicators refrain from taking part in any undertaking which the communicator considers to be unethical.

6. Professional communicators obey laws and public policies governing their professional activities and are sensitive to the spirit of all laws and regulations and, should any law or public policy be violated, for whatever reason, act promptly to correct the situation.

7. Professional communicators give credit for unique expressions borrowed from others and identify the sources and purposes of all information disseminated to the public.

8. Professional communicators protect confidential information and, at the same time, comply with all legal requirements for the disclosure of information affecting the welfare of others.

9. Professional communicators do not use confidential information gained as a result of professional activities for personal benefit and do not represent conflicting or competing interests without written consent of those involved.

10. Professional communicators do not accept undisclosed gifts or payments for professional services from anyone other than a client or employer.

11. Professional communicators do not guarantee results that are beyond the power of the practitioner to deliver.

12. Professional communicators are honest not only with others but also, and most importantly, with themselves as individuals; for a professional communicator seeks the truth and speaks the truth first to the self.

Note. Reprinted with permission from the International Association of Business Communicators.

TABLE 3.3. International Public Relations Association Code of Athens

CONSIDERING that all Member countries of the United Nations Organisation have agreed to abide by its Charter which reaffirms "its faith in fundamental human rights, in the dignity and worth of the human person" and that having regard to the very nature of the profession, Public Relations practitioners in these countries should undertake to ascertain and observe the principles set out in this Charter;

CONSIDERING that, apart from "rights," human beings have not only physical or material needs but also intellectual, moral and social needs, and that their rights are of real benefit to them only insofar as these needs are essentially met;

CONSIDERING that, in the course of their professional duties and depending on how these duties are performed, Public Relations practitioners can substantially help to meet these intellectual, moral and social needs;

And, lastly, CONSIDERING that the use of the techniques enabling them to come simultaneously into contact with millions of people gives Public Relations practitioners a power that has to be restrained by the observance of a strict moral code.

On all these grounds, all members of the International Public Relations Association agree to abide by the International Code of Ethics, and that if, in the light of evidence submitted to the Council, a member should be found to have infringed this Code in the course of his/her professional duties, he/she will be deemed to be guilty of serious misconduct calling for an appropriate penalty.

Accordingly, each member:

SHALL ENDEAVOR

1. To contribute to the achievement of the moral and cultural conditions enabling human beings to reach their full stature and enjoy the indefeasible rights to which they are entitled under the "Universal Declaration of Human Rights";
2. To establish communication patterns and channels which, by fostering the free flow of essential information, will make each member of the group feel that he/she is kept informed, and also give him/her an awareness of his/her own personal involvement and responsibility, and of his/her solidarity with other members;
3. To conduct himself/herself always and in all circumstances in such a manner as to deserve and secure the confidence of those with whom he/she comes into contact;
4. To bear in mind that, because of the relationship between his/her profession and the public, his/her conduct—even in private—will have an impact on the way in which the profession as a whole is appraised;

SHALL UNDERTAKE

5. To observe in his/her professional duties, the moral principles and rules of the "Universal Declaration of Human Rights";
6. To pay due regard to, and uphold human dignity and to recognise the right of each individual to judge for himself/herself;
7. To establish the moral, psychological and intellectual conditions for dialogue in its true sense, and to recognise the rights of these parties involved to state their case and express their views;

(cont.)

TABLE 3.3. *(continued)*

8. To act, in all circumstances, in such a manner as to take account of the respective interests of the parties involved; both the interests of the organisation which he/she serves and of the publics concerned;
9. To carry out his/her undertakings and commitments which shall always be so worded as to avoid any misunderstanding, and to show loyalty and integrity in all circumstances so as to keep the confidence of his/her clients or employers, past or present, and all of the publics that are affected by his/her actions;

SHALL REFRAIN FROM

10. Subordinating the truth to other requirements;
11. Circulating information which is not based on established or ascertainable facts;
12. Taking part in any venture or undertaking which is unethical or dishonest or capable of impairing human dignity or integrity;
13. Using any "manipulative" methods or techniques designed to create subconscious motivations which the individual cannot control of his/her own free will and so cannot be held accountable for the action taken on them.

Note. Reprinted with permission from the International Public Relations Association.

tomer, (4) manage for tomorrow, (5) conduct public relations as if the whole company depends on it, and (5) remain calm, patient, and good-humored. The Page Society's ethical code may be best summed up in its assertion that

> Real success, both for big business and the public, lies in large enterprise conducting itself in the public interest and in such a way that the public will give it sufficient freedom to serve effectively.[2]

The Arthur W. Page Society consists of senior management officials. Members are at the corporate senior vice president level, are the CEOs or presidents of public relations firms, or are leading public relations educators and researchers. Although they number about 300, they represent public relations at the highest level and have major input into both corporate and firm public relations campaigns. As with the PRSA, IABC, and IPRA codes, enforcement of the "Page Principles" is primarily voluntary. The *Public Relations Seminar* is another assemblage of senior-level public relations executives. Membership is about 250 people, many of whom also belong to the Page Society. The Seminar's main function is its annual conference, and it does not have a formal code of ethics.

What Is Missing Is a Discussion of Public Relations Research Ethics

What is missing from this discussion of pubic relations ethics? Research! *Nowhere in the codes of conduct do we find research ethics specifically mentioned.* You may read into the codes and principles that research should be conducted fairly, accurately, honestly, and representatively, but nowhere are such concerns specifically addressed. It is important, therefore, that we turn our discussion to the ethical conduct of research.

ETHICS AND THE CONDUCT OF RESEARCH

It is a sad state of affairs that we have to even discuss the ethical conduct of research. Prior to the mid-1960s there was general agreement that researchers—be they academics or practitioners—conducted research in an open and honest way. They treated the people they observed under varying experimental conditions or tallied responses to questions posed in surveys and focus groups honestly and fairly. All that changed when two sets of psychological studies were reported. The first, by Stanley Milgram, surprised many when research participants were asked to zap confederates (people who secretly are in league with the researcher) with progressively larger doses of electrical stimulation—and they readily complied.[3] The second was Philip Zimbardo's study of prisoners and prisoner conditions whereby students were recruited for a study but not told they would be "jailed" and mistreated.[4] In the first case, research participants were not told they could withdraw from the study; in the second, that they were actually a part of a research program which abused them.

The American Psychological Association (APA), in response to members' concerns, created its own code of ethics in dealing with human "subjects." This code set forth the ways in which research participants were to be treated (see Table 3.4). The American Medical Association (AMA) has a similar research code. The main thrust of both codes, however, was with experiments—which sometimes require deception—and the values highlighted were seen as primarily academic, not necessarily applicable to business research.

Even the stringent ethical standards set forth by the APA and AMA, however, proved insufficient protections for research respondents. The federal government, concerned that research participants were not being treated in a fair and honest manner, began to *mandate*

TABLE 3.4. American Psychological Association Code of Research Ethics

The decision to undertake research rests upon a considered judgment by the individual psychologist about how best to contribute to psychological science and human welfare. Having made the decision to conduct research, the psychologist considers alternative directions in which research energies and resources might be invested. On the basis of this consideration, the psychologist carries out the investigation with respect and concern for the dignity and welfare of the people who participate and with cognizance of federal and state regulations and professional standards governing the conduct of research with human participants.

a. In planning a study, the investigator has the responsibility to make a careful evaluation of its ethical acceptability. To the extent that the weighing of scientific and human values suggests a compromise of any principle, the investigator incurs a correspondingly serious obligation to seek ethical advice and to observe stringent safeguards to protect the rights of human participants.

b. Considering whether a participant in a planned study will be a "subject at risk" or a "subject at minimal risk," according to recognized standards, is of primary ethical concern to the investigator.

c. The investigator always retains the responsibility for ensuring ethical practice in research. The investigator is also responsible for the ethical treatment of research participants by collaborators, assistants, students, and employees, all of whom, however, incur similar obligations.

d. Except in minimal-risk research, the investigator establishes a clear and fair agreement with research participants, prior to their participation, that clarifies the obligations and responsibilities of each. The investigator has the obligation to honor all promises and commitments included in that agreement. This investigator informs the participants of all aspects of the research that might reasonably be expected to influence willingness to participate and explains all other aspects of the research about which the participants inquire. Failure to make full disclosure prior to obtaining informed consent requires additional safeguards to protect the welfare and dignity of the research participants. Research with children or with participants who have impairments that would limit understanding and/or communication requires special safeguarding procedures.

e. Methodological requirements of a study may make the use of concealment or deception necessary. Before conducting such a study, the investigator has a special responsibility to (1) determine whether the use of such techniques is justified by the study's prospective scientific, educational, or applied value; (2) determine whether alternative procedures are available that do not use concealment or deception; and (3) ensure that the participants are provided with sufficient explanation as soon as possible.

f. The investigator respects the individual's freedom to decline to participate in or to withdraw from the research at any time. The obligation to protect this freedom requires careful thought and consideration when the investigator is in a position of authority or influence over the participant. Such positions of authority include, but are not limited to, situations in which research participation is required as part of employment or in which the participant is a student, client, or employee of the investigator.

g. The investigator protects the participant from physical and mental discomfort, harm, and danger that may arise from research procedures. If risks of such consequences exist, the investigator informs the participant of that fact. Research procedures likely to cause serious or lasting harm to a participant are not used unless the failure to use these procedures might expose the participant to risk of greater harm or unless the research has great potential benefit and fully informed and voluntary consent is obtained from each participant. The participant should be informed of procedures for contacting the investigator within a reasonable time period following participation should stress, potential harm, or related questions or concerns arise.

h. After data are collected, the investigator provides the participant with information about the nature of the study and attempts to remove any misconceptions that may have arisen. Where scientific or humane values justify delaying or withholding this information, the investigator incurs a special responsibility to monitor the research and ensure that there are no damaging consequences for the participant.

i. Where research procedures result in undesirable consequences for the individual participant, the investigator has the responsibility to detect and remove or correct these consequences for the participant.

j. Information obtained about a research participant during the course of an investigation is confidential unless otherwise agreed upon in advance. When the possibility exists that others may obtain access to such information, this possibility, together with the plans for protecting confidentiality, is explained to the participant as part of the procedure for obtaining informed consent.

---

that certain things be done to ensure the fair treatment of "subjects" in both human nonhuman research. Enforcement was simple: if you failed to conduct ethical research, your grant funding was withdrawn. Since major research universities and major medical facilities base much of their budgets now on "extramural" funding, the enforcement of federal "human subject" guidelines has a major impact. Researchers at universities and medical centers that take in federal funds must now demonstrate how they will protect their participants and how their research conforms to the ethical standards set forth by the government.

What are the major code points of such research? First, and foremost, all research *participants must agree to actively participate in the research.* That is, you cannot "subject" a person to research without their expressed permission. In the academic and medical worlds this means having the participant sign an agreement to participate. Second, *the participant must be allowed to withdraw from the research project at any point* without penalty. This means that if you offer some kind of reward to research participants and they withdraw, you cannot withhold the reward (you must give at least a portion of it to the participants who withdraw). Third, *participants must understand what they are volunteering for*. That is, you cannot deceive research participants by telling them that you are researching one thing and then research something else entirely different (reminiscent of the old "bait and switch" routine). The only exception is in laboratory experiments, where deception is required to keep a participant "blind" to the real purpose of the study; in such cases, participants must be carefully and fully debriefed at the experiment's conclusion as to its real purpose and any potential future problems they might encounter.

Fourth, *the actual research must not harm the individual, psychologically or physically*, unless researchers have provided intervention programs to alleviate any harm inadvertently done. Fifth, *participants' actions, behaviors, and/or statements must remain confidential and anonymous*. If not, then measures must be in place that—with the exception of very specific legal situations—participant protection is guaranteed. (If, for example, you were conducting research on gangs as part of a community relations study and a participant said she was a gang member and, further, that she had committed a crime, you *must* report it to the local authorities if you do not have a waiver from the government.)

Finally, and while not a part of the federal code of ethics, APA strongly recommends that people who participate in research projects not be labeled as "subjects" (or, worse yet, "victims"). A subject, the APA points out, has no recourse but to participate—much as with Milgram's and Zimbardo's participants—and the label "subject" has a tendency to not only devalue the individual but also (again, as in Zimbardo's experiment) may make the researcher feel superior to the participant.

Research Ethics, Research Participants, and Public Relations

So, what does this have to do with public relations research? Given that public relations researchers (even academic researchers) conduct very little experimental research, what is the relevance to today's practice? Quite simply, public relations researchers research *people* through surveys, polls, focus groups, participant-observation, and in-depth interviews. Public relations researchers must keep in mind that their participants (or respondents) are volunteers who agree to participate in the research because they have been kindly and honestly asked for their opinions. Failure to practice ethical research leaves the participant with bad attitudes toward research in general and the practice of public relations in particular. Therefore, the practice of ethical research—either by practitioners or hired research firms—is essential to the industry. As in the earlier example of insistent telemarketing at dinnertime, how often have you been turned off by a research project that (1) assumes you will participate, (2) has no consideration for your time, and (3) fails to educate you about whatever is being researched?

The Ethical Public Relations Researcher

Whether you are conducting the research yourself or have hired someone else to do it, you are responsible for the ethical collection of data. You agree to the method, you agree to the questions being asked, and you agree with how the data will be managed. Therefore, you must not only understand research ethics but be prepared to practice them yourself.

The ethical public relations researcher will make sure that the following guidelines are observed:

1. Always remember that research participants are people who, like yourself, prefer to be treated honestly and fairly.
2. Always make it clear that participation is not required but, rather, strictly voluntary.
3. Make every effort to maintain the participant's confidentiality and anonymity, recording the data in such a way that it cannot be readily attributed back to the individual research participant.
4. If you offer some type of reward for participation, follow through and provide it—including the promise of summaries of the data either individually or published in a corporate newsletter or intranet page. Also, debrief participants when necessary and when requested if not necessary.
5. Investigate potential areas of harm to participants and be prepared to offer intervention programs to those who need them.
6. Strive to make the research experience an educational one for the participant, helping to make that individual a better member of society.

When in doubt, remember the Golden Rule: *Do unto others as you would have others do unto you.*

The Ethics of Data Collection

Part of ethical research relates to what you do with the data once obtained. Today's problems often stem from a lack of perceived anonymity and confidentiality. We will explore this in detail when we turn to the various methods for collecting data, but we must deal with such problems in general as part of our general discussion of ethics.

Surveys and polls tend to have similar problems. In almost all instances the researcher has a list of respondents (and those who did not respond) that can be *linked* to the data. It is important, then, to remove that link as soon as possible. Most research guidelines suggest that, once data have been collected, the link should be broken within 30 days of the end of data collection. In cases where you are returning to the same people for follow-up data, the link between data collections must be carefully guarded—under lock and key! A special problem is found in e-mail surveys and polls. Regardless of what you may believe, *there is no guarantee of confidentiality and anonymity in Internet or intranet research.* Therefore, it is important that you set up safeguards or that you engage a firm capable of conducting the research in a way that assures the requisite confidentiality. Using an Internet research firm does distance you, the researcher, from the data and makes it confidential from your point of view; legitimate firms will destroy any identifying link.

Interviews and focus groups also have problems with confidentiality and anonymity. This is particularly true when the data are recorded electronically. When preceding via these methods, ensure that the participants know and understand that you are recording their responses. If they have problems with that, they must be allowed to leave the research project (my own personal experience suggests that few, if any, participants actually withdraw from a study based on that—but they may do so if they do not trust the researcher). When transcribing the data, all names or identifiers must be replaced by some notation system that makes participants' comments confidential. In many cases absolute anonymity is hard to guarantee when using such informal methods as interviews and focus groups but efforts must be made to divorce respondents' real identities from the data collected. *The basic ethical principle is that the data gathered are held in strict confidence and as anonymously as possible.*

Ethical Concerns in Reporting the Data

The final element in any research program is the reporting of data—the findings of the particular researches. Ethical problems often arise in reporting the data, primarily in maintaining confidentiality and anonymity but also in keeping promises to those who participated. We turn to the concerns over confidentially and anonymity first.

All research reports should be as complete as possible. This means that the sample or population under study must be reported. Generally, such reporting requires that composite statistics be employed; averages and percentages provide readers with a feel for who participated in the research and allow for comparison with other studies. *In no instance should an individual's actual name, position, or any other unique identifier be used without first getting that individual's consent* (the same is true of organizations when case studies are reported). Generic identifiers or placeholders may be used, but only if the reader cannot deduce who specifically may have said what to whom about what.

This problem is much more problematic in corporate public relations research where we are interested in how employees feel about their organization, its culture, its leadership, and so forth. It is not uncommon for a senior manager to ask for information about specific comments that may appear overly negative or aimed at him. In these situations the researcher must not reveal the requested information, even if it may cause you harm. If you do enough research for a client long enough, sooner or later you may be asked to compromise a research participant's identity. Doing so once only makes it easier to do so again, thus violating the important principle that *the research participant is sacrosanct*.

Second, if you promise a participant something, you must follow through. It is not only ethical, but it says something about you as a researcher if you fail to follow through and your own organization's credibility suffers. If, for instance, you represent that the findings will be published, you must do all you can to ensure that they are. This is quite often a problem when the data you gather do not match the client's expectations. In such instances it is important that you educate the client, to make sure that the findings are not placed on some shelf and left to collect dust. If you are conducting research for a private client, however, you may have little control over the actual disposition of the research findings. Speaking personally in at least one case the author of this volume could not work again for the company that hired him because the promise made to him regarding publishing was broken, a promise he made to the research participants. Quite simply, going back to that company and collecting data would be hard, given the lack of credibility for both the researcher and the company among the employees who participated.

One incentive often used to get survey and poll participation is the offer of an advance copy or an executive summary of the results. Once the offer is made, the researcher is ethically obligated to follow through and send the copy or summary to participants. Failure to follow through does nothing to educate participants, as promised, nor does it leave them with a favorable impression about the research project. Moreover, it is an ethical obligation of the researcher to release the data to the media and public, according to the American Association for Public Opinion Research. The problem with this scenario for the public relations practitioner—or any other researcher—who is researching for a client, however, is that the research data and findings are often proprietary and hence not under the researcher's direct and continuing control. For the academic public relations researcher, publication or sharing of the conclusions with the public is much more commonplace.

WHO OWNS THE DATA?

Finally, there is an ethical problem relating to the ownership of data and research. When you conduct research for a firm or client or organization, they typically own the data and the conclusions; that is, the data are proprietary (which may also explain why you rarely see research, for example, about public relations' role in increasing the corporate bottom line). You have been paid to get and interpret that data; it belongs to them. In some instances, however, the researcher may be allowed to use the data in other ways—such as an academic researcher, who might request that certain otherwise private data be used as part of a case study or for specific educational purposes. Such situations are rare and must be part of any contract between the organization and the researcher. Further, any specialized data compilations that alter the character of the data in any way, such as through statistical transformations or different weighting procedures, must be fully reported and, if necessary, you should be prepared to explain them later without expecting of remuneration (unless, of course, your contract provides for continued consultation).

SUMMARY

This chapter has explored the ethics involved in conducting research in general and research in public relations in particular. Several codes of professional ethical conduct were presented. The ethics of conducting public relations *research* were examined in detail, including the fair treatment of research participants, ensuring the confidentiality and anonymity of data, the correct reporting of data, and the question of subsequent data ownership. Perhaps the best way to become an ethical researcher, however, is to treat the entire process in an ethical and honest manner. Treat the research participant as you yourself would like to be treated. Treat the data gathered as if it were your own attitudes and behaviors. Treat the research report as though you were discussing findings about yourself.

REVIEW QUESTIONS

1. Discuss what it means when someone says that public relations is ethical or is not ethical.
2. Are ethical codes, as exemplified in the IPRA's Code of Athens, the PRSA's Code of Professional Ethics, and the ABC's Code of Ethics for Professional Communicators enforceable? How?
3. How does public relations differ from marketing or advertising in terms of ethical codes?
4. Discuss what it means to be an ethical researcher. What practices should be followed? Why?
5. What ethical constraints are placed on the public relations practitioner when she finds information or data that does not fit with a client's perceptions?

PRACTICE PROBLEM

You have been hired to establish the "communication climate" of a large corporation. In conducting your research you have had to make several promises to research participants to get them to participate in focus groups and surveys, one of which is that the results will be made available to its own employees by the company. Your research finds that there are several major problems that seem to arise from senior management's ability (or lack of ability) to communicate with its employees. Your report is made, you are not only paid your fee, but given a bonus for "quick and concise work invaluable to the company." You are reminded by letter a week or so later, however, that the information and report you prepared are viewed as "proprietary" by the company and you are instructed not to release any information, findings, or conclusions to the "public" (including both employees and the media) without the company's permission. A local media representative, after talking to employees at the company, phones you and asks you to (1) comment on the company's "communication climate" and (2) share at least a portion of the results of the research you conducted for the company. What do you do?

NOTES

1. There are more general treatments of ethics, but all are found in general communication research methods *textbooks*. A general treatment is found in Don W. Stacks and John E. Hocking, *Communication Research*, 2nd ed. (New York: Longman, 1999), who treat ethics in the first section of their book. Other texts relegate ethics to later chapters, some almost as afterthoughts. See James A. Anderson, *Communication Research: Issues and Methods* (New York: McGraw-Hill, 1987); Lawrence R. Frey, Carl H. Botan, Paul G. Friedman, and Gary L. Kreps, *Investigating Communication: An Introduction to Research Methods*, 2nd ed. (Englewood Cliffs, NJ: Prentice Hall, 1999); Michael Singletary, *Mass Communication Research: Contemporary Methods and Applications* (New York: Longman, 1994); Roger D. Wimmer and Joseph R. Dominick, *Mass Media Research: An Introduction*, 7th ed. (Belmont, CA: Wadsworth, 2000).

2. "The Page Philosophy," *Membership Directory 1999* (New York: Arthur W. Page Society, 1999).

3. Stanley Milgram, "Behavioral Study of Obedience," *Journal of Abnormal and Social Psychology*, 67(1963), 371–378; Stanley Milgram, *Obedience to Authority* (New York: Harper & Row, 1974).

4. C. Hanley, C. Banks, and P. G. Zimbardo, "Interpersonal Dynamics in a Simulated Prison," *International Journal of Criminology and Penology*, 1(1973), 69–97.

Informal Research Methodology

Part I laid the foundation for the study of public relations research. Part II builds upon that foundation by closely examining five research methods identified primarily as informal in nature. By informal we mean that the data gathered from these methods cannot be confidently interpreted more broadly but rather are specifically restricted to the situations where the data were gathered. Informal methodology, however, offers the researcher several important advantages. First, informal methods offer an in-depth understanding of how certain people or organizations think and operate. Second, informal methods provide an ability to understand fairly comprehensively how *specific members* of a population feel about questions of value, better enabling researchers to elaborate more fully on their findings for the larger population; in other words, the data may serve as useful exemplifiers. Third, informal methods often provide a richer context in which the findings of formal research can be better explained. And, fourth, informal methods are often preferred when conducting environmental scans or monitoring in regard to a specific public relations problem.

Chapter 4, on historical and secondary research methods, examines sources of information that report historical and critical analyses of communication events. Secondary sources may include databases, newspapers, and industry reports. Next, Chapter 5 examines the case study, which is the in-depth analysis of an individual, organization, or event that provides specific detail as to how a public relations problem was solved. Most public relations case studies follow the RACE model or ROPE model, which was discussed earlier and will be further detailed later (see Chapters 1 and 5).

Three methods of conducting research are examined in Chapter 6: first, the most specific, the interview, then a more general approach, the focus group, and finally the most general informal research method, participant-observation. Each method offers differing levels of researcher control, from high (the interview) to nonexistent (participant-observation). All three are important ways to gather data, but the participant-observation method is usually restricted to corporate communication problems and environmental scanning.

Finally, Chapter 7 examines content analysis. Content analysis is both an informal method of conducting research and a way to measure qualitative data. As such, content analysis serves as both a jumping-off point to formal research methods and a way to analyze data gathered by informal methods. Quite simply, content analysis breaks down the rich stream of informal data into countable categories based on a prescribed categorization system. By using content analysis we can "count higher than one."

Chapter 4

Historical and Secondary Research Methods

The most difficult segment of many research programs is not so much the collection and analysis of the data but rather the setting up, or beginning, of the research process. This is especially true when the research being undertaken aims at something new not previously a part of your earlier research projects for that client. In Chapter 2 we labeled this part of the research process "environmental scanning" or "environmental monitoring." This chapter investigates that part of the research process aimed at *systematically* searching out available research. The descriptor "systematically" is purposefully employed here. Random searches of databases, newspapers, and organizational archives are insufficient to provide you with the depth or breadth of the materials that are available. Thus, you must have some sort of *search strategy* in mind when beginning any research project. Further, you must have some idea of how you will *analyze* the information and data, since many of your searches will produce data that must be carefully sifted through, and compared and contrasted, to "mine" its rich content fully.

This chapter is divided into two sections. First, we examine the gathering of data and some basic tests for historical credibility and timeliness. Given the recent rapid growth in databases, professional periodicals, and professional archives, it is almost impossible to list all the information sources you will use specifically. Instead, general areas and strategies will be examined. Second, we look at some of the analytical tools available for examining the data gathered. Some of the analytical tools are simply logical extensions of your current knowledge and are quite simple; others may employ sophisticated statistical analyses that are beyond the scope of this book. In either case, to be an intelligent user of research, you must know at least something about each.

GATHERING SOURCES OF DATA

All research begins with the answering of questions of definition. Historical research is often the first step in answering definitional questions and is necessary when answering questions of fact (it will help you to establish baselines or benchmarks against which to measure program or campaign results). The major questions that all researchers have to answer at this stage of research, however, are very general. "Where do I begin?" is the first question. This stage is particularly difficult for novice public relations practitioners because they have not yet mastered the body of knowledge underlying public relations and related business fields. They do not yet have a ready familiarity with the people, sources, or strategies best employed when seeking out the data (typically in the form of documents) to be used in the analysis of the problem.

The second question stems from the first—"When do I *end* my search?" The answer to this question depends on whether practitioners are specializing in a particular area (e.g., governmental, corporate, environmental public relations) or whether they move from area to area, depending on the client. Regardless, sooner or later they must say, "Stop! I've found enough information for now." Ten or 20 years ago the stop decision was fairly simple—you read all that was available. Today, however, that decision is much more difficult since the Internet and access to company intranets provide a constant flow of information that could be monitored. It is a wonder that more public relations firms have not set up their own management information systems to identify and monitor the flow of information now available to the practitioner.

So, to answer the first question, where do you begin? The answer is found in the library. Libraries are at their simplest document depositories, but (to borrow from an automobile maker's advertising campaign) definitely they are "not your Dad's" libraries. Libraries are still depositories—they are where we find the accumulated knowledge of the ages—but they are no longer physically constrained. Many of the documents you most need can now be accessed electronically. Rather than going to "the library" and looking up in a card catalog system the books and periodicals you need, today from your desktop computer, you can readily access data bases, download information of interest by key words or phrases, and store selections or whole documents in your hard drive. The material being accessed, however, has not changed nearly so much as has the ease of access and the time it takes to access huge volumes of information. We now turn to the various libraries you will access, then to the documents themselves, and finally to access methods.

Libraries

There are a number of libraries you will use. A library in this instance is a *formal storage place that contains a variety of types of documents.* Libraries can be public, academic, specialized, institutional, or personal (see Table 4.1). Availability and accessibility to these depositories ranges from the general public to only those people the individual collector invites to peruse his or her collection. *Public libraries* were once

TABLE 4.1. Types of Libraries
and Examples of Each

Public
Library of Congress
State
Country

Academic
University
College
Junior college/community college

Specialized
(Also found in Academic)
Silver Anvil
CBS Evening News
Presidential
Association

Institutional
General Motors
IBM
Edelman

Personal
Individual researcher or practitioner

general depositories of books, encyclopedias, and periodicals; they now can access a large variety of documents and databases.

Academic libraries are typically associated with research and are often called "research libraries." The types of documents found may include widely available books and periodicals but also more arcane research journals (academic libraries are evaluated not so much on the number of documents they contain but rather on the quality of those documents for advancing basic knowledge of the discipline). Many mass communication colleges, schools, and departments have their own libraries specifically holding advertising, broadcasting, communication, film, journalism, and public relations research journals, databases, and industry-related periodicals. Academic libraries also contain specialized collections (Vanderbilt University, for example, has almost a complete video collection of the *CBS Evening News*). Access to most academic libraries is often restricted to students or faculty of that particular university. In any case, to check material out you must have permission of the institution involved.

Specialized libraries can be typed according to whether their holdings are specific to an industry or topic area. For instance, the Public Relations Society of America has its own library (the PRSA Professional Development Center) devoted to public relations practices and theory. While access to information is not free, the sliding scale of fees is based on the amount of information you are seeking. Most contemporary U.S. presidents have their own libraries—such as the Reagan Library and Nixon Library in California, the Carter Library in Georgia, and the Johnson Library in Texas—and access is generally free, but documents must be examined and either photocopied or scanned on location. Most trade associations have specialized library collections that are available for modest fees. In addition, some companies will, in conjunction with an association, house certain specialized industry-related collections. Ketchum Public Relations, for example, houses materials on all Silver Anvil public relations campaign award-winning campaigns in its library.

Institutional libraries are found in most companies. Access to company documents (other than their annual reports) is greatly restricted to those who work for the particular company and often on a "need to know" basis. A special type of institutional library now emerging is associated with various newsletter firms, such as *pr reporter* and *O'Dwyer's Newsletter*. Again, access to documents may be restricted to those with a need to know or for whom special permission has been granted.

Finally, there are the *personal libraries* of public relations practitioners and academics. Personal libraries are most likely to contain very specialized documentation focusing on the interests of the particular owner. Almost all academic researchers maintain private libraries that contain books, journals, articles, convention papers, and other documents that they have collected over the years. These are accessible only through permission of the holder. The same is true of practitioners, who often sell or donate their papers and documents to academic libraries upon retirement.

Sources of Information

In general, there are three types of sources of information. *Primary sources* are the actual documents—studies, books, reports, and articles—as written by the researchers themselves. Primary sources are what we are looking for when conducting a library or document search: we want to see the actual report (and the original set of analyses). A primary source, then, is much in the nature of a treasure trove, or the mother lode. However, it is often impossible to get to the primary source for a variety of reasons, including a lack of knowledge of the general area or, perhaps lack of physical access to the actual data. Therefore, we must sometimes rely on secondary sources. A *secondary source* is a report on the findings of the primary source. While not as authoritative as the primary source, the secondary source often provides a broad background and readily improves one's learning curve. Most textbooks are secondary sources; they report and summarize the primary sources. One potential disadvantage of secondary sources, however, lies in the biases of the author. Most people wittingly or unwittingly bias their reporting according to their own beliefs and attitudes; thus, they may fail to mention a particular study or research program because it does not coincide correctly with their evaluation criteria. A third type of source of information is the tertiary source. A *tertiary source* reports on or summarizes the secondary source's report on the primary report. Tertiary reports should be approached with caution, since authors' biases can be further compounded in such reports.

When conducting historical and secondary research, you should strive to obtain as many primary sources as possible. In the case of secondary research, actual use of the original data, not just summaries as reported, is critical. If a research problem concerns a particular area, it is best to first identify the parameters of that area and problem through secondary sources and then systematically obtain and evaluate each primary source. In getting directly to the bedrock data, you become an "expert" in that given area, able to discuss and evaluate from personal experience with the original reports.

Documents

In general, there are three basic types of documents: books, periodicals, and databases. There are other documents that provide important information but are unpublished or unavailable to the general public: professional "white" or position papers and nonprinted documents. We cover them in order of their depth of analysis.

Books

A *book* is an in-depth analysis of a particular subject. It sets forth a historical, critical analysis of the topic under study. As such, most books are somewhat dated even before they are published. They represent, however, the most complete analysis available on that topic and may present data, theory, or analysis—or all three. Books are generally of two types. The first is for use by the general public. In academia such books would be considered textbooks, introducing the reader to the vocabulary and body of knowledge in a given area. Other books intended for the general public may be classified as either introducing the reader to some basic fundamentals, such as leadership, motivation, or business, or, alternatively, the "self-help" book. The latter often takes a particular theoretical perspective (often found first in academia) and elaborates on it in day-to-day situations. The second major type of book is the advanced treatment of a particular subject. Found in both academia (as a graduate-level text, perhaps) and in the general public, this book moves the reader from the basic concepts to an advanced understanding of the topic.

Books are essential in gaining an understanding of what the research is to be about. They present historical perspective, provide analytical insights, and offer sometimes timely advice. Books, then, set the baseline against which all other documentation is evaluated.

Periodicals

Periodicals are documents that are published on a particular cycle. Periodicals may be yearly, monthly, quarterly, weekly, daily, and so forth. We can break periodicals down into four groups: magazines, journals, newsletters, and newspapers. The *magazine* can be further defined as general consumption (e.g., *Newsweek, People, Time*) or specific to a company or industry (e.g., annual reports, company magazines). In terms of coverage, the magazine does not normally offer in-depth analysis but instead focuses on a variety of topics of interest to the reader. The *annual report*, is a specialized type of magazine, a document that most public relations practitioners either help to write or use in their research of a particular company or industry. Magazines are usually published on a weekly or less frequent cycle and typically include a publication date, volume number, and issue number. Thus, a publication might be dated December 27, 2000, and designated as Volume 12, Number 52, for example. These numbers would tell the reader that the information contained is valid through late December, has been published for the past 12 years, and is published weekly (there being 52 weeks in the year).

Journals are periodicals that are published on specific topics. *National Geographic*, for instance, is actually a journal—it is the "journal of the National Geographic Society." Journals are usually produced by a professional association and help members to keep up with theory and research in that particular field, such as the *New England Journal of Medicine*. In public relations, the Public Relations Society of America's *Strategist* is that society's journal. There are specific, research-oriented journals in public relations, with the *Journal of Public Relations Research*, *Public Relations Review*, and *Public Relations Quarterly* among the more nationally and internationally recognized. Date, volume number, and issue number also identify journals.

Newsletters are produced by special-interest or research groups that present and sometimes test ideas and news of interest to their members and practitioners. Four newsletters that impact on public relations are *pr reporter*, *Tactics*, *PR News*, and *O'Dwyer's Newsletter*. All offer weekly analysis of industry trends and practices. There are a number of other newsletters now available to public relations practitioners (e.g., the *Ragan Report* and the Lukaszewski Group's *Executive Action*), but *pr reporter*, *PR News*, *O'Dwyer's Newsletter* and *Tactics* probably are the industry's mainstays. Of the four, *Tactics* is produced by the Public Relations Society of America on a monthly basis, while the others are produced by private organizations. Thus, *Tactics* most closely represents PRSA's interests, while the other three are more general in their approaches and points of view.

Finally, we have the *newspaper*. Newspapers can be divided into two classes, general public and industry-specific. They also are published on a particular cycle, usually daily, but may be weekday-only, weekly, bimonthly, or monthly. Further, general public newspapers range from national (e.g., *New York Times, Washington Post, Los Angeles Times*), to regional (e.g., *Atlanta Constitution, Chicago Tribune, Denver Post*), to state (e.g., *Detroit News/Free Press, Miami Herald, Charlotte Observer*), to local (e.g., *Fort Valley* (GA) *Leader-Tribune, Cheboygan* (MI) *News, Milwaukee Journal*). Industry-specific newspapers might include *PRWeek* and *Ad Age*.

Databases

Ten years ago you would not have seen databases covered in an analysis of public relations documents. The ways in which databases have rapidly evolved, both in terms of ease of access and thoroughness of content, have made their inclusion necessary. A *database* is a set of documents made available for retrieval via computer. The earliest database, HUMRO, was created by the U.S. government in the early 1970s as a way to distribute unpublished documents on the humanities to a large audience. Given a set of code words ("key words"), the database was searched and author-title citations were provided. Later short abstracts were added. At that time the major database employed by most researchers seeking documents was the bibliography (sometimes "annotated" with a sentence or two about each document). Today databases are so wide-ranging that it would be impossible to list them all (see Table 4.2 for a selective listing). It is a mistake to even compare the earliest databases, such as HUMRO, with today's much more complex and detailed databases. The early databases were simply listings of periodicals, publications, or sources by date, while today's databases often offer a great deal more.

Perhaps the most important databases for informal research are "LEXIS/NEXIS" and "FirstSearch." LEXIS/NEXIS searches across a variety of business, newspaper, and legal documents. It is updated

---

TABLE 4.2. Selected General Information Sources and Databases

ABI/Inform	IMS (marketing/advertising statistics)
Agricola	Legal Resource Index
AP News	LEXIS/NEXIS
Applied Science and Technology Index	Magazine Index
Art Index	Marquis Who's Who
Book Review Index	MEDLINE
Business Periodicals Index	PR Newswire
CENDATA (U.S. Bureau	PsychINFO
of the Census)	PTS Forecasts
CIS (Congressional Information	PTS Marketing and Advertising
Service)	Reference Service (MARS)
COMINDEX	SciSearch
Donnelley Demographics	Sociological Abstracts
Dow Jones News/Retrieval	State Action Reporter
Education Index	Thomas Register Online
Electronic Yellow Pages	UPI News
Encyclopedia of Associations	Vu/Text (Knight-Ridder Inc.
GPO Monthly Catalog (Government	newspapers)
Printing Office)	

daily and is probably the most potent of the document database search engines available. Its database includes foreign and domestic documents and provides citations, short abstracts, and entire articles or opinions. The service is expensive; depending on the options selected, it may cost over $1,000 per half-hour to search. FirstSearch replaced the *Reader's Guide to Periodical Literature*. It covers periodicals, is updated on a regular basis, and is available on a fee basis.

Other databases are industry-specific and often offered for a fee by associations or private research firms. Many public relations practitioners use databases such as PR Newswire, Businesswire, Delahaye MediaLink, Burrelle's Information Services, ABI/Inform, Disclsoure, Dow-Jones News retrieval System, Dun & Bradstreet Million Dollar Directory, and newspaper databases to access public relations-related information and documents. The U.S. government also has a database of "government publications" and governmental documents that can be accessed online at no charge.

A specialized database kept by PRSA is the "Body of Knowledge." Originally a print-only listing of research articles and documents that relate to public relations, the Body of Knowledge is a computer-assisted research database updated regularly by public relations educators and practitioners.

Unpublished Papers

A final type of document is the *unpublished paper*. Unpublished papers are often called "white papers" or "position papers" in business and "convention papers" in academia. You often find the former on a variety of web sites and institutional databases, while the latter are typically found in the ERIC (Educational Resources Information Center) database available through most universities, colleges, and increasingly in public libraries. Papers present positions or in-depth analysis of events, research, or other topics and might be considered typologically to be somewhere between academic papers that have been presented and sometimes have gone through a formal review process and the ideas or positions of a particular person or organization.

Search Strategies

As we have seen, there are many different types of documents that may serve your purposes. Approaching the document search can be an intimidating process. At one time it was fairly simple—you went to the library or the newspaper "morgue" and read through the citations or gained access to a bibliography on the topic of interest. Today it is much more complicated and reaches beyond the scope of this book. As an overview, consider the search strategy established by Ward and Hansen in *Search Strategies in Mass Communication* (see Figure 4.1).[1]

Searching begins by answering several questions that deal with definition. What are the questions, concepts, and areas under study? What sources are available? Are they informal sources (people you know, things you see daily, networks available to you), institutional sources (sources you can access through personal contacts, the Internet, and so forth), or library sources? Further, Ward and Hansen argue that other forms of research become part of the search mix— interviews, focus groups, surveys. And, finally, the search strategy must encompass some way of establishing the veracity of the documents[3] obtained. Since we have covered how to get access to documents, and we will be covering the formal and informal research in later chapters, we now turn to assess the documents found.

Assessing Documents

There are at least three critical ways to establish a document's veracity.[2] The first is through the document's *content*. You assess content by asking the following questions: does it deal with what you need, are interested in, or add anything new? A second way to assess veracity is through *authority*. Here your assessment is based on who produced the document (to include who wrote and who sponsored the writing). One way to establish authority is whether the document has undergone some sort of *peer review*. Peer review, which is found primarily in academic research journals, means that recognized experts have reviewed the material and have established its accuracy. Authority is a rather difficult thing to establish on the Internet because anyone can start up an Internet site or web page and "publish" whatever they want. Therefore, it is important that such Internet sites provide information about the site's sponsor and ways to contact the webmaster for more information regarding the site.

Finally, there are *critical standards* that should be met in any document:[3] (1) Are the main issues or points clearly identified? (2) Are the writer's underlying assumptions or arguments generally acceptable? (3) Is the evidence presented adequate, evaluated clearly, and supportive of the writer's conclusions? (4) Is there a bias and does the writer or publisher address that bias? And, (5) how well is the document written and/or edited? Although these may be subjective judgments, they are important in establishing not only a document's veracity but also its usability.

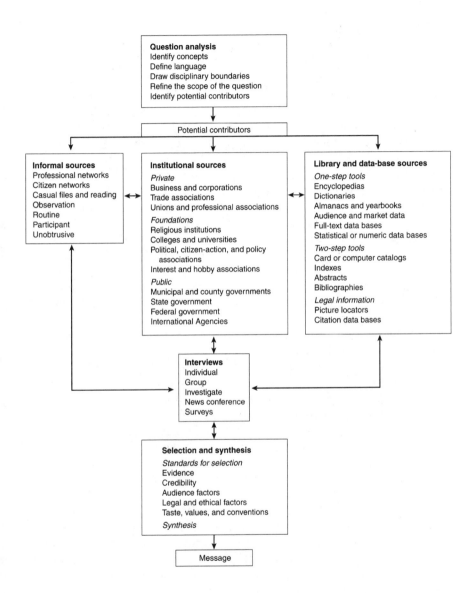

FIGURE 4.1. Documentary search strategy. From J. Ward and K. A. Hansen, *Search Strategies in Mass Communication*, 2nd ed. (New York: Longman, 1999). Reprinted with permission from the authors.

Search Engines

The Internet is a large and relatively uncharted area. To find websites of interest you must employ a special tool, a *search engine*. A search engine looks throughout the Internet for matches to your search criteria, which are words and phrases that are key to your topic. For instance, a search for "public relations" would produce a list of any Internet sites that included the words "public" and "relations." Therefore, you must either limit or extend your search through the use of *Boolean operators*—such words as "and," "or," or "not."

If you were interested in only "public relations," on most search engines you would put quotation marks around the phrase—otherwise you would get all the "hits" for both "public" and "relations," as well as "public relations." If you wanted a specialized aspect of public relations—say, public relations in the automobile industry—you would use "public relations" *and* "automobile," with the term "or" as a link between the two key words/phrases. This would give you all the locations for public relations and all the locations for automobile. Not a particularly efficient search. Using "and" instead of "or" would limit the search to just public relations and automobile.

What are the major search engines in use today? Although there are many, the major ones are Yahoo! (www.yahoo.com), AltaVista (www.altavista.com), Lycos (www.lycos.com), Google (www.google.com), excite (www.excite.com), and Direct Hit (www.directhit.com). Yahoo! and AltaVista are probably the most widely used search engines, covering a multitude of websites and newsgroups. Direct Hit ranks your search results according to what other people have selected as the most relevant and popular sites for your search request. Thus, you might use Yahoo! or AltaVista to "search the web" for general topics and then use Direct Hit to see how these topics rank in terms of use and popularity.

There are many specialized search engines, but often when listed they turn out to be commercial websites. Figure 4.2 shows the results of a Yahoo! search for the term "public relations search engines" (note the phrase has been enclosed in quotation marks). Among many other citations, the search engine found a website, RestaurantResults.com, that listed 10 public relations firms.

Obviously, search engine results must be evaluated carefully. Using the same search criteria for websites as for documents is an excellent way to begin testing for site veracity. In particular, look for a webmaster to whom you can turn. Sites with webmasters are generally serious undertakings, and the webmaster may be able to provide you with evidence of authority or credibility.

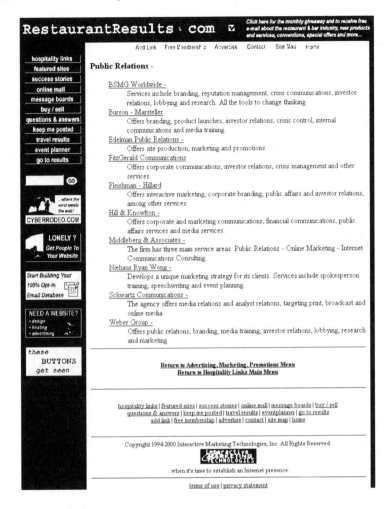

FIGURE 4.2. Results of Yahoo! search for "public relations search engines." Courtesy of CowboysCowgirls.com.

SECONDARY RESEARCH

Secondary research represents the analysis of findings already published. As part of your environmental scanning or monitoring task, secondary research analysis often is an important first step in determining whether earlier research still stands up to current standards and whether previously unavailable data can withstand further testing or even replication of existing testing. Secondary research can be conducted on both qualitative and quantitative data and analyzed specifically from a public relations perspective.

While there are certain obvious advantages to secondary research, there are also significant disadvantages. The major disadvantage lies in the fact that you have not collected the data yourself. You do not know exactly *how* it was gathered and whether it is *accurate*. You do not know if all the data were presented, or only that data of interest to the researcher or the particular company; you do not know if the data were "weighted" or "transformed" unless the report specifically provides that information.

The advantages gained through secondary research may be more than offset if the data are neither valid nor applicable to your particular research problem. Thus, you must carefully evaluate not only the data but also who designed the research study that gathered the data and how those data were gathered. Thus, much of what was discussed earlier applies here in terms of establishing the veracity of the data.

Sources of Data

In one of the better treatments of secondary research in general and public relations in particular, Brody and Stone break down secondary research sources into three types.[4]

Organizational Research

The first type is *organizational research*, which measures attitudes and opinions held by management and employees, customers, and shareholders. For instance, the organization may conduct yearly surveys of corporate culture—how managers and employees (for certain) but also customers and shareholders perceive the prevailing corporate culture. The late 1990s saw an increase of interest in establishing an organizational culture that lived up to the corporation's "mission, vision, and values." Access to such data provides a rich database from which to look for trends and problem areas.

Secondary research may be conducted on a variety of organizational data. Organizational research employs most major research methods, from interviews and surveys to focus groups and communication audits. A *communication audit* is a particularly intense method that combines attitude surveys, in-depth interviews, focus groups, and in many instances the keeping of journals that account for daily activities and thoughts. Other data may be "mined" in trying to understand the results of formal and informal research methods. For instance, data may be gathered from human resources that provide evidence of employee turnover, accidents on the job, and productivity levels; from accounting, financial data may provide evidence of periodic shifts in productivity and culture; from external communications, an examination of press releases and annual reports may provide information about long-term strategies. All these data may then be subjected to either statistical or logical analyses.

Industry Research

While organizational research focuses on a single company or organization, *industry research* looks at entire industries. Brody and Stone note that, although industry research comes from a variety of sources, it is obtained primarily from trade sources (e.g., newsletters, membership magazines, media releases of trade associations or groups, literature gathered at trade shows, meetings, or open houses, and industry-wide reports), governmental sources (e.g., government agencies such as the U.S. Census Bureau, Library of Congress, U.S. Government Printing Office, General Accounting Office, members of Congress), and third-party sources (e.g., customers, suppliers, competitors).

Stakeholder Research

Stakeholders are groups or people who are internal or external to the organization but who have common concerns or shared interests. Brody and Stone identify four such groups who may be approached for information concerning a public relations problem: prospective employees (sources include labor statistics, development agencies, chambers of commerce) and shareholders (sources include financial reports, stock reports, brokerages, and financial newsletters); government agencies (sources include the General Accounting Office and Government Printing Office, individual agencies' reports and testimony, and interviews with agency heads); and special-interest groups (sources include pamphlets and newsletters, speeches, reports published by special-interest groups, and analysis of media reporting on special interest group activities).

Data Analysis

Depending on the type of data gathered, secondary research uses almost all contemporary statistical analyses and logical testing. The major problem to be overcome in analyzing either qualitative or quantitative data, however, is whether the data gathered are comparable. This assumes, of course, that the data are valid in the first place. If the data being gathered come from one source and have been collected the same way over a period of time, then the data may be comparable and identified legitimate trends. If, however, the data are not comparable, then statistical tests are useless even if conducted correctly. The data still may be evaluated qualitatively, to see if particular outputs (e.g., press releases) were found. Such analyses may end up using content analysis (see Chapter 7) or case study methodology (see Chapter 5), but neither can be used to project to a larger group. Nor can the data be used to establish cause and effect. They simply describe.

Statistical testing can be very sophisticated. *Meta-analysis*, for instance, is a form of secondary analysis popular in academia that looks historically at how quantitative research findings can be evaluated regarding the effectiveness of a particular variable.[5] Let's say that you were interested in how particular types of press releases were preferred by particular industries. In conducting your documentary review you find that a number of studies have been conducted, studies that presented quantitative evidence of preference. By means of meta-analysis one could look at all the studies reported and venture conclusions about which press release types are preferred, if any, and by which industries.

SUMMARY

This chapter examined the first steps in any research program or campaign, finding the existing documents and sources and data that might help most in answering questions about definitions and facts. As public relations practitioners get better acquainted with a particular problem area—that is, specialize in a particular public relations area or function—they continually conduct historical/documentary research as a part of their environmental scanning or monitoring. They come to know the most significant and dependable information sources, and they access and read them daily. It is when a new or unexpected problem is faced that you must go back to square one and systematically evaluate old and new information sources.

Once a source has been identified, it may provide data already gathered. Rather than having to conduct new research, you can reanalyze that data via secondary research. In addition to providing insight into previous research, secondary research allows the researcher to answer different questions, relate one set of data to another, and in some instances provide baseline or benchmark data for future comparisons. Secondary research is a logical outcome of historical/ documentary research.

Both historical/documentary and secondary research are informal research methods. They do not provide evidence of current differences or definite relationships; rather, they offer evidence of potential differences and relationships and often serve to move from simple description to the prediction of the outcome for a particular variable. They cannot, however, be used to extend findings to a larger population; only formal research methods can accomplish that. Their importance, however, is found in the information provided, information that may be used in further informal analyses, such as in developing a case study or conducting a participative study. We turn next to the case study as an informal method that enables us to explore in rich detail "good" and "bad" public relations programs or campaigns.

REVIEW QUESTIONS

1. How would you go about finding information about global warming and its impact on "quality of life"?
2. Is there still a reason for going to the library? If so, which of the many different types of libraries do you think are the most important today?
3. Is the Internet a reliable source of information for public relations practitioners? Why or why not? What criteria would you use to establish an Internet site's reliability and validity?
4. Explain how you would undertake to conduct a research study based on secondary data analysis. Assume that the secondary data you are to evaluate consist of annual reports and that the subject of your analysis is stakeholder concerns about the particular industry that you are studying.
5. What is meant by the statement "depending on the type of data gathered, secondary research uses almost all contemporary statistical analyses and logical testing"? What are the potential problems associated with secondary data analysis?

PRACTICE PROBLEM

The local chamber of commerce wants to better understand how the public perceives local attractions. You have been hired to conduct a historical and secondary research of the local attractions. The attractions are located in a large metropolitan area, are accessible via local airports and railroad stations, as well as three major interstate highways (two of which intersect near one of the attractions). The area has four newspapers (one daily), three television stations (two affiliated with national networks), one cable company, and 16 radio stations (all formats covered). Further, the chamber of commerce has 20 years of surveys and focus groups available for review. How would you go about conducting the research project? What limitations would you emphasize in making your report?

NOTES

1. Jean Ward and Kathleen A. Hansen, *Search Strategies in Mass Communication*, 2nd ed. (New York: Longman, 1999).
2. Don W. Stacks and John E. Hocking, *Communication Research*, 2nd ed. (New York: Longman, 1998), pp. 90–92.
3. Mona McCormick, *The New York Times Guide to Reference Materials*, rev. ed. (New York: Times Books, 1985).
4. E. W. Brody and Gerald C. Stone, *Public Relations Research* (New York: Praeger, 1989), pp. 87–96.
5. Stacks and Hocking, p. 94.

Chapter 5

Case Studies

There is no more descriptive approach to public relations than the case study. A case study describes and analyzes a person, organization, or event in detail. How much detail the case entails depends on the problem and the data available to the researcher. Public relations case study are often seen as analogous to business case studies, such as those published by the Harvard School of Business. Along these lines, you might find the public relations case studies of Notre Dame's College of Business Administration particularly relevant. The case study is an obvious extension of secondary research, although when researching a case study other informal methods also may be employed, particularly interviewing and in some instances focus groups and participant-observation.

THE CASE STUDY DEFINED

Although case studies are highly valued in public relations, current public relations research books do not include them as methods. This may be because the focus of public relations research over the past decade has been on social science method, or formal research methodology. *Case studies*, as noted above, are *in-depth studies of particular people, organizations, events, or even processes*. They provide a richly detailed and complete understanding of the case under study. Case studies are found in most *applied* disciplines, from business to law to advertising to medicine to public relations. They offer insight into good and bad practice. A case study also helps us to understand theory, but theory as applied to specific situations. As such, a case study represents what Earl Babbie calls *grounded theory*.[1] Grounded theory seeks to understand social phenomena based on the patterns, themes, and common categories found in daily interaction. Grounded theory, then, attempts to explain everyday activity and may result in theory based in practice, not abstract relationships between concepts and constructs.

Advantages and Disadvantages

An obvious advantage of the case study method is that what is being studied has already occurred. The case study looks back in an attempt to explain through the use of direct observation, participatory informal research, and secondary research what and why something occurred and, in the case of public relations, how that outcome was managed. The case study, then, provides detail only found in hindsight and presents it in such a way as to establish what strategies worked and why. Thus, the case study in public relations can examine the way the problem was stated and the initial research gathering stages based on environmental scanning and monitoring; the strategic communication planning based on stated objectives; the communications themselves, the actual outputs; and the evaluation of the entire program or campaign. Furthermore, case studies can be used to evaluate policy, something that the formal research method is not very good at.

Case studies are not, however, limited to the study of campaigns, although the vast majority of cases published do study campaigns as exemplars of good or bad public relations. Indeed, the Silver Anvil is awarded annually by the Public Relations Society of America to the best public relations campaigns as demonstrated through the case study method in public relations. Case studies can look at the impact of particular individuals and organizations on particular industries. Such cases might examine in detail Edward Bernay's impact on public relations practice or how the "Committee on Public Information," often called the Creel Committee, influenced contemporary public relations practice in the United States. The goal of most case studies, then, is to describe and provide examples. A secondary goal, at least in public relations, is to provide a grounded theory of how public relations works, one that can then be tested by formal research methods.

If the case study has a major disadvantage, it is its inability to generalize in its findings. An important distinction between informal and formal research is the ability of the latter to project findings to larger populations. The case study, because it is an in-depth analysis of a particular phenomenon, cannot do this. For example, a case study of an IBM East Coast plant's culture cannot be generalized to one of its West Coast plants. The two plants, although operating under the same company rules and structures, are surprisingly different. If, on the other hand, the case study examined IBM's approach to corporate culture in general, then you might look at both coasts as examples of where the cultural approach worked and why. In too many instances a case study is used not as an example from which to help find communication strategies that may be adapted to a particular problem but instead as a solution to the *current* problem and not as a guide to alleviating the uniqueness of the problem.

Quite simply, a case study provides examples of what worked or did not work in a very specific instance. Obviously, times change and what worked in one case may still work in another, but probably only with major revisions determined by the unique circumstances.

THE CASE STUDY IN PUBLIC RELATIONS

Even though the case study is an informal research method, still it should be approached systematically. Most public relations case studies follow a ROPE or RACE outline (see Chapter 2); that is, they systematically examine each stage of a public relations campaign, from initial statement of the problem through final evaluation. Some case studies are less linear in nature and include a feedback phase. Such an approach implies that case studies are but a snapshot of public relations, especially when public relations is approached as a proactive process that actively seeks out and identifies potential problems and opportunities.

Three Approaches to the Case Study

A review of public relations cases published in textbooks, research journals, and professional archives suggests that the public relations case study can be approached in at least three ways. The first is *linear* and suggests that the case is a unique entity unto itself. That is, the case demonstrates good or bad public relations practices (usually good) that are time- and space-dependent, thus taking on a specific historical perspective. The second is *process-oriented* and suggests that the case is but a snapshot of the larger public relations process. Here the case is seen as representative of a process of public relations and that the case may provide insight into similar situations and solutions. The third ap-

proach is *grounded* somewhere between the first two, taking on a formal structure—such as the MBO or programmed approach—but also
indicating process.

The Linear Case Study

Probably the best-known case study approach is associated with Jerry
A. Hendrix (see Table 5.1).[2] Hendrix's ROPE (Research, Objectives,
Programming, Evaluation) approach is *linear* and begins with the research background on the client or organization, the case is defined as
either a problem or an opportunity, and the relevant publics are specifically targeted. It then moves to an analysis of the research objectives,
defining them as either impact objectives (informational, attitudinal,
and behavioral) or output objectives (distribution or execution). Next,
the actual campaign planning and execution are examined in detail.
And, finally, the case is evaluated based on the achievement of both
impact and output objectives. This approach suggests that each case is
independent of all other cases and provides a historical case study perspective.

Process Case Study

Allen H. Center and Patrick Jackson suggest a similar process in build-
ing a case study.[3] They begin with "fact-finding and data-gathering" to
define and clearly state the specific problem or opportunity. Second,
they evaluate the "planning and programming to devise and package
a [public relations] strategy." Third, the actions and communications
employed to execute the campaign strategy are examined. And, finally, the results are evaluated, assessed, and feedback provided as to
whether or not the campaign in whole or part has been successful and
whether to continue it as is, refine it and continue, or discontinue it.
Unlike Hendrix, Center and Jackson see public relations as always an
ongoing process (see Figure 5.1), and their case analyses reflect that approach.

The Grounded Case Study

A third way to approach the case study is to ground the process
through some systematic process that implies process but follows a
specific form, such as an MBO outline or program plan (see Chapter 2).
In this approach you would first research and define the situation and
the problem. Second, you would list and evaluate the objectives. Third,
you would examine the target public(s). Fourth, you would present

TABLE 5.1. Hendrix's ROPE Outline

R $\rightarrow$ O $\rightarrow$ P $\rightarrow$ E

Outline of the public relations process

I. Research
   A. Client/organization: background data about your client or organization—its personnel, financial status, reputation, past and present PR practices, PR strengths and weaknesses, opportunities
   B. Opportunity/problem: proactive or reactive PR program; long-range or short-range campaign
   C. Audiences (publics): identification of key groups to be targeted for communication
      1. Desired research data: each targeted audience's level of information about your client/organization; image and other relevant attitudes held about your client/organization and its products or services; audience behaviors relevant to your client/organization; demographics, media habits, and media-use levels of each targeted audience.
      2. Research procedures: nonquantitative and quantitative

II. Objectives
   A. Impact objectives
      1. Informational objectives: message exposure, comprehension, retention
      2. Attitudinal objectives: formation of new attitudes, reinforcement of existing attitudes, change in existing attitudes
      3. Behavioral objectives: creation of new behavior; reinforcement of existing behavior; change in existing behavior
   B. Output objectives: distribution or execution of uncontrolled or controlled media

III. Programming—planning and execution of:
   A. Theme (if applicable) and message(s)
   B. Action or special event(s)
   C. Uncontrolled media: news releases, feature stories, photos; controlled media: print, audiovisual, interpersonal communication, PR advertising
   D. Effective communication using principles of: source credibility, salient information, effective nonverbal and verbal cues, two-way communication, opinion leaders, group influences, selective exposure, and audience participation

IV. Evaluation—ongoing monitoring and final assessment of:
   A. Impact objectives
      1. Informational objectives: measured by publicity placement, surveys
      2. Attitudinal objectives: measured by attitude surveys
      3. Behavioral objectives: measured by surveys and observation of behaviors
   B. Output objectives: measured quantitatively by simply counting the actual output.

Note. From J. A. Hendrix, *Public Relations Cases*, 4th ed. (Belmont, CA: Wadsworth, 1998). Reprinted with permission from Wadsworth, an imprint of the Wadsworth Group, a division of Thomson Learning.

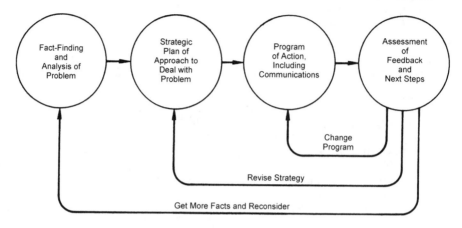

FIGURE 5.1. Center and Jackson's approach. A. H. Center and P. Jackson, *Public Relations Practices: Managerial Case Studies and Problems*, 5th ed. (Upper Saddle River, NJ: Prentice Hall, 1995). Reprinted with permission from Pearson Education, Inc.

and examine the strategies that were to be employed. Fifth, you would spell out the tactics to be employed. Sixth, you would set up the timeline or calendar for the campaign. Seventh, you would provide the campaign or program budget. And, eighth, you would evaluate the campaign by demonstrating how the strategy and tactics yielded measurable outcomes.

Answering Research Questions

The case study allows the researcher to systematically answer all four of the basic research questions that public relations researchers ask.

Questions of Definition

The process of researching the problem or opportunity and the situation requires both environmental scanning and monitoring. Thus, the public relations researcher employs historical/documentary research in an attempt to see what variables may be influencing or may influence the problem, opportunity, or situation. This basic research provides a basis for not only defining those variables but also operationally defining them according to the problem, opportunity, or situation. Questions of definition also provide clues to existing research that may be accessible and may help us to better understand what the problem, opportunity, or situation is.

Questions of Fact

In the case study questions of fact are those that have been tested and found to impact on the problem, opportunity, or situation. Case studies report in retrospect what was found, not what might be found to differ. Thus, questions of fact serve as a guiding force that may be later evaluated as to their appropriateness or the way they were correctly or incorrectly interpreted. Case studies often look at the existing data presented in the campaign; thus, they may actually amount to secondary research analyses.

Questions of Value

The case study, as an informal, basically qualitative method, allows the researcher to say how well the case was handled. In retrospect you can evaluate how well campaign objectives were stated and whether they led to strategies and planning that were easily understood and obtainable. At this stage of the research, you can say whether the outcomes were clearly operationalized and how well they were measured throughout the campaign or program. The actual outputs—messages—can be evaluated as to their appropriateness and effectiveness based on subjective measures of liking, value, artistry, and the like. (Formal research does not address appropriateness, only whether the messages worked and how well they worked.) Thus, the case study provides a richness of understanding not available in other, formal methods.

Questions of Policy

Of all the research methods examined in this book, only the case study allows you to answer questions of policy. Why? Because you have the advantage of hindsight. Were the goals met in a way that best suited the problem, opportunity, or situation? Or, stated differently, were the client's needs met by the campaign that was conducted? And, if so, how well and where was the strategy on-center or off-base? An excellent example is found in Hill and Knowlton's campaign for the Citizens for a Free Kuwait. It turned out that Hill and Knowlton's client was the royal Kuwaiti family and the Citizens for a Free Kuwait was a front group. In testimony before Congress it was alleged that Iraqi soldiers had removed babies from incubators and left them to die on the ground. The testifying witness ("Nayriah," a 15-year-old girl) was later identified as the daughter of the Kuwaiti Ambassador's daughter then living in Washington, DC. Should they have taken on the client and, more importantly, should they have misled the American people and Congress? Clearly, questions of ethics provide compelling case studies.

Case studies, then, are clearly in the unique position of providing answers to the four basic research questions that all public relations practitioners ask. They do so, however, after the fact and in retrospect. Thus, their explanatory power is found in understanding what worked or did not work through description. In many instances the case study provides valuable insight into similar problems. In other situations the case study may be the first step in forming a theoretical position on public relations strategy and planning, one that can be tested in the field or in the laboratory.

CONDUCTING THE CASE STUDY

The case study is basically an historical review of a public relations campaign, the analysis of a situation and how it was handled, or an examination of someone or some company that influenced public relations. As such, it generally relies on (1) documents that were used to plan and execute the campaign or manage the situation or the thoughts of the individual or company, (2) secondary research on data provided or obtained that relate to the case, (3) interviews with participants when possible, and (4) sometimes actual participation in the situation itself. Because there are similar underlying elements in any case study, regardless of approach, our examination of how to conduct a case study will proceed in a somewhat linear manner: statement of the problem, research methods and the research process used in preparing the case, the case topic's stated objectives, the actual strategy and how it was carried out, and evaluation of how the problem, opportunity, or situation was handled.

Stating and Defining the Problem

Each case study begins with a formal introduction that defines and states the problem, opportunity, or situation. What, for instance, prompted the communication campaign? Was it anticipated (proactive public relations) or unanticipated (reactive public relations)? In the case of the latter, why was it not anticipated? Where were the blind spots? Where it was anticipated, how was it anticipated? Each requires that the problem, opportunity, or situation and the variables that have led up to its occurrence be carefully and completely defined.

An example might be a case study of the travel and tourism industry, specifically one airline's campaign to become the major carrier in a particular market.[4] What led up to the campaign? In this case the airline, American Airlines (AA), was expanding into Central and South America, a new market, by purchasing the routes once flown by Eastern Airlines (now defunct). The opportunity was to expand into a new market; the problem was how to do so without alienating current passengers and while also attracting new passengers. The situation thus provided an opportunity to expand American's market, but it had to overcome the problems of differing cultures and the previous airline. Because Eastern had been in such dire financial straits, the purchase of the routes had been widely anticipated. As such, the case study details the successful implementation of a campaign that led to full airplanes and also the acceptance of the American Airlines corporate culture by former Eastern employees.

Research

The research phase began with a review of all published accounts of the airlines in question. This historical review looked at why Eastern Airlines was unable to maintain its routes as well as why the American Airlines felt it could maintain and expand its service to Latin and South America. Further, it helped to better understand American Airlines's position in the travel industry and the airline industry in particular. The documents examined came from a variety of sources. Many came from a LEXIS/NEXIS search of American Airlines in both the English and Spanish language media (LEXIS/NEXIS contains foreign as well as American media). Others came from American Airlines itself: media releases, annual reports, and internal memoranda made available to the researchers. A qualitative secondary research was undertaken of all the documents. Further, interviews with American Airlines management were conducted at several sites, including American Airlines headquarters in Dallas, its Latin American hub in Miami and in the major cities American was to begin serving or had served in the region (Mexico City had been serviced by American for over 50 years, offering the first penetration into the "Latin" market). Finally, the researchers were allowed to participate in one of the "familiarizing" sessions American set up with Latin/South American media in Miami.

Research was also undertaken on the primary, secondary, and intervening publics that the campaign would target. The primary publics were business passengers and stockholders. Secondary publics included all American Airlines employees, from management to pilots to janitors, and the leisure travel passenger. Perhaps most important, however, were the intervening publics: national and local politicians, national and local media, the military, and regional airlines who might feel an economic pinch from American's penetration into the region.

Objectives

Once the research has been conducted, both goals and objectives must be identified and stated. Goals are the general results that the campaign seeks to attain. Objectives are specific and fall into a number of classes, but are dependent on the definition of the problem (see Chapter 2).

In the American Airlines case, the goal was to successfully penetrate the Latin/South American travel market and acclimate its new employees to American's corporate culture (referred to as "The American Way"). A second goal was to become more closely identified with the local country's culture and create a greater sense of community. Specific informational objectives were to publicize American's entry into the new market(s), to get the business traveler to consider American for travel between major Latin/South American airports, and to change the perception of American as a regional to an international airline (through the use of both the Dallas and Miami hubs). The attitudinal or motivational objectives were to change the perception of American Airlines from a North American ("gringo") company to one that accepted and participated in local culture, to make business travelers (and leisure travelers whenever possible) think positively of American Airlines when they thought of travel, and to create "The American Way" attitude among all employees. Finally, the behavioral outcomes were to open new routes within a certain time frame and to increase the company's market share in the travel market.

Communication Strategy

In the next phase of the case study, the communication strategy that was planned and employed is presented and the tactics employed as outputs are identified and discussed. In this phase examples should be provided that show how the planned strategy was actually executed. Here interviews with the people who created the outputs often provide extra data that further explain why certain tactics were preferred over others or why one tactic was chosen for one public and another for a second public. At this phase any themes or overarching messages are identified and their use traced through the actual campaign or program.

In the American Airlines case the strategy could be broken into separate activities. First, American's top management visited each of the new route destinations and met with employees (former Eastern employees were retained or hired back as much as possible) and national and local government officials and the military (the military often controls much of what happened in the markets American was entering, so excluding them from the campaign could have been a serious mistake). Second, opinion leaders—national and local officials and media representatives—were brought to Dallas and Miami for "familiarizing" with "The American Way" and to see how their markets were being integrated into the larger American route structure. The "fam" trips also provided participants greater understanding of how American operated and resulted in numerous articles being written in local and national media about business and leisure travel. Third, American offered to sponsor local festivals and special events, using local employees as the contact points (they, then, became an intervening public). Fourth, local employees were provided orientation sessions on "The American Way."

Evaluation

Finally, the campaign must be evaluated. How well did it do? Did it meet its goals? Which objectives were met and how were they measured? How were the results used?

In the American Airlines case the goal of moving into the market rapidly was met and, based on confirmed reservations and actual travel statistics, American became the dominant carrier in both Latin and South America for the business traveler and made inroads into the regional leisure travel market. Second, based on an analysis of local and national coverage of both American Airlines and the travel industry in general, American was capably portrayed as a partner in the local community. Third, based on corporate research, the new employees largely adopted American's corporate culture, "The American Way," as their own work ethic and expressed preference for American's values, vision, and mission.

SUMMARY

Although the case study as an informal research method is found throughout public relations education and practice, very little explanation of the case study method appears in the literature. The case study provides a richness of data and understanding that is not available through other methods. The case study's major advantage is the ability to explain in hindsight what and how well the public relations campaign or program was done. Case studies can run hundreds of pages and should utilize data from historical/documentary research, interviews, and existing quantitative data. Finally, the case study, when approached from a grounded perspective, may actually result in new theory, theory grounded not in conceptual and abstract associations but in actual practice. The case study does have a significant disadvantage in that it *cannot be generalized* to other problems, situations, and opportunities with any degree of validity or reliability. This limitation is overcome, however, when case studies are used as examples of how good or bad public relations has been practiced.

REVIEW QUESTIONS

1. What is a case study, and how does it help public relations practitioners understand public relations problems?

2. Can a *good* case study be used to generalize to a similar problem, or is the case study limited to an understanding of a specific concern or problem that could be used to develop communication strategies? Why?

3. Differentiate between the three different types of case studies found in public relations.

4. Is the process by which one goes about conducting a public relations case study any different from other methods, formal or informal? Why or why not?

5. Suppose you have conducted a case study on the 2000 presidential election. What limitations are placed on your interpretations of the data you gathered and the logic you used in creating the case?

PRACTICE PROBLEM

In conducting research for a financial client you have come upon a case study conducted by a public relations educator that examined how a national company with a problem similar to your client's dealt with the negative publicity associated with the arrest and conviction of a bank's senior vice president for stealing several million dollars from trust funds. The case study suggests that there are three different ways to reduce negative publicity, each taking a different tack with a different target audience. Your client also has seen the case and wants you to come up with a plan of action based on the case for them. They want no other research to be conducted, insisting that the case "neatly lays out all the problems and the solutions we need." How would you explain where the case study fits into your proposed research campaign? What would you say are the advantages offered by the case study and what are its limitations in regard to your client's problem?

NOTES

1. Earl Babbie, *The Practice of Social Research*, 9th ed. (Belmont, CA: Wadsworth, 2001), pp. 285–286.
2. Jerry A. Hendrix, *Public Relations Cases*, 4th ed. (Belmont, CA: Wadsworth, 1998), pp. 43–44.
3. Allen H. Center and Patrick Jackson, *Public Relations Practices: Managerial Case Studies and Problems*, 5th ed. (Upper Saddle River, NJ: Prentice Hall, 1995).
4. The examples provided here are found in Marie Fernandez, "American Airlines and the Triumph of the Latin American Market: An Integrated Marketing Communications Approach," master's thesis, University of Miami, 1997; and Don W. Stacks, "A Look at Tourism Through a Multi-Dimensional Model of Public Relations," *World Futures, 57* (2001), 189–201.

Chapter 6

Informal Methods
of Observing People

Informal research often involves dealing with people and observing their reactions and statements in response to some stimulus. That stimulus may be something in the environment over which you have no control; something used to get a reaction from a group of people, over which you have limited control; or something used to get a reaction from an individual, where you maintain a fairly high degree of control. As Stacks and Hocking point out, informal methods of research can be divided into three areas, differentiated by the amount of control you have over the research situation and by the number of people you are observing.[1]

Public relations research often entails employing several research methods. As discussed in Part I, the best approach to any problem, opportunity, or situation is to triangulate both informal and formal methods. The same holds true *within* informal methodologies. Because of the high costs associated with in-depth interviews, practitioners are increasingly resorting to focus groups to obtain informal participative data from their publics. While focus groups may be less expensive to run, it is still important to obtain information from key stockholders, shareholders, and gatekeepers; therefore, the in-depth interview is still an important method. Finally, participant-observation is underemployed in public relations. Understanding everyday behavior and deviations from that behavior provides an important advantage, especially for practitioners who practice proactive public relations. (True participant-observation research is also very costly, both in terms of time and money; however, over a period of time the method offers you a valuable informal way of gathering data.)

This chapter introduces the first research methods that involve direct interaction between researchers and other people. We begin by looking at the most controlled of situations, where a researcher sits with another individual and asks carefully crafted questions that often provide the lead for follow-up questions, that is, the *in-depth interview*. We then move from one-on-one interviews to what has been described as "group interviews," the *focus group*. Finally, we look at an informal method that most corporate public relations practitioners should engage in daily but one that offers only limited, if any, control and puts you in a situation where you may be a part of the research situation or environment, namely, *participant-observation*.

There is one more quality that differentiates between in-depth interviewing and focus groups and the participant-observation method. The first two methods rely on *systematic observation*, where the researcher carefully constructs questions in the form of a discussion guide or interview schedule, to include probing questions where necessary, based on historical/documentary research. The last, participant-observation, is not done systematically but *participatively;* in participant-observation you as the researcher are part of the process you are observing; you influence and are influenced by the daily activities in which you are participating. As with the case study, the participant-observation method is *grounded research*—that is, it is based in everyday activity.

Our systematic examination of informal participative methods moves from the most controlled to the least. Thus, we begin by looking at the in-depth interview, then the focus group, and finally participant-observation.

IN-DEPTH INTERVIEWS

An in-depth interview differs significantly from what most people think of when they hear the word "interview." An interview is a fairly short questionnaire that allows for both closed (e.g., yes/no) and open (e.g., "What do you think about . . . ?") responses about some topic of interest (i.e., the "interview" is typically associated with survey research). *An in-depth interview is much longer, follows a schedule of questions, and is a method in and of itself.* In-depth interviews are best used when answering questions of definition, value, and policy.

Advantages and Disadvantages

The in-depth interview is usually conducted when you have identified one or more people whose knowledge or participation in an event will shed significant light on whatever topic or problem is of interest. The in-depth interview, like all informal research methods, provides rich detail and the ability to understand what the individual being interviewed really thinks about something.

As a method, in-depth interviewing's major advantages are twofold. First, it allows the interviewer to get an understanding of not only the problem being researched but also the person being interviewed. Second, it allows for introspection on the part of the interviewee and is still controlled by the interviewer. Perhaps the best examples of in-depth interviews are found in the one-on-one type of interviewing that television interviewer Barbara Walters has employed. What differentiates public relations in-depth interviews, however, is not an emphasis on personality (unless, of course, you are writing about a certain individual within the corporation for publication) but rather on perspectives on a particular problem.

The major disadvantages to in-depth interviewing include the high costs and heavy time commitments, difficulties in gaining access to the interviewee, and the vast amount of historical/documentary research necessary to conduct a *good* in-depth interview. Additionally, the method does not allow for generalizability to larger populations.

Costs and Time

In-depth interviews are extremely costly, both in terms of monetary outlays and time expended. Because you get much better insight into the interviewee if you conduct the interview within his or her environment, costs associated with travel must also be factored in. In dealing with an international public relations problem you may have to travel to some of the most expensive cities or to some of the most difficult places in the world. In addition to travel costs, there is the possibility that you may actually have to pay interviewees for their time. Finally, there are costs associated with the transcription of interview notes or recordings. Time is also a major disadvantage. In the actual time it takes to interview one individual in depth (a minimum of one hour and most likely several hours will be dedicated to the interview itself), you could have conducted between 5 and 15 telephone interviews or 10 to 30 poll-type interviews. Factor in the time it takes to get to the interview location and you can see why time becomes a major disadvantage.

Background Research

Determining whom to interview and what questions to ask is a daunting task in many instances. Part of the problem may be simply in correctly identifying the key players or decision makers. Environmental scanning and monitoring may provide clues as to who should be interviewed, but you also need to conduct documentary research into others important to the problem. Background research is important because the in-depth interview may take strange and surprising turns based on how the interviewee responds to set questions, and alternative lines of questioning must be in the interviewer's mind. Many would-be in-depth interviewers fail at their task when they get answers they were totally unprepared for and, as a consequence, significant lines of questioning are missed.

Limited Access to the Interviewee

Difficulties in gaining access to the interviewee are also a disadvantage. Identifying the significant players is difficult in many instances. Getting access to the interviewees after they have been identified can prove problematic, since most important figures are unwilling to give up the hours (even occasionally days) it may take to conduct the actual in-depth interviews. Further, as many novice interviewers may discover, interviewees often cut short interviews in which they feel that the interviewer is asking obvious questions or clearly demonstrates insufficient preparation or insufficient knowledge about the problem, the interviewee, or both.

Conducting the In-Depth Interview

Assuming that you have done your preparatory homework carefully and have also correctly identified those who need most to be interviewed, how is the interview accomplished? An in-depth interview requires three steps: setting the location, creating the interview schedule, and analyzing the data.

Location

Where the in-depth interview is conducted is important. In the best of all worlds, the interview should be conducted at the interviewee's office or home. This provides a certain comfort zone for the interviewee and provides insight into his or her personality. The nonverbal elements of an in-depth interview are often overlooked, but how interviewees decorate an office or house, the number of "filters" they employ to keep others away (secretaries, lack of a phone or computer, and the like), the "trappings" displayed (such as certificates, photographs, trophies) tell you much about the person you are interviewing. These nonverbal elements often provide clues about similar interests that can be used to establish a bond between interviewer and interviewee.

Interviews are often conducted in "neutral" locations. If the location is "on-sight," is on the interviewee's property, you can still gain insight into the individual. Many times, however, interviews are conducted in hotel rooms or meeting rooms. Such neutral locations may make the interviewee feel less threatened, but do not provide you much information about the "real" person. *The key, then, is to conduct the in-depth interview at the interviewee's location.*

Interview Schedule

As noted earlier, in-depth interviewers do not use questionnaires, relying instead on an *interview schedule*. The interview schedule is not a time schedule but a list of questions that drive the interview (see Figure 6.1 for an example). Generally, in-depth interviews are conducted via an interview schedule with few close-ended questions prepared, and those questions are of one of two types, funnel or topical.

A *funnel question* moves the interview from one particular question to the next based on the response to the funnel question. Sometimes the funnel question takes the interview from the general to the specific, seeking a basic understanding of what the interviewee knows about the problem or situation or opportunity. In other instances the funnel question serves to move from one set of prepared questions (*topical questions*) to another. For instance, a funnel question may ask, "Were you on the scene when X-problem occurred?" If the interviewee responds affirmatively, the interview might move to what the interviewee saw, thought, and what his actions were and the later implications or ramifications (all *topical questions*). If he answered negatively, the interview might move to what the interviewee heard or thought and what he believed the actions and implications were.

An important element of in-depth interviewing is the *probe question*. The probe question seeks greater understanding of responses to funnel or topical questions. A probe question might be, "And what did you feel after that?" or "Why do you believe this occurred?" or "Can you think of any other things that may have occurred?" The probe question takes the interview into different areas and often provides extremely rich information.

Hello, my name is _____ and I'm here as part of a study that is looking at XYZ's stakeholder base. I'd like to ask you a few questions dealing with your perception of XYZ, both in terms of your personal view and how you think others view the company. XYZ has underwritten this study and has given your name as an influential stakeholder. Let me assure you that your name will not be used in the final report without your permission and that your anonymity will be maintained at all times. Would you mind if I use a tape recorder for this session? If not, I'll rely on handwritten notes. As an incentive for participation, I'll send you an executive summary of the results of the study. Can we begin?

1. First, tell me a little about yourself. What do you think it is that made you what you are today? How does this compare with others whom you consider to be your peers?

2. What brought you to XYZ? What is it about XYZ that first attracted you to it?

3. Why do you think that XYZ is placed where it is in the market? Does it have a special niche that it has taken advantage of?

4. Peters and Waterman suggest that niche corporations and companies often fail because they cannot move out of the niche that they created for themselves. Do you think that XYZ might fall into such a trap?

5. There has been a lot of media coverage about XYZ's newest acquisitions. How would you evaluate that coverage? Is it what you think XYZ needs at this time?

6. If you had to describe XYZ to a potential customer, what would you say? What adjectives best describe the company?

7. I know that XYZ's senior management thinks highly of you; what is your opinion of them? Where are they on target? Off target? If there were to be a change in senior management, what would it do to your evaluation of the company?

8. Finally, think ahead a few years. Where do you think XYZ will be in, say, five years? Ten years? Will it survive the decade?

Thank you. You've been most helpful. My next step will be to transcribe our conversation. Would you mind looking it over after transcription for errors? If you want to elaborate on your comments, that would be fine. I'll send you a copy of the executive summary as soon as it is ready. Thanks again for your time and trouble.

FIGURE 6.1. Sample of an in-depth interview schedule.

The interview schedule provides you with the control necessary to direct the interview. It is extremely important that you direct the interview and not let the interviewee conduct a "self-interview." Inexperienced interviewers, especially when interviewing people they respect and admire, often will let the interviewee control the interview, leading to a one-sided and often superficial interview. Keeping to the schedule helps to reduce this problem.

Analysis

The third step in the in-depth interview is to analyze the data gathered. Since in-depth interviews often take hours to complete, it is best to *record* the entire interview. If you plan to record the session, you must first get the interviewee's permission (and it is best if you can get them to sign a consent agreement or at least indicate on tape that they agree to mechanical recording; many states require that an individual be told they are being recorded, if not the individual doing the recording can be taken to court—as Linda Tripp found out when she unobtrusively recorded her conversations with Monica Lewinsky). If the interviewee will not agree to be recorded, you must rely on handwritten notes. Either way, the notes or recordings must be transcribed in order to conduct any formal analysis. Formal analyses can be conducted qualitatively or quantitatively.

Qualitative analyses rely on the background data you gathered prior to the interview and are subjective in nature, often requiring the subjective evaluation of not only what was said but also *how* it was said. Experienced interviewers sit down immediately after the interview session and record their initial impressions. Was the interviewer uncomfortable with some questions? Was there any deception in the answers? What nonverbal behaviors were observed? What about the interviewee's physical surroundings—were there certain things that helped to understand him or her better?) *Quantitative analyses* examine the data and reduce them to numbers wherever possible, usually also employing content analysis (covered in Chapter 7). For example, you might count the number of times allusions to X occurred or perhaps the number of times the interviewee hedged in answering the questions.

A final part of the analysis is to identify significant responses to questions to be cited in the final report. These quotes provide further understanding and clarification about the problem, opportunity, or solution, as seen by the interviewees. Often those interviewed will see things differently, and direct quotations enable you to establish how such differences were expressed.

Summary

The in-depth interview is the most controlled of all informal research methods, but it is also the most expensive. As with any informal method, its results cannot be generalized to other situations or problems, but they do provide an in-depth understanding of what others saw, thought, and/or how they acted in regard to the situation or problem. Case studies often use the in-depth interview to provide a level of understanding not found in most other formal or informal methods. We turn next to a second informal way of gathering data that has been sometimes called "group interviews," namely, the focus group.

FOCUS GROUPS

Perhaps the best way to look at focus groups is to think of one interviewer conducting a simultaneous interview with as few as 3 and as many as 20 interviewees. The typical focus group, however, is generally run with between 5 and 10 participants. A focus group in reality is a controlled group discussion where the group leader (called a "moderator") skillfully asks questions to the group and then probes for better understanding and agreement among group members. The focus group is not as controlled as the in-depth interview, but in this informal method you can direct questions and expose issues and determine how deeply you want to address the problem, opportunity, or solution. The focus group is used primarily when you want to answer questions of definition, value, or policy.

Advantages and Disadvantages

Focus groups provide a fairly quick and relatively inexpensive way to get at questions or concerns. The method is often employed as a precursor to formal methods, such as surveys, which are significantly more expensive to conduct.[2] While the in-depth interview allows the interviewer to probe the responses of a single interviewee, the focus group allows members to "tag" off each other's responses, often providing extensive insight into the topic of discussion. As Stacks and Hocking point out, "The focus group provides data that tend to be holistic and its outcome often is greater than the sum of its participants."[3]

The method's disadvantages include potential overreliance on the moderator's ability to control the group—to draw out reticent members and control overly talkative members—and, like the in-depth interview, the heavy commitment in time taken to conduct the focus group. Another disadvantage stems from the voluntary nature of participant involvement. Volunteers are not "normal" in that they may be participating for some ulterior reason. Yet, when members are not volunteers, and instead are selected for some particular reason, they may be afraid to speak up or may use silence as a weapon for being taken away from work. Hence, you may have to pay members for participating or provide other incentives (gifts, products, and so forth).

Conducting the Focus Group

Conducting a focus group involves seven steps. First you must choose which of two types of focus groups you will conduct, the traditional focus group or the "known group" focus group. Second, you select and train your staff—typically a moderator and an assistant run a focus group. Third, you create your discussion guide. Fourth, you select your participants. Fifth, you set up the room in which the group(s) will meet. Sixth, you conduct and record the session(s). And, seventh, you transcribe and analyze the data.

Costs

There are any number of research organizations that conduct focus groups. Whether you hire such an organization or conduct your own sessions, focus groups are not inexpensive. In general, be prepared to pay between $3,000 and $4,000 *per group*. Further, for each segment of the public studied, there should be at least *two* focus groups conducted. (The second group is used to establish whether the first group's responses are representative of the population segment; if the two groups differ, then a third group should be run. This is true for even homogeneous populations.)

Costs associated with focus groups can be broken into four areas. First, and most importantly, is the moderator. This is the person who will ensure that your discussion guide is followed and, based on experience, will deftly take the group in the directions needed. A moderator typically costs between $1,000 and $4,000 *per group*, and a *good* moderator may cost up to $5,000 per group. Moderators often bring an assistant with them to help conduct the focus groups at their own cost.

Second, the costs for actually running the focus group will depend on how you are recording the focus groups. Recording is often a necessity, and at a minimum a good recording setup is required: omnidirectional microphones or multiple microphone sets are the key here. Video recording is more expensive, but you get the advantage of actually seeing the focus group, but confidentiality is a problem and at the *start of the session* video recording may inhibit participation. Not all researchers support the use of recording equipment, mainly due to the moderator skill needed to make participants comfortable enough to talk while being recorded. Experience suggests, however, that once the focus group gets into the questions most participants forget that they are being recorded. A good moderator will take participant reaction to recording into consideration and map his or her communication strategies around those who are reticent due to the recording of the session. A rule of thumb is to tell participants upfront that they will be recorded and then describe what will happen to the recordings after the data has been analyzed (it is best to erase them after transcription; in the transcripts individual participants' names are never used—pseudonyms or initials are often used instead).

Third, the costs associated with transcription of the focus group must be considered. Although most clients request verbatim transcripts, most never really read them. Transcription of the focus groups can account for as much as 40% of the research costs.

Finally, there are the costs associated with participant selection; most of the time participants are paid for their time, either with cash, the product being discussed, or gift certificates. Corporate focus group participants are often provided a free meal and/or other compensation.

Types

The most common type of focus group brings selected individuals together in small groups based on *parameters* defined by a particular problem, opportunity, or situation (e.g., demographic and psychographic characteristics).[4] This type of focus group typically is formed either by random selection of participants from a larger population (public) or through a call for volunteers from that population.

The second type of focus group is called a *known group focus group*.[5] This type of focus group is used when researching in an organization where you want someone from each level—the lowest to the highest—to participate. The advantage to this group is twofold. First, all levels of the organization are represented; second, the participants are selected for particular reasons (they may be opinion leaders, they may represent certain factions, and so forth). The primary disadvantage, however, is also twofold. First, because participants are interacting with people who may be their superiors, there is a tendency to keep their attitudes and opinions to themselves out of fear of retaliation. To overcome this, participants answer questions anonymously by writing their responses, usually during a morning session, and then the lists of "answers" are used as the actual discussion guide in an afternoon session. Second, the known group method is much more expensive to conduct. A known group focus group could actually be conducted by beginning with the initial stage data responded to electronically—through the Internet or corporate intranet, for instance—and then the members could meet face-to-face to discuss responses to the questions asked.

In reality nearly all participants in focus group are *volunteers*, and volunteers bring with them reasons for participating that may yield problems during the actual discussions. The importance of employing a trained moderator becomes apparent in such situations.

Staffing

As indicated, the focus group minimally requires a moderator and perhaps an assistant. Sometimes a stenographer will be hired to record the group, but this is usually done through audio and/or video recording. If a known group technique is employed, then at least three additional assistants will be employed to help the moderator summarize the written answers or comments from the first session and transcribe them to larger sheets of paper or poster board to be taped to the walls of the room and then help maintain the materials during the afternoon session. If the first stage is conducted electronically, answers or comments can be duplicated and passed out among group members, thus reducing the extra time needed to transpose from one medium to another.

Discussion Guide

A discussion guide must be created. A good discussion guide consists of an introductory statement and about 10 questions, divided into four types: introductory, key, probe, and transition (see Figures 6.2 and 6.3).[6] *Introductory questions* are icebreakers and are used as the first question asked and immediately after the break. *Key questions* are the ones that concentrate on what the focus group is exploring. In general, you can ask between five and seven key questions in a 2-hour focus group. *Probe questions* are questions that you have prepared for the moderator's use and are of importance to your understanding of the problem, opportunity, or situation. A good moderator will rephrase probe questions as needed. *Transition questions* provide both a break and a transition between introductory and key questions.

It is a good idea to go over the entire discussion guide with the moderator, getting his or her input into the final discussion guide. A

Good afternoon/morning, and welcome to our session. Thank you for taking the time to join our discussion of X's culture. Our discussion will examine X's focus, mission, and orientation. My name is Don Stacks; I'm a professor of communication at the University of Miami. Assisting me is Bill Adams, a professor of communication at Florida International University.

We want to hear how you as managers see X's culture. This study has targeted the corporate function within the service area. Although there have been similar studies conducted, this study is unique in that it will focus on the corporate function. You were selected by Human Resources because of your background and managerial position. We will be conducting several other focus groups with other members of the X family, but we wanted to begin with you because of your experience with the company, and we want to tap into those experiences.

Today we'll be discussing your thoughts and opinions about X as a place to work, your perceptions as to its mission, and its focus. Based on these discussions, a cultural survey will be created and used to assess X's corporate culture. There are no right or wrong answers, just possible differing points of view. Please feel free to share your point of view even if it differs from what others have said. Keep in mind that we're just as interested in negative comments as positive comments, and at times the negative comments are the most helpful.

Before we begin, let me suggest some things that will make our discussion more productive. Please speak up—only one person should talk at a time. We're tape recording the session because we don't want to miss any of your comments. We'll be on a first-name basis, and in our later reports there will not be any names attached to comments. You may be assured of confidentiality. If anyone wishes to withdraw, please do so now.

My role here is to ask questions and listen. I won't be participating in the conversation, but I want you to feel free to talk with one another. I'll be asking you about 10 questions, and I'll be moving the discussion from question to question. There is a tendency in these discussions for some people to talk a lot and some people not to say much. But it is important for us to hear from each of you this afternoon/morning because you have different experiences. So if one of you is sharing a lot, I may ask you to let others talk. And if you aren't saying much, I may ask for your opinion. We've placed name cards to help in remembering names. Let's begin by finding out something more about each of you by going around the group. _____, let's start with you: tell us something about yourself that is not work-related, something that gives us an idea of who you really are. . . .

FIGURE 6.2. Sample of a focus group moderator's opening statement.

Opening: Tell us something about yourself that is not work-related, something that gives us an idea of who you really are.

Introduction: How many different businesses have you worked for since you began your full-time working career?

PROBE:

How many were energy-related?
What specific jobs?
What led you to leave those positions?

Transition: Think back over those years and make a list on the notepad in front of you of those businesses. Include in that list the two or three things that you liked most about each job and the two or three things you liked least about each job. Bill will make a list of the likes and dislikes on the flip pad.

LOOK FOR:

Elements that deal with leadership
Elements that deal with trust
Elements that deal with company direction
Elements that deal with customer focus
Elements that deal with team environment
Elements that deal with feedback
Elements that deal with job satisfaction
Elements that deal with career development
Elements that deal with performance rewards
Elements that deal with being well treated
Elements that deal with empowerment

PROBE each participant as to how these differ or do not differ from X.

Key: On your note pad, jot down three to five words that you believe would sell X to a new employee at the managerial position.

LOOK FOR: action verbs, adjectives, adverbs

PROBE each for the underlying meaning of each word and how it relates to X's overall mission.

Key: Now, jot down three to five words that you believe would sell X to a new employee in a nonmanagerial position.

LOOK FOR: action verbs, adjectives, adverbs

PROBE each for the underlying meaning of each word and how it relates to X's overall mission.

BREAK

Transition: During the break you had some time to reflect back on the questions and discussion we've just completed. Is there anything you'd like to add to what was said?

PROBE: Are there things we missed? Are there things we glossed over that, on second thought, are important and should be brought up with the group?

(cont.)

FIGURE 6.3. Sample of a focus group discussion schedule.

Key: Each of you has a sheet of paper that requires you to make some evaluative judgments. Please take a few minutes and rate the items. Note that there are two sets. The first asks you to rate X as it is NOW. The second asks you to rate X as it SHOULD BE. When we're finished rating, Bill will list your evaluations for discussion. Please do not put your names or any other identifying marks on the sheets. I will be collecting them for further analysis.

PROBES:

Where do we agree?
Are there differences of opinion in our group?
Did anything you saw or heard surprise you?
Would you change any of your scores now, after you've listened to others?

Key: Suppose X was a family.

How would you describe that family?
How do the various brothers and sisters act?
Is the family a warm and caring family?
Can you identify the grandparents? If so, how well did they do in bringing up their children?

FOLLOW-UP QUESTIONS:

What strengths does this family have?
What's needed to improve this family?

Key: We've looked at all the elements that produce a culture. Based on this discussion, how would you describe X's culture?

PROBE:

Its leadership (vision, integrity, empowerment, action)
Its operating philosophy (customer orientation, commitments, speed, competition)
Its structure (customer-focused, flat, team-based, effective)
Its rewards (aligned to business, results-based, competitive but variable, flexible benefits and varied recognition, leveled [X/team/ individual] rewards)
Its identity (fast, flexible, customer-oriented, providing value, a good place to work and have work for you, employee empowered and developed)

Ending: Of all the things we discussed regarding X's culture, which one is most important to you?

Summary: Bill will summarize the key points made in our discussion.
(Begin with findings, what was said, follow with what was not said.)
Is this summary complete? Does it sound OK to you?

Final   Is there anything that we should have talked about but didn't? This is
question: the first in a series of groups that we are doing. Do you have any advice on how we can improve?

good moderator can offer incredible insight into the process, something you should pay attention to.

Participant Selection and Recruitment

Participant selection and recruitment are an important aspect of any
focus group, regardless or type. Some research questions require a random sampling of a particular group (see Chapter 9 for an in-depth discussion). In general, random sampling requires that all participants in
a population have an equal chance in being chosen. Being chosen,
however, does not mean that potential participants will show up.
When randomly sampling from a large population, employ the "rule
of 10"—for every participant you need, contact 10^7; that is, for two focus groups of 7 participants each, you should contact 140 potential participants. How many will actually show up will be determined by (1)
interest in the topic and (2) what the respondents will receive for participating. Although you may seek random sampling, what you actually have is a volunteer group, and volunteer groups are what make
focus groups an informal research method. If you should happen to re-
cruit more than the 14 required for two groups (and not all that say
they will show up will actually do so), then you can expand the groups
or have a third group ready in case the two groups significantly differ
in their discussions. (*Focus groups should have between 5 and 12 members
and never more than 15 participants.*)

Recruitment within an organization is generally less problematic.
Selection may be done in concert with management or done randomly;
again, the rule of 10 should be followed. Recruitment for known
groups, however, may be easiest. In known groups recruits are asked
to participate by top management and generally agree to participate.
Again, some type of incentive is often required.

Room Preparation

A focus group environment is one that is conducive to communication.
First and foremost, participants must not feel threatened by the room
or location. When conducting employee focus groups, for instance,
avoid using a conference room located next to a manager's office—as
you might expect, employees may be reticent to say much that close to
"management." Focus groups are generally held around tables where
all participants have eye contact with the moderator and one another
(see Figure 6.4). Thinking of the table setup as a clock, the moderator
should be at 12:00 and the assistant should be at the 1:00 position. Participants take on hour positions. Using a table allows participants

FIGURE 6.4. Focus Group Room Setup.

something to write on; generally pads of paper and at least two pencils per participant should be provided. Any audio and audiovisual equipment should be set up directly behind or in front of the moderator or slightly off to his or her side.

The room should be comfortable and quiet. A conference room often works well, although focus groups have been run in a variety of locations, from offices to hotel rooms. Participants should have room to spread out and access to refreshments. A bathroom should be close by, preferably connected to the room for minimal disruption. The moderator should check out the room prior to beginning each focus group. If a known group is being conducted, you will need walls to tape up or pin up poster board or flipchart paper during the second session. Nametags should be prepared and randomly placed around the table. Only first names should be used to help maintain confidentiality.

Finally, the recording equipment should be placed and tested. Research firms will rent out focus group rooms in which the recording equipment has been hidden from view. They may actually have two-way mirrors behind which cameras are available for recording, although the ethics of two-way mirror use would require that participants know that they are being observed, just as with audio or video recording. Make sure that the recording equipment is working properly and that it is recording from all parts of the room. Any audiovisual stimuli should be tested (e.g., advertisements or videotaped materials) and any computer-assisted materials pretested and set up for use.

Conducting the Focus Group

The actual conducting of the focus group rests on the moderator's shoulders. The first thing the moderator should do is double-check all recording equipment and any stimulus materials to be used. Once participants have been seated, the moderator should introduce him- or herself and whomever is assisting, discuss the fact that the session will be recorded, ensure confidentiality, and tell participants that they may withdraw if they want without penalty (this is ethically important, especially so if you are working with an organization). Moderators usually use a scripted introduction for this.

Next, the moderator asks the first, icebreaking question. Typically participants are asked to introduce themselves and to share some experiences. This does two things; first, it gets names and voices recorded and, second, it means that all participants will have said at least something, reducing the likelihood that they will subsequently be silent. The next question may be transitional, or it may be a key question. Approximately an hour into the session a *short* (5-minute) break should be scheduled, and afterwards a transitional question should be sufficient to bring the group back to task. Known groups will typically break after the first session which may last two hours or more, have lunch, come back and discuss for an hour, break, and then discuss for the rest of the afternoon. Moderating a known group is more difficult because the discussion will be much less guided by preplanned questions during the second session.

There are two problems moderators often confront in focus groups. The first is the nonparticipant. A good moderator will get each participant to join in the discussion, often phrasing a probe question to a particular individual. The moderator's awareness of both verbal and nonverbal interest cues (e.g., raised eyebrows, posture, stares) is important in keeping all participants in the discussion. Second, the moderator must know how to handle the overly communicative participant or the participant who wants to dominate or control the interaction. A good moderator will use humor and frankness when trying to work with these participants. In the end, however, the moderator may have to thank and excuse the dominating personality early, telling him or her during the break that the remaining time must be devoted to others' contributions.

After the session is completed, the moderator should thank all participants and answer any questions he or she can. If several other groups are scheduled, it is a good idea to ask participants not to discuss what was talked about with others who may be participating.

Analyzing the Data

Analysis of focus group data occurs in three phases. First, the moderator and researcher get together and discuss what the moderator felt was the outcome. It is best to tape record these "review sessions." Second, the tapes are listened to and transcribed if necessary. Transcription takes both time and money (often costing $25 a page or more) so both should be planned for if utilized. Third, the discussions are systematically analyzed, often employing both logical analyses of answers and formal content analysis (see Chapter 7). Often a 3- to 5-page summary of each focus group is written and used in the final analyses. Like most public relations research, the findings may be incorporated into a larger report where other data collection methods have been employed. When conducting employee focus groups or groups with a stake in the study, it is a good idea to share with participants a brief summary of the study's results.

The data reported are usually stripped of any participant identification, thus ensuring confidentiality. Anonymity is seldom guaranteed because answers and transcripts or the actual tapes themselves do not allow for total anonymity. If possible, destroy all tapes—both audio and video—after the data have been analyzed and the report(s) written.

Summary

Focus groups offer you a way to conduct research on a larger scale than the in-depth interview. Focus groups are an important methodology and should be used in conjunction with other informal and formal methods. The focus group enables the problem, opportunity, or situation to be discussed in great detail, often leading to surprising results as people "tag" on to others' responses. Focus groups have two limitations. First, you cannot generalize from them to larger groups or publics. Second, they are dependent upon the skill of the moderator and his or her ability to work with participants. The data gathered in focus groups are important in understanding why and how well things are perceived. Because of this—and because in-depth interviews are so expensive—focus groups are being used with greater frequency in public relations research.

PARTICIPANT-OBSERVATION

Participant-observation is an informal method that is not often formally employed in public relations research. Indeed, it takes considerable time to conduct, provides very little timely information if approached as a planned part of a specific campaign or program, and is quite expensive to conduct. As such, participant-observation is not usually found in research conducted by public relations firms; it is found instead in corporate public relations. Even in corporate public relations, however, it is approached nonsystematically and really from an environmental monitoring or scanning approach. An advantage to either a formal or an informal participant-observation is that it allows you to get to know a particular public or group, getting out and talking to and observing members of your target public, their community, their culture. As Melvin Sharpe has noted, "Certainly we have seen too many examples of culturally insensitive communication programs and cultural research . . . [that a simple, informal participant-observation] would have helped."[8] It is important, however, to know the general underpinnings of the method. Participant-observation helps answer questions of definition, value, and policy.

Advantages and Limitations

The major advantage of the participant-observation method is that it provides you with an understanding of how people behave in their day-to-day activities.[9] It provides you with an understanding of how people perceive the organizational roles, rules, and routine. Importantly for proactive public relations, it provides clues to when problems will arise and often suggests intervention strategies. Participant-observation is something that all corporate practitioners should be familiar with. An excellent case in point is what Polaroid Corporation CEO Gary DiCamillo did when he assumed the corporate helm during the mid-1990s. Besides interviewing employees and others he visited Polaroid's locations, walked the various plants and headquarters, and joined in discussions about Polaroid with employees and managers. Through his participant-observation research (now an active research program that he and his top executives conduct on a yearly basis) he was able to find out what was right, what was wrong, what Polaroid's strengths and weaknesses were, and what should be his priorities in the coming years.[10]

The chief disadvantage consists in the amount of time and associated costs it takes to complete an actual participant-observation study. Thus, our approach is more oriented toward understanding the participant-observation method as a way of conducting daily in-house environmental scanning. (It should be noted that public relations firms might most likely employ the method internally and when working with long-term clients.)

Conducting Participant-Observation

Conducting a formal participant-observation study requires three things. First, you must understand the expected rules, roles, and routines for your environment. Second, you must participate in the daily activities of those you are observing and take notes. Third, you then compare the observations noted to those expected. In other words, you must know what is expected and why and then be able to identify deviations from those expectations. This involves getting out of your office and "walking the site."

Understanding the Work Site and Environment

All organizations and groups have both formal and informal expectations. For instance, most beginning workers soon find out what the expected daily routine is, even though it may not be formally set forth in the corporate handbook. The same is true of working with clients—the more you know about their expectations, the better you can serve them. What are the expectations and how do you gain understanding? Answering these questions deals with the question of definition. Where you find the answers lies in the employee handbook and your experience with the corporation or others you have worked with. What are those expectations? They are found in the formal and informal rules, roles, and routines.

Rules are written and unwritten behaviors that are expected on the job. Employee handbooks and contracts between clients and organizations spell out the formal rules for doing business. Formal rules may include when the workday begins and ends, when and how long lunch and other breaks are, dress codes, and so forth. Informal rules are the unwritten expectations we have, of always being at your desk, of making sure that new employees have been mentored, who can speak to whom without getting permission first, and so forth. Rules set forth the norms of conduct.

Roles are both formal and informal. Formal roles are assigned, such as rank and duties. Informal roles are assigned by or taken by others. Informal roles are such things as cheerleader, gadfly, and quarterback. In many cases the formal and informal roles people take on complement one another; in others, they contradict one another.

Routines are the typical things that are done. They reflect the interaction of rules and roles. A daily routine may be that certain people gather around the coffee room and chat before work, then break into their work units, unite once a week for a meeting, have lunch with certain people, work on particular things at particular times that become predictable, and leave early or late or on time.

In each environment—both in terms of the larger corporate and the smaller unit work environment—you should be able to create a model of daily activity that provides a "reality check" for normalcy or typicality. It is this that you use in your environmental scanning.

Participating and Observing

The participant-observer engages in conversations and observations daily with members of the population being observed. This may mean walking the plant floor in corporate public relations or meeting regularly with a client at the client's convenience. During your interactions you look for typical and atypical behaviors and note them. Note taking is not done during the interaction, since that activity might change the behaviors of those with whom you are interacting. Instead, you should keep two sets of notes, one mental and the other written. Immediately after a daily visit to a particular unit, jot down in a log what you observed and whether it was typical. The key is to observe, remember, then later record on a timely basis unfailingly.

Analyzing the Data

Analysis involves comparing the noted interactions and behaviors to those expected. Where interactions indicate that roles have shifted, rules have changed or are being broken, and routines are being disrupted, you have identified a potential problem area that needs to be addressed. Your "data" are the observations, and your "logic" is whether the data fit with the normal operations of the unit, organization, or the expected client–firm relationship. Atypical observations may point to potential intervention strategies and serve to drive tactical public relations strategies.

Summary

Participant-observation is a method that provides true environmental scanning or monitoring data. It requires communicative interaction and a keen eye for subtle changes. Not found much in formal public relations practice, the good practitioner should be a practiced participant-observer. In many instances, what was observed may lead you to conduct in-depth interviews or focus groups or pursue a formal research method, such as surveys or polls.

SUMMARY

This chapter has examined three informal methods of data gathering. They differ primarily in the amount of control they offer the public relations researcher, from high control to basically no control. The in-depth interview provides information that is rich in detail and provides insight into how a particular person or persons viewed some problem, opportunity, or situation. The focus group is less controlled but still provides an understanding of how people perceived a problem, opportunity, or situation; it also allows people to interact and come up with ideas or solutions or insights that one-on-one interviews rarely find. Finally, participant-observation is an informal method that provides you with no control over the observations; in fact, you are a part of the interaction. All three methods answer questions of definition, value, and policy. Each provides a depth of analysis not available with formal methods.

REVIEW QUESTIONS

1. Why would public relations practitioners want to consider participative methods as a way to conduct research? What advantages do these methods give you as a researcher over other methods?

2. How does the concept of control operate as you move from in-depth interviews to focus groups to participant-observation methods?

3. How is the in-depth interview different from the door-to-door or participant survey?

4. When would you use a focus group, and what type of questions does a focus group answer that cannot be answered by other methods?

5. The text notes that participant-observation is often left out of public relations research typologies. What importance does having an understanding of how people operate—their norms, roles, rules, and routines—in daily interaction relate to an understanding of public relations or of specific public relations problems?

PRACTICE PROBLEM

Your assignment is to write a major article for your company's annual report. Your CEO wants to know how you plan to research the article. What would you tell him or her about the use of participative methods when told to research "the day-to-day activity employees engage in to ensure that stakeholders and stockholders are getting value for their investments"? Provide a rationale for conducting in-depth interviews and focus groups—specifically, with whom, and where would you conduct the research? What would participant-observation add to your article?

NOTES

1. Don W. Stacks and John E. Hocking, *Communication Research*, 2nd ed. (New York: Longman, 1999).
2. Jim Grunig and Lauri Grunig, "Focus Group Research in Public Relations, Part II," *pr reporter*, No. 3 (February 22, 1999), pp. 1–6.
3. Stacks and Hocking, p. 202.
4. See Thomas L. Greenbaum, *Moderating Focus Groups* (Thousand Oaks, CA: Sage, 2000).
5. Stacks and Hocking, p. 202.
6. David L. Morgan and Richard A. Krueger, *The Focus Group Kit* (Thousand Oaks, CA: Sage, 1998). The kit contains six volumes: "The Focus Group Guidebook," "Planning Focus Groups," "Developing Questions for Focus Groups," "Moderating Focus Groups," "Involving Community Members in Focus Groups," and "Analyzing and Reporting Focus Group Results."
7. Stacks and Hocking; Roger D. Wimmer and Joseph R. Dominick, *Mass Media Research: An Introduction*, 6th ed. (Belmont, CA: Wadsworth, 2000), pp. 97–100, suggest that you plan to contact 150% of the participants you think you will need.
8. Melvin Sharpe, in reviewing the first draft of this chapter, February 2001.
9. Mark Hickson, III, "Participant-Observation Technique in Organizational Research," *Journal of Business Communication, 11* (1974), 37–42, 54.
10. Gary DiCamilllo, "The Power of Corporate Listening," presentation at the annual meeting of the Arthur W. Page Society, Charlestown, SC, October 2000.

Chapter 7

Content Analysis

There are times when it is important to systematically evaluate data gathered by means of informal methodologies. Content analysis enables us to look at qualitative data in a quantitative manner. As a method, content analysis allows us to break up the information we have obtained from in-depth interviews, focus groups, and participant-observation into units that can be placed into categories that can be *counted* and thus quantified. Public relations researchers have employed content analysis for years when they have counted the number of certain types of press releases, the number of times a client's name has made its way into print, or when examining the readability of public relations messages.

Although some have characterized content analysis as a formal research method,[1] it actually serves as a transition between informal and formal methodologies. It is an informal method in that the data it operates on are basically *qualitative* deriving, from responses to open-ended questions or from observing certain messages in certain media. It is a formal method, however, in that it can be used to establish an observational tool that meets a requirement of social science research, randomly sampling a larger population to count the number of times a particular phenomenon occurs; thus, it can answer a question of *fact*.

DEFINING THE METHOD

Content analysis *is a systematic, objective, and quantitative method for researching messages.*[2] It is particularly appropriate for the analysis of documents, speeches, media releases, video content and scripts, interviews, and focus groups. The key to content analysis is that it is done objectively; you can give others the same content and based on your "rules" they will find the same results. Further, the content is treated systematically. That is, those "rules" are applied in a consistent manner across all messages. Finally, the messages are transformed from qualitative statements to numbers, data that can be quantified and compared against other data. In so doing, you have created a system that can describe the message(s) under study with a degree of reliability and from which validity also can be assessed.

ADVANTAGES AND LIMITATIONS

The major advantages to content analysis are found in its ability to objectively and reliably *describe* a message or group of messages and its application to advanced statistical analyses. Second, content analysis provides both logical and statistical bases for understanding how messages are *created*. Content analysis focuses on the messages or communications actually produced in practice and in that regard may be considered a major methodological tool that bridges informal and formal methods. Its major disadvantage is that it requires that the actual messages be recorded for analysis.

CONDUCTING A CONTENT ANALYSIS

There are several steps involved in conducting content analysis. First, as in all research methods, a documentary/historical search of research relevant to your problem, opportunity, or situation must be conducted. Second, the content must be identified. Third, the actual units to be counted must be specified. Fourth, the system through which you will categorize the units must be created and pretested. Fifth, messages must be selected. And, sixth, the actual counting of units and their placement into categories must be accomplished, and the reliability of that process must be ascertained.

Why conduct a documentary/historical search? The major reason is to have some idea as to what kind of content has been analyzed in previous research, thus giving you clues as to your coding scheme's units and category structure. The search may also provide information regarding what to expect from previous research and how to best describe the content being analyzed.

Content

Content analysis can be conducted on two levels. Most content analyses are conducted on what has been called *manifest content*. Manifest content is what you actually see and count. Manifest content may be the number of times specific financial figures are given in an annual report, the number of times the active voice is used in a series of press releases, the number of times a particular client is mentioned in the mass media, or the size of photographs used in a magazine or number of column inches published about your client. It also might include responses to "fill-in-the-blank" questions (called a "cloze procedure"), such as "Red as a _____" or "When you think of public relations, the first thing that enters your mind is _____." Manifest content, then, is *it*, that is, the actual word phrase, character, item, or space or time measure counted.

Latent content is more qualitative and deals with the underlying or deeper meanings of the message. These themes become what is measured; but, because they are attitudinal in nature, they are typically more difficult to count and must be measured via some scale or other measurement system.[3] At least one content analysis theorist, Ole Holsti, suggests that content analysis should be conducted only at the manifest level.[4] Latent content might include how good or bad, attractive or unattractive, a particular message or photo was, whether it conformed to a campaign theme, and so forth. Latent content is hard to count; therefore it has reliability and validity problems.

Manifest content may be seen as reflecting the answers that questions of definition and fact seek. It is easily defined, quantified, and counted. Latent content may be seen as reflecting both questions but also addressing questions of value. Although much more difficult to define and quantify, it provides insight into the value of the communication or message under study.

Units of Analysis

Units of analysis are the things that are actually counted. As such, much care needs to be taken when defining exactly what it is you are counting. Most research uses Bernard Berelson's five units of analysis (see Table 7.1).[5] Note that four of the units are manifest in nature, that is, they are things that are easily definable and countable. The fifth, the theme, is latent and must be operationally defined. An *operational definition* is one that you, the researcher, create. In terms of definition, manifest content may be considered *denotative* (it has a dictionary defi-

TABLE 7.1. Units of Analysis

Symbols/words
Company name
Logotypes
Articles of speech

Characters
Race
Stereotypical roles
Occupations

Themes
Slogans
Sexuality
Campaign theme reported

Time/space measures
Column inches of story
Airtime during news programming
Size of photographs in print

Items
Advertisement
Editorial
Speech

nition most of us can agree upon), latent content is *connotative* (its definition is more in line with specific usage). Manifest content can be categorized as words, characters, physical measures of time and space, and items. Latent content is categorized as themes or theses.

Manifest Units of Analysis

Suppose for a minute that you were concerned whether your client, a hospital, was getting sufficient coverage in the media. What kinds of manifest units of analysis might best be employed? As noted above, there are four types of manifest units of analysis. The first is the *word* (or *symbol*). Words or symbols may include nouns, proper nouns, parts of speech, or may take on the form of symbols (both nonverbal and physical, i.e., a smile or a cross). What kinds of words or symbols might you look for? The obvious choice is the hospital's name, "Mercy Hospital." But Mercy is also the area's only trauma center, has specializations in heart organ transplants, and is affiliated with a major medical teaching center. Therefore, other words or symbols that might be used include "trauma" or "trauma center," "heart," "heart surgery," "organ transplant," and so forth. The second manifest unit of analysis is the *character*. A character is usually defined an individual or role. Character units of analysis in the Mercy Hospital case might be "patients," "surgeons," "nurses," and so forth or particular doctors, nurses, or administrators who represent the hospital. *Time and space measurement* is the third manifest unit of analysis. Here you would be looking at the amount of airtime given to Mercy Hospital in the media, to include not only paid advertising but also stories picked up from your media releases. Finally, there are *item* manifest units of analysis. The "item" is an entire message itself. Perhaps you have done a major campaign on the hospital's use of a new technique; stories that focus only on that technique would be considered an "item."

More than one unit of analysis may be employed in a content analysis. You might be interested several units of analysis. A word of caution about employing multiple units of analysis must be injected here. Content analysis is best used when you have defined down to the core the most important units. Including too many units of analysis often results in reduced research reliability and validity. It may be best to conduct several content analyses—one looking at words and characters, another concerned with time and space, and yet a third on specific items.

Latent Units of Analysis

Latent content units of analysis delve into deeper aspects of the message. While manifest content is found on the surface of the message, latent content analysis explores the message's depth. The latent unit of analysis is called the *theme* or *thesis*. You may be concerned that your client, Mercy Hospital, is not being covered "fairly" in the local media. Indeed, you are concerned that it may be receiving overly "negative" press coverage. Your content analysis would then focus on the themes of "fair news coverage" and "negative news coverage." In constructing your theme or thesis unit of analysis, you would carefully define what you consider to be "fair" and "negative" news coverage. Not everyone must agree with your definitions, but they must be able to see how they relate to your research questions, "How fairly is Mercy Hospital being covered by the local media?" and "How much of this coverage is negative?" Fairness might be defined as stories that include both sides of any issue, when hospital administrators have been interviewed, and when the coverage appears to be objective (again, define this term). Negativeness might be defined as stories that put the hospital in a bad light.

Clearly, theme or thesis units of analysis are hard to define—thus Holsti's assertion that they are best left alone. However, there are ways to quantify in a reliable manner themes and theses, such as with "rating scales" (more will be said about this in Chapter 8) that ask coders to rate the stories on a scale of 1 (very negative) to 7 (very positive). A word of caution: theme or thesis units of analysis often yield low reliability statistics.

Most latent content analyses examine only one theme or thesis. However, you might be interested in one or two manifest units of analysis along with the particular theme. For instance, a theme such as sexuality in print advertisements might also employ sex of character and size of story as manifest units of analysis.

Category Systems

Once you have selected your units of analysis, you must now consider where you will place them. Each unit of analysis must be placed into the appropriate category. Sex, for instance, can be categorized fairly simply as either male or female. Verbs can be categorized as to whether they are active or passive, nouns as proper or not, and so forth. Choosing an appropriate category system is as crucial as clearly defining your units of analysis. If your category system is sloppy or unclearly defined, then reliability suffers.

To create a systematic category system you follow five simple guidelines.[6] First, *the categories must reflect the purpose of the research.* If we are concerned with media reporting, our categories must reflect the media and how stories are reported. If we included categories for finance and bed counts, those categories would *not* reflect the study's purpose. Second, *the categories must be exhaustive.* Here media categories might be daily newspapers, weekly newspapers, radio news, and television news. This leads to the third guideline, *all categories must be mutually exclusive.* The use of the category "other" makes most category systems exhaustive and mutually exclusive. There may be some media that you had not planned for; such instances would be placed in the "other" category (which might include Internet reports). Quite simply, each instance must be placed in one—*and only one*—category. *When the "other" category exceeds 10 percent of the total number of instances, it should be re-examined and the category system redefined for that content variable.*[7] If this should occur, then you must go back to the beginning and reclassify each instance into the new categories.

Fourth, *placement of instances in one category must be independent of the other categories.* Placing an instance in one category must not influence or be influenced by the other categories in use. Placing a newspaper in the category "weekly" should not be influenced by the category "daily;" they are truly different, as different as radio is from television. If not, then the categories must be redefined. Finally, *all categories in your system must reflect one classification system.* If your classification system is "news," then quasi-news programming or magazines will not be considered.

As you might guess, category system creation can become quite complex. There are, for instance, different types of daily newspapers— those that do not include weekends are still daily—so you may have subcategories, such as 7-day and 5-day papers. What about television news in relation to different *timeslots*? These considerations must be taken into account early in the category-forming process.

Sampling

Once an exhaustive and exclusive category system is in place you must decide what content you will actually examine. If you have access to all possible documents over the time period of interest, then sampling is not a concern. You simply conduct your content analysis on all the messages. Usually, however, there are too many messages to evaluate. In such instances you will have to draw a sampling of those messages. Although sampling will be covered in detail in Chapter 9, a quick overview will help distinguish probabilistic sampling from nonprobabilistic sampling.

Probabilistic sampling occurs when every message in a population of messages has had an equal chance of being studied. It allows you to (1) generalize from the content sampled to the larger population of content and (2) estimate the amount of error you may anticipate in sampling from that population. There are three types of probabilistic sampling found in content analyses: simple random, systematic random, and systematic stratified random sampling. *Simple random sampling* occurs when you choose at random the content to analyze from the population (you take all the media and randomly select—like a lottery sample of numbers from a single population of numbers, except that you return each number to the population each time and then select again—the key here is that *each* selection has an equal chance, or probability of being chosen each time you select). Its advantage is that it is easy to conduct; its disadvantage is that it may not be representative of the larger population. *Systematic random sampling* occurs when you choose every *n*th instance from the population (you take your population of messages and sample, say, every 10th message). The advantage here is again simplicity; the disadvantage is that you need a complete listing of all messages. *Systematic stratified random sampling* goes one step further and selects from subsets within the population (you choose certain media outlets and then choose within them by an interval of *n*th instances). The advantage of this sampling method is increased representation of the sample due to the fact that you are selecting from a known population (usually a list); the disadvantage is it requires increased knowledge of the population.

Nonprobabilistic sampling occurs when you choose messages from a population for a particular purpose. It occurs when you do not have access to all messages or when you are only looking for certain messages. If for instance you only have access to five of nine media outlets, your selection of messages, even if you chose all the messages, would not represent the actual population of messages. Nonprobabilistic sampling does not allow you to generalize to the larger population; instead, the conclusions drawn from the content analysis simply describe what you found in the messages you examined.

The decision as to whether to employ probabilistic or nonprobabilistic sampling is determined by both the availability of data and what your research aims are. In many instances, nonprobabilistic sampling is all you need—you are simply looking to describe the messages you have. In others, you want to be able to generalize out to the larger body of messages.

Coding

Once you have your units of analysis defined, your category system in place, and possess the messages to be content analyzed, you must code them. *Coding* occurs when you identify and place the messages into your category system. Coding is the way you quantify the messages, when you distinguish between the units of analysis. In general, simple coding schemes are the most reliable, although simple schemes are not always possible. If we take seriously Holsti's admonition to code only manifest content, then coding becomes simple: we simply code what we see. If one of our categories is sex, then we code as female, male, or other. Why "other"? Suppose we are trying to see if female reporters are covering a shoe brand more than male reporters in a nationwide promotion; can you identify each reporter as male or female based on name alone—and do you have the ability to contact all reporters? If not, then Lee and Robin would be coded as "other."

Most coding schemes reflect simple differences (what we will distinguish as "nominal data" in Chapter 8). If we were interested in what made a good press release, we might examine the use of nouns (proper/nonproper) and verbs (active/passive). Simple differences do not indicate ordering, simply grouping. If we were interested in which automobiles were being advertised most, we would simply distinguish between the different manufacturers or models. If, however, we were interested in something that was ordered or ranked, from good to bad or inexpensive to expensive, for instance, our coding would result in "ordinal data" as opposed to "nominal data." Thus, we might code a media release as good, average, or bad or an automobile as inexpensive, moderately expensive, or expensive.

Ordered or ranked coding is usually found when measuring latent content, but scalar or interval coding is often used as well. As such, it requires that the coders make judgments regarding the underlying theme. Sexual innuendo and violence are two latent units of analysis that often require complex coding decisions to be made based on often questionable definitions. These decisions—coding quantification and definitions—often cause problems for coding reliability and validity.

Validity

Validity refers to whether you are actually coding messages they way they should be coded. Put another way, validity asks whether your coding system is measuring accurately what you want to be measured. Three things impact on coding validity and whether the content analysis conducted truly measures what you intended it to measure. First, what are *the units of analysis and how are they defined*. The definitional process is crucial when conducting a valid content analysis. If you are looking at "sex" as a unit of analysis, defining it as gender may not provide a valid definition (biological sex—male/female—is different from gender, which would be defined as masculinity or femininity and is more difficult to "observe"); "ethnic origin" is very difficult to define, especially in such cities as Los Angeles or Miami, where "Hispanic" can take on several different meanings. Second, what is the *category system*? If the categories are not treated systematically and in the end are neither exhaustive nor exclusive, then they may not reflect the purpose of the content analysis. Most category problems are found in overstuffed "other" categories or when units of analysis are inappropriate for the content (such as using simple counts of passive versus active language in an annual report rather than a thematic analysis of "indecision" which is latent in terms of content in the annual reports of successful companies). Third, *validity is often compromised by the process in which the actual messages are gathered for analysis*. Sampling, or lack thereof, is a major concern. Failing to take into account weekly community newspapers may invalidate your study if you chose to sample only *daily* newspapers or, alternatively, if you did not realize that you were looking at television news story content during a "sweeps" week (which is not truly characteristic of most weeks)—these are but two common examples where sampling problems could cause concern about the validity of the content analysis.

Reliability

While validity is often seen as a subjective call, reliability can be measured. More specifically, coding reliability can be measured. Reliability refers to *the amount of error coders make when placing content into categories*. Manifest content analysis, which examines particular words, symbols, characters, items, and space and time measures, is more reliable than latent content analysis, which examines themes or theses. Even simple counts of words, such as the number of times the word "the" occurs in a particular message, will result in some error in counting, thus reducing reliability. Try to count out the number of characters on this page. Now, count them again. Did you get the same number? In so doing you have established *intracoder* reliability. If someone else counted the same page, you would have established *intercoder* reliability. All content analyses must be coded either by two independent coders or by one coder coding the same material twice, usually after a time interval.

By coding the material at least twice we can establish the coder reliability. Reliability is determined on a .00 to 1.00 continuum and yields a *reliability coefficient*. A coefficient of .00 means that the coders were totally different in how they placed content into categories, while 1.00 means that they coded the content identically. "Good" coder reliability is obtained when coders agree on coding content at least 90% of the time (i.e., has a reliability coefficient of .90 or higher). Computing coder reliability is fairly simple. Although there are several different reliability formulae, two are used most often (see Table 7.2). Holsti's reliability formula takes the number of coding decisions agreed upon by the coders and divides it by the number coding decisions per coder:[8]

$$\text{Reliability} = \frac{2M}{N_1 - N_2}$$

Where M is the total coded items agreed upon, N is the total items for coder 1, and N is the total items for coder 2. A more conservative reliability formula takes into account the possibility that the coders agreed on their coding due to chance.[9] Scott's *pi index* works off Holsti's reliability and adds a computed "expected agreement" to be compared against the "observed agreement."

$$Pi = \frac{\% \text{ observed agreement} - \% \text{ expected agreement}}{1 - \% \text{ expected agreement}}$$

As seen in Table 7.2, Scott's pi is lower than Holsti's reliability coefficient, having factored out chance agreement between coders.

TABLE 7.2. Reliability Coefficient Example

Holsti's intercoder reliability

$$\text{Reliability} = \frac{2M}{N_1 + N_2}$$

For two coders, each codes 100 newspapers looking for the number of times your company is depicted *positively* in the "letters to the editor" section of each paper. The two coders agree on 86 of the 100 newspapers:

$$\text{Reliability} = \frac{2(86)}{100 + 100} = .86, \text{ or a coding reliability of } 86\%$$

Scott's pi index

$$Pi = \frac{\% \text{ observed} - \% \text{ expected agreement}}{1 - \% \text{ expected agreement}}$$

where % expected agreement is the sum of the squared observed outcomes.

Assuming that you have coded 100 local television news programs for coverage of your event with the following category system and the outcomes:

Event reported positively	45%
Event simply reported	35%
Event reported negatively	10%
Other	10%

Intercoder agreement (Holsti) = .92

% expected agreement = $(.45)^2 + (.35)^2 + (.10)^2 + (.10)^2 = .335$

$$Pi = \frac{.92 - .335}{1 - .335} = .878$$

USES

While most content analyses can be easily conducted by hand, they are laborious and often result in unintended error. The computer has changed all of this, and special content analysis programs have been written. Early programs, such as *The General Inquirer* and *SLCA* (Syntactic Language Computer Analysis), required tedious retyping and internal coding.[10] Newer programs, such as Diction,[11] take scanned or typed-in text and conduct sophisticated manifest content analyses. The output from a Diction analysis of a speech is found in Figure 7.1. As you can see, it provides a rich depth of analysis of the message and the writer's approach to the message and its content. Other uses of content analysis include readability indices (found in almost all word processing programs, including Microsoft Word and WordPerfect), typically conducted on the entire message or subsections cut and pasted into new files; the Flesch–Kincaid readability score for the screen text depleted was computed to be 12.0 (see Figures 7.2 and 7.3).

SUMMARY

Content analysis allows the public relations researcher to employ some pretty sophisticated statistical analyses on qualitative data. It does so by converting qualitative data into quantitative data that can be counted. Content analysis begins by establishing just what it is you want to count (the unit of analysis), sets up a systematic categorization system, and then counts the number of units that fall into each category. Content analysis can be effectively used when examining public relations messages for their frequency, construction, and content. When randomly sampled from a larger population, content analysis allows us to make reliable conclusions about the content under analysis; it is a transitional step to formal methodology.

Text file (President Richard Nixon's final speech in office, 8/1/74)

> You did what you believed in, sometimes right, sometimes wrong, and I only wish that I were a wealthy man at the present time. I've got to find a way to pay my taxes. And if I were I'd like to recompense you for the sacrifices that all of you have made to serve in government. But you are getting something in government and I want you to tell this to your children, and I hope the nation's children will hear it, too, something in government service that is far more important than money. . . .
>
> . . . . And I think of her, two boys dying of tuberculosis, nursing four others in order that she could take care of my older brother for three years in Arizona and seeing each of them die. And when they died it was like one of her own. Yes, she will have no books written about her, but she's a saint. Now, however, we look to the future.

Standard Dictionary Totals

Variable	Frequency	% of words analyzed	Normal range Low	High	Standard score	Out of range
Numerical Terms	5.03	1.01	0.30	15.04	−0.36	
Ambivalence	26.66	5.33	6.49	19.21	2.17	*
Self-reference	22.13	4.43	0.00	15.10	1.86	*
Tenacity	36.22	7.24	23.32	39.76	0.57	
Leveling Terms	7.04	1.41	5.02	12.76	−0.48	
Collectives	10.56	2.11	4.04	14.46	0.25	
Praise	15.28	3.06	2.77	9.59	2.67	*
Satisfaction	4.02	0.80	0.47	6.09	0.26	
Inspiration	4.19	0.84	1.56	11.10	−0.45	
Blame	3.02	0.60	0.06	4.16	0.44	
Hardship	9.05	1.81	1.26	10.48	0.69	
Aggression	3.02	0.60	1.07	9.79	−0.55	
Accomplishment	10.06	2.01	4.96	23.78	−0.46	
Communication	10.06	2.01	2.21	11.79	0.64	
Cognition	14.08	2.82	4.43	14.27	0.96	
Passivity	2.01	0.40	2.10	8.08	−1.03	*
Spatial Terms	9.05	1.81	4.17	19.85	−0.38	
Familiarity	113.68	22.74	117.87	147.19	−1.29	*
Temporal Terms	16.60	3.32	8.36	21.82	0.22	
Present Concern	15.09	3.02	7.02	16.60	0.67	
Human Interest	69.06	13.81	18.13	45.49	2.72	*
Concreteness	21.13	4.23	10.70	28.50	0.17	
Past Concern	5.03	1.01	0.97	6.19	0.56	
Centrality	1.01	0.20	1.19	7.54	−1.05	*
Rapport	1.01	0.20	0.42	4.26	−0.69	
Cooperation	0.00	0.00	0.36	8.44	−1.09	*
Diversity	3.02	0.60	0.07	3.81	0.58	
Exclusion	1.01	0.20	0.00	4.31	−0.52	
Liberation	1.01	0.20	0.00	4.72	−0.43	
Denial	6.04	1.21	2.57	10.35	−0.11	
Motion	0.00	0.00	0.17	4.35	−1.08	*

FIGURE 7.1. Diction example. *Note.* From R. P. Hart, *Diction 5.0* (Thousand Oaks, CA: Sage). Reprinted with permission from Sage Publications

Flesch Reading Ease score

Rates text on a 100-point scale; the higher the score, the easier it is to understand the document. For most standard documents, aim for a score of approximately 60 to 70.

The formula for the Flesch Reading Ease score is:

$$206.835 - (1.015 \times ASL) - (84.6 \times ASW)$$

where ASL is the average sentence length (the number of words divided by the number of sentences) and ASW is the average number of syllables per word (the number of syllables divided by the number of words).

Flesch–Kincaid Grade Level score

Rates text on a U.S. grade-school level. For example, a score of 8.0 means that an eighth grader can understand the document. For most standard documents, aim for a score of approximately 7.0 to 8.0.

The formula for the Flesch–Kincaid Grade Level score is:

$$(.39 \times ASL) + (11.8 \times ASW) - 15.59$$

where ASL is the average sentence length (the number of words divided by the number of sentences) and ASW is the average number of syllables per word (the number of syllables divided by the number of words).

FIGURE 7.2. Readability scores and interpretation in Microsoft Word.

REVIEW QUESTIONS

1. Why is content analysis especially relevant to public relations practice?
2. Assume that you are asked to conduct a content analysis of the competition's annual reports from 1960 to present. List several potential units of analysis and how you would code them.
3. Why do we want a coding reliability greater than .90? What's so magic about a 90% reliability figure?
4. What is the difference between coding reliability and coding validity?
5. How is content analysis a "transitory step to formal methodology"?

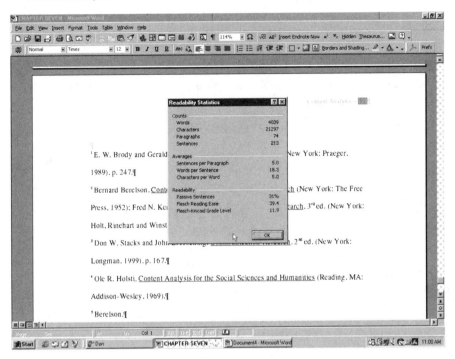

FIGURE 7.3. Screen shot of content analysis. Reprinted with permission from Microsoft Corporation.

PRACTICE PROBLEM[12]

The management of a large corporation producing chemical products for agricultural use viewed the media as biased in their attitude toward this industry. How would you conduct a content analysis of major *newspapers* to see if the coverage was biased or balanced? What would be your time frame? What units of analysis would you use? What category system is suggested in the problem? How would you go about actually coding the news content? What would the results provide that might influence the corporation's media relations campaign? Finally, what limitations would you place on your findings, and what suggestions for further research as part of a proactive public relations media campaign might you make?

NOTES

1. E. W. Brody and Gerald C. Stone, *Public Relations Research* (New York: Praeger, 1989), p. 247.
2. Bernard Berelson, *Content Analysis in Communication Research* (New York: The Free Press, 1952); Fred N. Kerlinger, *Foundations of Behavioral Research*, 3rd ed. (New York: Holt, Rinehart & Winston, 1986).
3. Don W. Stacks and John E. Hocking, *Communication Research*, 2nd ed. (New York: Longman, 1999), p. 167.
4. Ole R. Holsti, *Content Analysis for the Social Sciences and Humanities* (Reading, MA: Addison-Wesley, 1969).
5. Berelson.
6. Holsti.
7. Roger D. Wimmer and Joseph R. Dominick, *Mass Media Research: An Introduction*, 6th ed. (Belmont, CA: Wadsworth, 1997).
8. Holsti.
9. W. Scott, "Reliability of Content Analysis: The Case of Nominal Scale Coding," *Public Opinion Quarterly, 17* (1955), 321–325.
10. P. Stone, D. C. Dunphy, M. S. Smith, and D. M. Ogilivie, *The General Inquirer: A Computer Approach to Content Analysis* (Cambridge, MA: MIT Press, 1966); H. Waylan Cummings and Steven L. Renshaw, "SLCA III: A meta-theoretic approach to the study of language," *Human Communication Research 5* (1979), 291–300.
11. Roderick P. Hart, *Diction 5.0* (Thousand Oaks, CA: Sage, 1999).
12. This problem was suggested by Melvin Sharpe in an early review of the manuscript.

PART III

Formal Research Methodology

Public relations research has grown tremendously over the past two decades. From reliance on simple counting of outputs to an analysis of outcomes, the public relations practitioner has begun to work with sophisticated social scientific methodology and statistical tools. This movement from what we have been discussing as informal to formal methodology opens a window for advanced understanding and analysis of the public relations process. Further, it provides practitioners with ways of stating within certain degrees of confidence that their campaign or program results were based on the systematic collection and interpretation of data. Further, that confidence can be established *quantitatively*.

Part III begins with an examination of *measurement*. Chapter 8 explores the quantification process. It begins by looking at what data are (nominal, ordinal, interval, and ratio) and how reliability and validity are established. The chapter then presents the basics for measuring attitudes and beliefs, the creation of measurement scales that are used in the collection of data, and the general underlying principles for creating them. The general problems associated with establishing and measuring public relations outcomes are then discussed.

Chapter 9 explores in depth the concept of sampling from a larger population to a group of people representative of that population. While this concept was briefly examined in Part II, this chapter discusses probability and nonprobability sampling, different sampling techniques, and how to establish what we will call "sampling accuracy" and "sampling confidence" (how much error we will accept in sampling from a population and the degree of error we can expect at most from respondents, respectively).

Survey research is examined in Chapter 10. The chapter distinguishes between surveys and polls and discusses the two major types of surveys conducted in public relations. Pragmatic concerns—such as how the survey is conducted, the writing of survey questionnaires and types of questions asked, the training of interviewers, and how to maximize response rates—are examined. Finally, the problems and promises of new technologies and their use in survey research, as well as the limitations on interpretation, will be examined.

Experimental method is then examined in Chapter 11. The experiment is the ultimate methodology employed in both the natural and social sciences. It is differentiated from all other methods by the amount of control over the variables under study. Most public relations practitioners will never conduct an experiment, but most will find their practice either impacted or informed by experiments. Some will represent companies and others work for companies that conduct experiments on a daily basis and may have to explain their findings to the general public. It is important that the practitioner understand the experimental method, its advantages, and its limitations.

Chapters 12 and 13 introduce the concepts of statistical reasoning and confidence. Chapter 12 looks at descriptive statistics. Descriptive statistics found in public relations practice include frequency counts, percentages, proportions, means, medians, modes, ranges, variances, and standard deviations. These statistical tools tell us about the observations taken on the people selected for research. They cannot be generalized to the larger population. Chapter 13 examines inferential statistics, something that practitioners rarely see in research reports but which are the basis for decisions regarding the researcher's confidence that the results obtained—and any differences found—were because they actually existed and not a mere chance occurrence. Basically, descriptive statistics say, "This is what I found when observing or asking these questions"; inferential statistics say, "I'm this confident that what I observed occurred because of the campaign or program and not by chance occurrence." Statistics enable us to describe and predict within established degrees of confidence the world around us.

Chapter 8

Measurement
in Public Relations

Measurement is the process by which we observe things seen and unseen. It almost always includes a comparison of sorts: press release *A* is longer than press release *B*, males like object *X* more than females, more people of *X* characteristic attended event *Y*, and so forth. Notice how imprecise these comparisons are. What do we know about how we made these comparisons or decisions? This chapter looks at how we measure and how much confidence we can place on that measurement's reliability and validity. It begins with an examination of four basic *levels of measurement*, then moves to how we can establish a measure's *validity* (does it measure what we say it measures?) and *reliability* (does it measure the same way every time?). The chapter then explores how we can measure things that are unseen: attitudes and beliefs. Here, we will explore the underlying rationale for commonly used *attitude scales* and how to construct and evaluate them.

Measurement is essential when we try to understand why people behave as they do. Basic to this understanding of behavior is what drives them to behave. As public relations has moved from the tactical to the strategic, as the practitioner has become part of the decision-making process, questions as to the value public relations provides in establishing and maintaining relationships have become a focal point. As such, we will examine the progress being made in *measuring relationships* as a way of establishing overall public relations value to an organization or client.[1]

UNDERSTANDING MEASUREMENT

Measurement occurs when we observe something. Formal measurement requires that as precisely as possible we state how we were measuring what we observed. The distinction between informal and formal measurement will become more apparent in Chapter 12, when we look at describing and understanding data. For our purposes now, however, it is important to understand that how we define what we are measuring determines (1) how precise we will be in explaining what we have observed and (2) which analytical tools (statistics) are appropriate for the type of measurement we need. For instance, when we say that one account is "big" and another is "small," how do we know what big and small are? Formal measurement lets us decide exactly how to approach this language problem by stating what level of measurement we are using when observing.

Measurement Levels

Observations can be made at one of four levels: nominal, ordinal, interval, or ratio. The four levels can be further summarized into two distinct classes, categorical or continuous. In general, *categorical measurement* occurs when our observations (*data*) are placed into classes to be counted, and *continuous measurement* occurs when our data are based on some continuum. Categorical data are fairly simple and are language-based (e.g., "tall," "Ford," "profitable"); continuous data are more complex and assume that observations, while falling into classes, are equidistant apart (e.g., such measures as inches, miles, degrees of temperature). Further, observations made as continuous can be reduced to categorical, but categorical data cannot be transformed into continuous data; this assumption is one that we often find violated when research is conducted in the field. *Public relations research uses both classes and makes observations at all four levels.*

Categorical

Categorical measurement puts observations into classes. Content analysis, with its categorization schemes, comes immediately to mind as an example of a method that effectively employs categorical observation. The most basic measurement we can make places data into simple classes with distinction made only as to differences. *Nominal measurement* observations include sex (male and female, with neither seen as better than the other), size (large and small, again with no distinction made as to which is better), and race (Caucasian, African American,

Hispanic, Latino, Asian American, Pacific Islander, Native American, and so forth, with no distinction made as to which is best). *Ordinal measurement* places observations in some type of order. Age and income are prime examples of ordinal measures: under 18, 19 to 25, 26 to 50, 51 and older; under $10,000, $10,001 to $50,000, $50,001 to $100,000, $100,001 and higher. Note that the categories are exclusive—you cannot be in two categories at the same time—and can be arbitrary in their span—the differences between classes need not be similar (thus, 1–18 in one class, 19–25 in another). The key here is that the classes are different and they represent some order (age increases, as does income, but no assumption is made as to the differences between categories, except their order).

Continuous

Continuous measurement assumes that the distance between classes is equal and observation occurs on a continuum. *Interval measurement* assumes that the distances between observations are equal all along the continuum. Thus, age and income can be observed as interval measurement when we ask how old someone is (the distance between ages 1 and 2 is 1 unit, between 1 and 35 is 34 units, between 35 and 70, 35 units). Note that we can reduce these observations later into distinct classes or even simple classes (e.g., old and young). *Ratio measurement* adds the requirement of an absolute zero point to the continuum. That is, not only are the classes equidistant on the continuum, but the continuum now has an absolute (as opposed to an arbitrary) zero point. Age could be observed as ratio measurement if we know exactly when we were born; income can be ratio measurement if you assume that $0.00 means that you have no income at all (and you could have negative income). Based on this distinction, a thermometer measured in degrees Fahrenheit (F) or Centigrade (C) is not ratio, but interval—the continuum for 0° is either 32°F or 0°C, which is when water freezes. (The total absence of warmth in Kelvin [0K], a ratio measure, is −459.67°F.)

Advantages and Disadvantages

Each level of measurement has advantages and disadvantages. Categorical observations are simple to make but difficult to interpret (just what is "larger"?). Continuous observations are more difficult to make but are easier to explain (e.g., the difference between 1 mile and 10 miles). Continuous observations may be reduced ("collapsed") downward from ratio to interval to ordinal to nominal. Finally, continuous observations, when summed and described, offer more information than categorical observations. It is important to note that *percentage* is not a continuous output, although it is typically reported as 0% to 100%. Percentage is based on categorical data and therefore must be treated as categorical rather than continuous data (something we will explore in greater detail in Chapter 12 and an assumption that is violated by many out of ignorance as to how the observations were defined).

Reliability and Validity

One of the cornerstones of formal research methodology is the ability to state the reliability and validity of the measures employed in gathering data. Regardless of the type or level of measurement used to collect data, measurement can be evaluated as to its reliability and its validity.

Validity

Validity refers to whether a measure is actually measuring what you defined it to measure. Validity is closely related to the question of definition; indeed, how we operationally define a variable impacts on the measure's validity. There are four types of validity, each a little more rigorous in turn. The first is commonly called face validity. *Face validity* occurs when you operationally define the measurement as measuring what you say it measures. Face validity is accepted on your credibility as a researcher. Thus, after much research into a problem, opportunity, or situation, if you decide that a certain measure is valid but have not tested it further, it is said to have face validity based on your knowledge of the area.

Content validity provides a little more rigorous test of a measure's validity. *Content validity* occurs when you ask others who have studied the area—preferably experts in that area—to review your measure. They provide a second level of validity, that of the impartial judge. Still, however, your measure's validity is based only on the authority and credibility you and your judges possess.

The third type of validity, *criterion-related validity*, is established when your measure is shown to be related to other established measures or if it successfully predicts behavior. Criterion-related validity is found through pretesting your measure against known measures and seeing if it can predict scores. This type of validity requires the measure to be used in conjunction with other measures and their results statistically analyzed.

Finally, *construct validity* is obtained through an analysis of how the measure is actually used. Construct validity is obtained through observation or statistical testing. Most attitudinal measurement schemes (*scales*) are composed of a number of statements (*items*) that people react to. These scales usually have more than one underlying concept being measured (most credibility measures, for example, are broken into different subparts—dimensions such as extroversion, dynamism, sociability, composure—which can be measures of particular aspects of credibility or can be summed to create a composite measure[2]), and the measure's validity is established through a statistical procedure called "factor analysis" (see Chapter 12).

Reliability

Reliability is the ability of a measure to measure the same thing comparably over time. A reliable measure is one that is stable—it does not fluctuate without reason. An example of reliability might be a bathroom scale. Each time you step on it, the scale should give you a weight. Your scale is reliable if you step on it twice in immediate succession and get the same result. Whether that measure is precisely accurate in conveying what you weigh, however, has not been determined; that is the domain of validity. If the scale was off by 5 pounds (or your watch was off by 5 minutes) but still gave you the same measurement in quick succession each time, then it is reliable.

Reliability looks at the error found in measurement. All measurement has some error attached to it. Your measure may not be constructed correctly—you might be measuring with a slightly short ruler, for instance. This would be considered *instrument error*. You or the people you are measuring may not be using the measure correctly—perhaps you are measuring with a meterstick instead of a yardstick. This would be considered *application error*. The key to measurement reliability is *maximizing systematic error* (*known error*) and *minimizing random error* (that which is *unknown*). Random error is nonsystematic and reduces the measure's reliability.

There are a number of ways to establish a measure's reliability. Repeated use is one. This is *test–retest reliability*, where you measure the same thing twice and see if the two tests obtain the same results. When we employ measures that test knowledge or retention, we may opt for *split-half reliability* or *internal consistency reliability*. Split-half technique randomly takes a measure and has some participants take one portion and others take a different portion of the measure and compare results between groups. If you were interested in measuring

how well job applicants could edit a press release and you had four releases in your test that had similar errors, you might test the measure's
reliability by giving some coworkers two releases and others the other
two releases and then grade each set and compare results. Internal
consistency is found when you have the same question or statement
twice; if both are answered correctly, then you have evidence of the
measure's internal reliability or consistency.

Reliability is almost always reported as a statistical coefficient.
Holsti's reliability coefficient and Scott's pi coefficient (discussed in
Chapter 7) are two examples. In general, *good* reliability estimates are
coefficients of .70 or higher. *Great* reliability estimates are coefficients
of .80 or higher. *Excellent* reliability estimates are coefficients of .90 or
higher. Two statistical tools that provide reliability estimates for attitudinal measures are the coefficient alpha for continuous data and the
KR-20 for categorical data. Each will provide general reliability estimates and also provide information about the measure's reliability if
certain items are excluded from the measure (see Figure 8.1). We will
explore these in more detail in Chapter 12.

Summary

Measurement is found on four levels (nominal, ordinal, interval, and
ratio) broken into two classes (categorical and continuous). How you
define your measurement will later determine how you analyze the
data gathered from your measures. All measures can be assessed for
their validity and reliability, and indications of how each was assessed
should be found in all research reports. A good measure is both valid
and reliable; however, reliability must be present or validity cannot be
obtained. We will explore this notion further in the next section.

MEASUREMENT SCALES

Much of what we attempt to measure in public relations is not readily
observable. That is, public relations often deals with perceptions,
knowledge, and attitudes toward a problem, opportunity, or situation.
As we will see later, current measurement research in public relations
is attempting to create measures to evaluate public relations effectiveness as an outcome associated with "relationships." Trying to understand what people think and why they think about something requires
that you tap into their attitudes about that "thing" or object. The only
way to do so is through measuring attitudes and through the creation
of measurement scales.

Coefficient alpha

```
     R E L I A B I L I T Y   A N A L Y S I S   -   S C A L E   ( A L P H A )
                                                        N of
Statistics        Mean        Variance      Std Dev    Variables
for SCALE         7.8452      5.1114        2.2608         3

Item-total Statistics
                        Scale         Corrected      Alpha
        Scale Mean if  Variance if   Item-Total     if Item
        Item Deleted   Item Deleted  Correlation    Deleted
GP1       5.8452        3.2389          .3838         .6479
GP2       5.0516        2.4475          .5453         .4297
GP3       4.7937        2.3238          .4692         .5486

Reliability Coefficients
N of Cases = 252.0        N of Items = 3
Alpha = .6493
```

KR-20

```
     R E L I A B I L I T Y   A N A L Y S I S   -   S C A L E   ( A L P H A )
                                                        N of
Statistics        Mean        Variance      Std Dev    Variables
 for SCALE       17.6102       .7584         .8709          9

Item-total Statistics
                          Scale
          Scale Mean    Variance      Corrected       Alpha
          if Item       if Item       Item-Total      if Item
          Deleted       Deleted       Correlation     Deleted
WORK1      15.6705        .5999          .2758          .5439
WORK2      15.6372        .6435          .3403          .5305
WORK3      15.6736        .5905          .2893          .5397
WORK4      15.6497        .6420          .2512          .5498
WORK5      15.6538        .6199          .3004    .     .5357
WORK6      15.6289        .6998          .1773          .5668
WORK7      15.6362        .6583          .2893          .5426
WORK8      15.6642        .6208          .2425          .5538
WORK9      15.6674        .6052          .2747          .5439

Reliability Coefficients
N of Cases = 962.0        N of Items = 9
Alpha = .5745
```

FIGURE 8.1. Example of reliability estimates: coefficient alpha and KR-20. SPSS runs the KR-20 under the "alpha" option for dichotomous data, in this case, yes/no. SPSS for Windows version 10.07, 1999, Chicago, IL. Reprinted with permission from SPSS, Inc.

Measuring What You Cannot See

It is a commonly held belief in the social sciences that behavior can be
explained and predicted by knowledge of an individual's or a public's
attitudes.[3] Attitudes have been described as an individual's "predisposition to behave." In terms of behavior, it is difficult to observe one individual's behavior—let alone hundreds of individuals' behavior. We
just do not have the time or the resources to follow people around and
observe how they actually behave. Therefore, we attempt to predict
behavior through an understanding of what individuals think about
the object of the behavior. If an employee, for instance, believes that he
or she is empowered by her company to take risks without punish-
ment then he or she should take risks. We can observe how much risk
he or she takes and then compare it to the individual's responses to an
attitudinal measure that may have empowerment as one of several
variables affecting the employee's perceptions of the company's culture.

When we measure an attitude, however, we are actually measuring people's opinions—their evaluation of how they will behave based
on (1) knowledge about the behavior in question, (2) how they feel
about the behavior in question, and (3) how they think they will behave prior to having to behave. An attitude, then, can be assessed according to these three criteria (an attitude's cognitive or evaluative, affective or potency, and connotative or activity dimensions).[4] Our
assumption is that when provoked by some stimuli—typically questions or statements—people's responses to the statements are indica-
tive of their intended behaviors. Attitude, then, serves as an *intervening
variable* that (1) can be measured and (2) can predict behavior.

There are several ways of measuring attitudes. We will explore
two that are used in the majority of public relations research, especially
when conducting surveys. Before that, however, we need to discuss
some important scale construction considerations and then look at the
two types of attitude scales commonly employed in public relations research.

Attitude Scale Construction

It is important to distinguish again between a measurement scale
and a simple measurement. A simple measurement consists in collecting a single data point, whether age, sex, political affiliation, or
purchasing power, for example. The data point can be measured on
any measurement level. Most polls consist of simple measures that

are fact-based and inquire about specific behaviors. Surveys, on the other hand, are much longer and attempt to understand in some detail not only what an individual may or may not do but also *why*. Surveys (as we will see further in Chapter 11) often ask about peoples' attitudes and beliefs.

An attitude scale is composed of a number of individual *items*. An item is a question or statement that people respond to based on certain criteria. As noted earlier, attitudes consist of several dimensions; some attitude scales attempt to identify the subdimensions behind the attitude that is the object of concern (e.g., as with credibility). Such identification is accomplished by carefully crafting scales and subscales that are valid and reliable measures of the attitude object. Since we cannot see an attitude, we must rely on opinions—verbal expressions of the attitude—that are given in response to some stimulus (the item). Most often these responses are recorded by marking on paper the participant's reactions to individual items.

Creating an attitude scale requires that you follow several steps. Failure to follow these steps may invalidate the scale, make it unreliable, or yield false conclusions.

1. Attitude scales assume that the level of measurement is at the interval level.
2. To assess an attitude, the scale must allow for a "no attitude" or "neutral" response, thus *all* attitude scale items must possess an odd number of responses (3, 5, 7, 9, 11) whereby the midpoint is 0 (i.e., from +1 through 0 to –1).

Attitudes and beliefs are typically measured through a "strongly agree" to "strongly disagree" continuum. Because not all people have an attitude about all attitude objects, there must be an option for "neutrality" on the continuum. Interval-level data assumes that each point is equidistant from the next, that is, "strongly agree" is as far from "agree" as "strongly disagree" is from "disagree." This makes sense. However, "disagree" is not equidistant from "agree" because there is no room for a response of "neither agree nor disagree." The data are not interval (thus fail to meet the first requirement), and do not allow for neutrality (SA = A and D = SD, but A ≠ D. Nor is the response "no response" the same as neutral. No response is the same as "refuse to answer."

3. To assess reliability, all attitude scales must include at least two items per scale or subscale.

A single item by itself cannot provide reliability estimates. There is no variation to observe; therefore, we do not know whether the participants responded to the question systematically or randomly.

Public relations researchers most often employ one of two types of measurement scales, either Likert-type measures (see next section) or semantic differential measures. Each has advantages and disadvantages.

Scale Types

Before turning to the two scale types found most in public relations research, it is important to go back and look at one of the first measurement scale types devised. In 1929 Thurstone and Chave developed what was to become known as the "equal appearing interval" scale, or the *Thurstone scale*.[5] What distinguishes Thurstone scales from others is the ability to have predefined values associated with scale items. Further, Thurstone scales can be used to measure most samples with high degrees of reliability and have been proven to be highly valid. Why, then, are they not used today? Walking through the six steps required to construct a Thurstone scale should provide the answer:

1. Conduct a *thorough* research of the attitude object, identifying all possible beliefs and values held toward the object.
2. Create *several hundred* positive, neutral, and negative item statements about the attitude object. Edit them for redundancy, and make sure that they represent degrees of evaluation toward the attitude object from one end of a continuum to the other.
3. Select a large number of people from the population you wish to research (usually 25 or more) and ask them to sort the statements into 11 piles that reflect their favorableness toward each statement, from very unfavorable (1) to very favorable (11).
4. Calculate each item's average value. This will result in an average item score from 1.00 to 11.00 (e.g., 1.22, 6.33. 7.58, 10.59). Once each item's value has been determined, examine the range of scores *each* item received from the sorters. You will want to use only those items on which the sorters are in agreement (for instance, an average of 6 for item *X*, with the majority placed in piles 5, 6, or 7).
5. Select the 25–50 "best" representative items for further analysis. These items must reflect the entire continuum, from 1.00 to 11.00. Have two or three "judges" examine the items to ensure that they reflect the measure's continuum. Those items that the judges cannot agree upon are then removed from consideration.

6. Finally, choose 10–20 items that represent points along the continuum and reproduce them in random order on paper. Respondents are asked to circle the items they agree with and you then add up their item scores (*not* listed on the page) and divide by the number of items they circled for the scale score. For example, if they chose items whose values were 1.22, 3.44, and 2.66, their score would be 7.32 ÷ 3 = 2.44, that is, at the "very unfavorable" end of the continuum (note, too, that you can check the respondent's score for reliability be looking at the pattern of responses; since all were closely congregated in this case, you can conclude that this respondent's score was reliable).

Thurstone scales take quite a long time to create. If you think there are underlying attitudinal dimensions, you must repeat the last five steps for *each* subdimension. The time spent, however, yields an attitude scale that is very valid and highly reliable. Further, you can choose different items from the final pool of items and use them at different times, thus reducing the possibility that one attitudinal assessment will influence another. When confronted with a problem that has been examined in the past, however, you may find that one or more Thurstone scales have already been created. A good source for such scales is Delbert Miller's *Handbook of Research Design and Social Measurement*.[6]

Because public relations researchers do not normally have the time required to create Thurstone scales, they often turn to two scales that can be created quickly and easily assessed for measurement reliability and validity: Likert-type scales and semantic differential-type scales.

Likert-Type Scales

The *Likert-type scale* was developed in 1932 by Rensis Likert.[7] Likert-type scales, also known as *summated rating scales*, are composed of a series of item statements that are reacted to on a continuum of predesignated responses. A typical Likert-type scale consists of several items (usually between 2 to 10 per underlying dimension) reacted to on a 5-point scale, usually "strongly disagree," "disagree," "neither disagree nor agree," "agree," and "strongly agree." Likert-type scales, however, can range from a 3-response continuum ("agree," "neither agree nor disagree," "disagree") to as much as an 11-response continuum. A modification of response types uses numbers rather than words or phrases, usually bounded at each end by the extremes of the continuum (see Figure 8.2).

Statement	Response				
	Strongly Agree	Agree	Uncertain	Disagree	Strongly Disagree
Public relations is an excellent career.	Strongly Agree	Agree	Uncertain	Disagree	Strongly Disagree
Public relations is a career.	Strongly Agree	Agree	Uncertain	Disagree	Strongly Disagree
Public relations is no career at all.	Strongly Agree	Agree	Uncertain	Disagree	Strongly Disagree
Public relations is an excellent career.	Strongly Agree	5	4 3 2	1	Strongly Disagree
Public relations is a career.	Strongly Agree	5	4 3 2	1	Strongly Disagree
Public relations is no career at all.	Strongly Agree	5	4 3 2	1	Strongly Disagree
Public relations is an excellent career.	Strongly Agree	9	8 7 6 5 4 3 2	1	Strongly Disagree
Public relations is a career.	Strongly Agree	9	8 7 6 5 4 3 2	1	Strongly Disagree
Public relations is no career at all.	Strongly Agree	9	8 7 6 5 4 3 2	1	Strongly Disagree

FIGURE 8.2. Examples of Likert-type scales.

The basic assumptions of the Likert-type scale are that (1) the scale responses are interval in nature, (2) the ends of the continuum being measured are bipolar, and (3) there is a neutral point. The first assumption is controversial, unless the scale or subscale has two or more items, because people can are responding to *categories*. Remember, the scale is also called a summated rating scale; therefore there must be at least two items to sum. If the "scale" has only one item, then it cannot be summed and the data are reduced to the ordinal level of categorical data (and the scale is no longer of the Likert type). Second, the bipolar ends of the continuum must be truly opposites. Strongly agree and strongly disagree are equal opposites on the scale. What about a continuum that had "excellent" at the positive end? The negative bipolar would have to be "terrible." (The scale responses would be: Terrible, Bad, Neither Good Nor Bad, Good, Excellent.) This causes problems for some people, especially those who do not want respondents to associate "terrible" with their product or service. However, using "bad"—or worse, "poor"— instead of "terrible" would skew responses in a positive direction by subtly indicating how you want respondents to react.

The third assumption requires that some midpoint be defined. While we have used "neither disagree nor agree," it could just as easily be "uncertain" or "neutral." The key, however, is that the response be included in the continuum, not placed off to the side. Without a neutral response the measurement level drops to categorical and the data must be treated as ordinal. The continuum can best be thought of as running from + through 0 to –. Thus, for a five-response continuum, Strongly Agree to Strongly Disagree, the actual scoring could be on a continuum of 5 (strongly agree) to 1 (strongly disagree) with 3 being neutral. Or, it could be scored as +2 (strongly agree) to –2 (strongly disagree) with 0 being neutral. For data entry ease and interpretation, the items are usually scored from 5 (high) to 1 (low).

Likert-type scales are constructed in four steps:

1. Research the attitude object and identify any underlying dimensions and their associated beliefs and values.
2. Generate a large number of item statements that range from one end of the continuum you will use to the other end of the continuum.

   a. Each item must reflect one and only one reaction.
   b. Items that are ambiguous or have two possible reactions (are "double-barreled") must be rewritten to be explicit.
   c. Items should include statements that are the opposite of each other (see Figure 8.2).

3. Establish the items' content validity through the use of judges who will look for items that are not well written or do not reflect the attitude object you are assessing or the subdimensions you think build to the attitude object's assessment.
4. Select the items to constitute the scale and place them in *random* order on the measurement scale.

The Likert-type scale's reliability is assessed through the *coefficient alpha*. Because people are reacting to predetermined responses, acceptable reliability should be between .80 and 1.00. Validity is partially obtained through the process of creating the measure itself, with researcher face validity and judges' content validity already established. Construct validity can be assessed in two ways. If time allows, pull a random sample from the population you wish to measure (at least 10 people per item in the measure) and conduct a pretest. The pretest data then are submitted to "factor analysis," and the dimensional structure is obtained (see Chapter 12). Factor analysis examines how the different items "load" together on a measure. Like reliability, "good" factors are produced by (1) at least two items that "load" at ±.60 and (2) do not "load" on other factors greater than ±.40, thus producing a "clean" dimension (see Figure 8.3).

Because respondents can readily comprehend simple predesignated responses, the Likert-type scale is an excellent measurement scale for use with mail or telephone or person-to-person interviews or polls. A Likert-type scale, It can be constructed quite quickly, and reliability and validity can be ascertained without much problem. There is, however, the problem associated with responding with preset answers and whether the measurement level is actually interval. To overcome these problems, public relations researchers often employ a second measurement scale, the semantic differential.

| | Factor Loadings | | |
Item	1	2	3
I like public relations.	.89	.32	.01
Public relations is a good career.	.22	.79	.36
Public relations is a terrible career.	.36	−.86	.23
Public relations is an arm of marketing.	−.32	−.22	−.72
I dislike public relations.	−.92	.01	.22

FIGURE 8.3. Hypothetical factor analysis.

Semantic Differential Scales

The *semantic differential-type scale* is similar to the Likert-type scale except that *there are no predesignated responses to react to.* Instead, participants react by placing a mark on a continuum bounded by two bipolar adjectives or phrases. The semantic differential scale was developed by Osgood, Suci, and Tannenbaum in 1957 as a way of measuring *meaning associated with attitudes or beliefs.*[8] They suggested that we evaluate attitude and belief objects in semantic space, space that they further defined as occurring in three attitude dimensions: evaluation, potency, and activity. *Evaluation* is the cognitive, knowledge-based component of an attitude and has been used in the vast majority of studies of attitude change and persuasion. *Potency* deals with our affective responses to an attitude object, that is, how much we like or dislike it. *Activity* deals with the behavioral dimension of the attitude, that is, how we plan to behave toward it. Figure 8.4 depicts an abbreviated version of Osgood, Suci, and Tannenbaum's three

My Company

Evaluative dimension

Good	___:___:___:___:___:___:___	Bad
Beautiful	___:___:___:___:___:___:___	Ugly
Dirty	___:___:___:___:___:___:___	Clean
Valuable	___:___:___:___:___:___:___	Worthless
Unpleasant	___:___:___:___:___:___:___	Pleasant

Potency dimension

Large	___:___:___:___:___:___:___	Small
Fast	___:___:___:___:___:___:___	Slow
Weak	___:___:___:___:___:___:___	Strong

Activity dimension

Active	___:___:___:___:___:___:___	Passive
Sharp	___:___:___:___:___:___:___	Dull
Slow	___:___:___:___:___:___:___	Fast

FIGURE 8.4. Example of Osgood, Suci, and Tannenbaum's semantic differential scale. Original work as reported in C. E. Osgood, G. J. Suci, and P. H. Tannenbaum, *The Measurement of Meaning* (Urbana: University of Illinois Press, 1957). Reprinted with permission from University of Illinois Press.

subscales and their items in relation to an attitude object, namely "My Company."

As illustrated in Figure 8.4, participants are reacting to only one statement in this semantic differential-type scale. The statement could be a complete sentence, a phrase, or a word or concept. For instance, Figure 8.4 asks participants to evaluate the attitude object "My Company." Responses would indicate how they cognitively perceive their company (evaluation dimension), how they react to it (their gut feelings) (potency dimension), and how they will behave toward their company (activity dimension). Reactions are measured by asking participants to respond by placing a mark (usually an "X") in the space between the bipolar descriptors that best reflects their evaluation. Because participants are not reacting to statements with predesignated responses, instructing the participant on how to respond is extremely important. For instance:

Below you will find a statement and several scales. Respond to each scale by placing an "X" somewhere between the two terms. The closer your mark is to one of the two terms, the more you feel that term applies to you. A mark in the middle indicates you have no opinion about the statement. Please make sure that you have marked *each* scale.

Public Relations

Active	____:____:____:____:____:____:____	Passive
Beautiful	____:____:____:____:____:____:____	Ugly
Dirty	____:____:____:____:____:____:____	Clean
Good	____:____:____:____:____:____:____	Bad
Large	____:____:____:____:____:____:____	Small
Light	____:____:____:____:____:____:____	Heavy
Sharp	____:____:____:____:____:____:____	Dull
Slow	____:____:____:____:____:____:____	Fast
Weak	____:____:____:____:____:____:____	Strong

Note in the actual layout of the measure that some of the bipolar terms have been reversed. This is to ensure that a "response set" or a "Christmas tree" effect has not occurred, where a participant has responded by simply marking down one column (this is a problem when respondents mark the zero-point all the way down).

After the measure has been completed, the items are then coded. As with the Likert-type scale, each item is systematically coded from low to high (usually 1 at the low level and, in this case, 7 on the high end, with 4 being the neutral point). When coded, any mark within the two colons is coded as being within that interval; if the mark is on the colon you must throw that response out. Just as with the Likert-type scale, you could code from +3 through 0 to –3, but the scales are typically coded 1 to 7 or higher. (Note: when you code the items that have been reversed, you must reverse the numbers in your coding, i.e., 7 = 1; 6 = 2; 5 = 3; 4 = 4; 3 = 6; 2 = 5; 1 = 7.) After each item has been coded, you sum the subscale items to create a dimension score which can then be averaged to bring the score back to a 1–7 continuum (e.g., scores of 4, 5, and 6 would equal 15 (4 + 5 + 6), or an average of 5 (15 ÷ 3). Semantic differential scales are not limited to 7 responses; they can range from a minimum of 3 to 11 or more responses to the bipolar terms.

The semantic differential's reliability is computed with the coefficient alpha. Good reliability estimates are .70 and higher. We accept a lower reliability because participants have no labels with which to react to. Validity is determined in the same manner as in the Likert-type scale, face and content validity done through researcher and judge judgment and construct validity through factor analysis, using the same criteria discussed earlier.

While the Likert-type scale can be used in almost any data-gathering method, the semantic differential-type scale requires that participants actually complete the scale in person. This means that participants must have the measure in front of them to place their marks. This is possible in face-to-face interviews and mail questionnaires but is almost impossible in telephone surveys.

Common Misuses in Practice

The most common mistake found in the field application of Likert-type and semantic differential-type scales is the use of an *even* number of responses. With the Likert-type measure the neutral point is often left out, the assumption being that a participant's "don't know" or "refuse to answer" is somehow covered by assuming DK or RTA = neutral. A second mistake is to take the average of all participants' responses to one item; the data are no longer interval but ordinal, and averages (and other continuous statistics) are inappropriate. What to do when someone fails to respond is often a problem, best treated by defining it as "missing" in your analysis; this removes those who failed to respond for that particular scale from later analysis but is better than simply assuming that no response equals a neutral response. It also would be helpful for others if all researchers used a common scaling technique for Likert-type and semantic differential-type scales, with 1 always being the low end of the continuum, thus reducing confusion when comparing results among various studies.

AN EXAMPLE IN PRACTICE

The Commission on Public Relations Measurement has been working for a number of years to come up with a common metric to measure public relations value. In 2000 Grunig and Hon published a monograph through the Institute for Public Relations that attempted to create a measurement scale for public relationships value (see Figure 8.5).[9] What they were attempting (and are continuing to attempt) to do was to establish a common metric for the measurement of public relations effectiveness, as operationalized as relationship value. The public relations relationship measure reported in Figure 8.5 is the outcome of their measurement research.

SUMMARY

This chapter has explored how we measure and quantify data collected in formal methodology. We began by looking at what data and measurement were, defining four basic levels of measurement that could be placed into two distinct classes, continuous and categorical measurement. The chapter then defined and laid out how public relations researchers deal with attitude assessment through the creation of measurement scales that are both valid and reliable. Finally, three measurement scale types were examined: Thurstone-type scales (seldom used), Likert-type scales, and semantic differential-type scales.

For each item below, enter the number from 1 to 9 that best represents the extent to which you believe each item describes each organization.

Strongly Disagree		Disagree		Neither agree nor disagree		Agree		Strongly Agree
1	2	3	4	5	6	7	8	9

Items	General Electric	NRA	Social Security	Microsoft	Red Cross
1. This organization treats people like me fairly and justly.					
2. This organization and people like me are attentive to what each other say.					
3. I have no desire to have a relationship with this organization.					
4. I am happy with this organization.					
5. It bothers me when this organization ignores my interests.					
6. Whenever this organization gives or offers something to people like me, it generally expects something in return.					
7. Sound principles seem to guide this organization's behavior.					
8. This organization believes the opinions of people like me are legitimate.					
9. I can see that this organization wants to maintain a relationship with people like me.					
10. The organization fails to satisfy the needs of people like me.					
11. I don't consider this to be a particularly helpful organization.					
12. This organization doesn't make me feel obligated to repay it for what it does for me.					
13. This organization does not mislead people like me.					
14. The management of this organization gives people like me enough say in the decision making process.					
15. I would rather work together with this organization than not.					
16. Both the organization and people like me benefit from their relationship.					
17. This organization does not especially enjoy giving others aid.					

(cont.)

FIGURE 8.5. Public Relations Relationships Value Questionnaire. Reprinted with permission from the Institute for Public Relations.

FIGURE 8.5. (continued)

Items	General Electric	NRA	Social Security	Microsoft	Red Cross
18. I keep track of benefits I have given this organization to make sure I get as many benefits in return.					
19. Whenever this organization makes an important decision, I know it will be concerned about people like me.					
20. In dealing with people like me, this organization has a tendency to throw its weight around.					
21. I feel a sense of loyalty to this organization.					
22. I feel people like me are important to this organization.					
23. This organization helps people like me without expecting anything in return.					
24. When this organization receives benefits from others, it repays them right away.					
25. This organization can be relied on to keep its promises.					
26. When I have an opportunity to interact with this organization, I feel that I have some sense of control over the situation.					
27. Compared to other organizations I value my relationship with this organization more.					
28. In general, I believe that nothing of value has been accomplished between this organization and people like me.					
29. This organization is very concerned about the welfare of people like me.					
30. This organization seems to keep track of what it has done for people like me and what we have done in return in order to keep an "even" relationship.					
31. I am very willing to let this organization make decisions for people like me.					
32. This organization has the ability to accomplish what it says it will do.					
33. This organization really listens to what people like me have to say.					
34. I feel that this organization is trying to maintain a long-term commitment to people like me.					
35. Most people like me are happy in their interactions with this organization.					
36. I feel that this organization tries to get the upper hand.					

(cont.)

FIGURE 8.5. *(continued)*

Items	General Electric	NRA	Social Security	Microsoft	Red Cross
37. Even though people like me have had a relationship with this organization for a long time it still expects something in return whenever it offers us a favor.					
38. I believe that this organization takes the opinions of people like me into account when making decisions.					
39. This organization is known to be successful at the things it tries to do.					
40. This organization won't cooperate with people like me.					
41. I could not care less about this organization					
42. Most people enjoy dealing with this organization.					
43. I feel that this organization takes advantage of people who are vulnerable.					
44. This organization will compromise with people like me when it knows that it will gain something.					
45. I think it is important to watch this organization closely so that it does not take advantage of people like me.					
46. This organization has much knowledge about the work that it does.					
47. I believe people like me have influence on the decision-makers of this organization.					
48. There is a long-lasting bond between the organization and people like me.					
49. Generally speaking, I am pleased with the relationship this organization has established with people like me.					
50. I think that this organization succeeds by stepping on other people.					
51. This organization takes care of people who are likely to reward the organization.					
52. I feel very confident about this organization's skills.					

REVIEW QUESTIONS

1. Differentiate between measurement and behavior. How do both relate to public relations?

2. There are four "levels" of measurement. How do they differ? Provide an example of each measurement level that might be found in daily public relations activity.

3. When public relations practitioners measure "opinions," they are really measuring "intervening variables" such as values, beliefs, and attitudes. Define each intervening variable, and provide measurement statements that would reflect each; use as your opinion object the term "public relations."

4. Explain how a Likert-type scale can reflect both ordinal and interval measurement. Why are Likert-type statements often mismeasured when used to measure interval variables?

5. What is the relationship between measurement reliability and measurement validity? Can you have validity without reliability? Why or why not?

PRACTICE PROBLEM

As the resident measurement specialist, you have been asked to create an opinion measure that will provide information on your company's employee perceptions of the new management team. What are the major dimensions of importance to your measure? How would you create, first, a Likert-type measure of employee opinion and, next, a semantic differential-type measure of employee opinion? Once these were created, how would you assess both measures' reliability and validity?

Assume that you have created your measure with three subdimensions: organizational trust, managerial responsibility, and benefits. After establishing face validity and content validity, you test the measure on an employee sample and find your three subdimensions via factor analysis. A reliability analysis via the coefficient alpha finds subdimensional reliability to be: organizational trust, .78; managerial responsibility, .64; and benefits, .92. Further, you have also asked the sample to respond to a known general measure of organizational satisfaction (assuming that trust, responsibility, and benefits are related to satisfaction) and have found correlations ranging from .42 to .76. What can you infer about your measure?

NOTES

1. Linda Childers Hon and James E. Grunig, *Guidelines for Measuring Relationships in Public Relations* (Gainesville, FL: Institute for Public Relations, 1999); and Walter K. Lindenmann, *Guidelines and Standards for Measuring and Evaluating PR Effectiveness* (Gainesville, FL: Institute for Public Relations Research and Education, 1997).
2. For more on credibility and its dimensions, see Charles Self, "Credibility," in Michael B. Salwen and Don W. Stacks (eds.), *An Integrated Approach to Communication Theory and Research* (Mahway, NJ: Erlbaum, 1998), pp. 421–442.
3. See, for example, any number of persuasion texts for more on this. A good introductory text is Erwin P. Bettinghaus, *Persuasive Communication*, 5th ed. (New York: Harcourt College Publishing, 1997).
4. Charles E. Osgood, G. J., Suci, and Percy H. Tannenbaum, *The Measurement of Meaning* (Urbana, IL: University of Illinois Press, 1957).
5. L. L. Thurstone and E. J. Chave, *The Measurement of Attitude* (Chicago: University of Chicago Press, 1929).
6. Delbert Miller, *Handbook of Research Design and Social Measurement*, 5th ed. (Newbury Park, CA: Sage, 1991).
7. Rensis Likert, "A Technique for the Measurement of Attitudes," *Archives of Psychology, 40* (1932), 1–55.
8. Osgood, Suci, and Tannenbaum.
9. Hon and Grunig.

Chapter 9

Sampling Messages and People

One of the major differences between formal and informal methodology is formal methodology's ability to generalize to a larger population. This is particularly true with survey and poll methods where we draw *representative samples* from larger populations and then generalize results back to the larger population. Formal methodologies permit one to generalize findings because of the way the methodologies select research participants or materials.

This chapter examines the process of selecting messages and people for research. Why "messages and people"? Often we do not have the access or time or money to contact *every* respondent or work with *every* message in a population of individuals or messages. In these instances we must rely on a smaller segment of that population; we get that smaller segment by *sampling* from that population.

Sampling is the science of systematically drawing a valid group of objects from a population reliably. This chapter explores three different ways of collecting respondents or content. First, we can conduct a *census* of the population. Second, we can conduct a *nonprobability sample* of the population. Third, we can conduct a *probability sample* of that population. In the first case, we do not need to generalize—we've used *all* members of the population. In the second, we cannot generalize because we have not randomly selected our sample, instead relying on those available. In the third, we can generalize because we have within an agreeable degree of error *randomly sampled* from the population.

SAMPLING

Public relations research often includes survey and polling methods for gathering information about a public's attitudes, beliefs, and behavior or the message content to be studied. It is usually impractical to study all the messages or contact all the people in a public; therefore, we resort to selecting messages or participants based on some criteria. We can do so scientifically or nonscientifically.

Unfortunately, public relations research is often constrained by time limitations. Although it would be ideal to have a week or even a month to research and draw a sample, it may be that you are on a 24-hour deadline. Today's 24/7 world of the Internet and rapid access to a large number of people has made research results needed "overnight." This often leads to an excessive amount of nonprobability samples— and the increased errors that come with them. This problem can be overcome by carefully planning needed research within a campaign or program; today, as in the past, we often react to a situation that suddenly requires research rather than being prepared to proceed under a planned proactive campaign. That, quite simply, is the state of affairs (and always has been).

Scientific sampling occurs when the selected group of people or messages represents the entire population from which it is drawn. *Nonscientific sampling* occurs when the sampled group is not representative of the entire population of people or messages. Scientific sampling, also called *probability sampling*, allows for generalization of the selected group to other members of the larger group. Nonscientific sampling, also called *convenience sampling*, only allows for descriptions based on the people or messages actually studied.

A convenience sample of respondents—people at a local festival you are promoting—selected only on the first day of a three-day festival, for instance, does not represent all festival goers, only those who attended the first day. The sample may have been chosen for pragmatic reasons (you may not have enough interviewers to survey people beyond that time, or this is the only time festival organizers will allow you to contact festival goers), but even if you randomly selected participants, you could only describe first-day festival attendees.

Regardless of the type of sampling employed, there are four important elements that underlie any sampling technique. These elements, dealing with sampling theory, define and establish the parameters of surveying. The first is the *universe*, or the general concept of who or what will be sampled. As Broom and Dozier point out, the universe is a relatively abstract term,[1] but it is an important one. Based on how we define our universe, the *population*, or the message types or the people to be sampled, is clearly specified and described (it could be registered voters, press releases for a particular product or service, or households with satellite dishes). Thus, before we can state what our population is, we must first look at the universe from which it will be drawn. For instance, the universe may be all colleges and universities in the United States and the population of interest only those that are private. Once the population has been described, the sampling frame is defined. A *sampling frame* is a list of *all* the messages or people to be surveyed (e.g., all households connected to satellite dishes with two or more televisions sets in the income range of $25,000–$50,000 in a particular geographic area). The *sample* consists of the actual messages or people chosen for actual inclusion in the research. The *completed sample* consists of those messages selected and analyzed and the people who actually responded to the survey.

PROBLEMS—ERRORS—ENCOUNTERED IN SAMPLING

There are two other sampling elements that need to be defined. *Coverage error* is the error produced in not having an up-to-date sampling frame from which to sample. For example, in a media relations project recently carried out for a client, the population was defined as writers covering a particular industry and the sampling frame was a listing of the fax numbers used to distribute media releases to writers about a particular company. The coverage error identified here was that the fax list was old; in many instances the writers were no longer with the media outlets identified (and in some cases the media outlets did not even cover the industry). You probably occasionally get mail addressed to someone else at your home—this is coverage error. *Sampling error* is the error produced when you do not sample from all the members of the sampling frame. Sampling error occurs when messages or people are inadvertently selected from a subset of the population. Sampling error can be estimated but only for samples selected through scientific probability sampling. For convenience, nonprobability sampling the question is moot—you have not sampled from the larger population but only from a specific subset. For instance, sampling from *available* employees for a focus group is a subset of the total population of employees. Finally, *measurement error*, the error found when people misunderstand or incorrectly respond to questions, is closely allied to sampling error. Measurement error can be statistically estimated and taken into account. (For a listing of sampling elements and definitions, see Table 9.1.)

TABLE 9.1. Sampling Elements and Definitions

- *Universe*—the general concept of who or what will be sampled
- *Population*—the message types or the people to be sampled, as defined and described
- *Sampling frame*—a list of *all* the messages or people to be surveyed
- *Sample*—the actual messages or people chosen for inclusion in the research
- *Completed sample*—messages selected and analyzed and the people who actually responded to the survey
- *Coverage error*—error produced in not having an up-to-date sampling frame from which to sample
- *Sampling error*—the error produced when you do not sample from all the members of the sampling frame
- *Measurement error*—the error found when people misunderstand or incorrectly respond to questions (found primarily when sampling people)

Reducing Coverage Errors

Reducing coverage errors is important to both probability and non-probability sampling. Coverage errors are often unseen and unpredictable. In part they are a result of poor or incomplete documentary/historical research. They also result in problems with sampling frames and an insufficiency of messages and/or people. Don A. Dillman suggests any sampling procedure should include a "coverage analysis of potential sample frames."[2] The primary coverage error problem lies in incomplete or out-of-date sample lists. Although the computer has made such lists easier to create, they require substantial maintenance. Dillman suggests that you answer four questions when conducting a coverage analysis[3]:

1. Does the list contain everyone in the population?
2. Does the list include names of people who are *not* in the study population?
3. How is the list maintained and updated?
4. Does the list contain other information that can be used to improve the sampling?

Depending on how you answer these questions, you will be aware of potential coverage problems and can possibly correct them.

A major problem occurs when you must sample from a population for which there is no sampling frame listing available. This generally occurs when you sample from the general population and not one that is defined by some association, company, or directory. This is particularly true when the sample is drawn from telephone directories, of which unlisted or unpublished numbers may be as high as 25% of the total listings.[4] Although there are other ways to obtain lists, the quality of such lists is always an open source of coverage error. Add to this the problem of contacting specific individuals or collecting specific messages, and coverage errors can be a real problem. For example, although a survey may be mailed to a specific individual with a specific title, there is no way of knowing if that person or someone else actually completed it; there is no way to adequately ascertain *who* completed mail surveys.

Reducing Sampling and Measurement Errors

Sampling errors occur when the sample drawn from a population does not accurately reflect that population. These errors are generally reduced through probability sampling and can be estimated by statistically determining how large a sample needs to be to result in "acceptable" sampling and measurement error. Although we will go into this in greater detail later, a sample that can be drawn with 95% confidence that it reflects the sampling frame and yields no more than 5% error in response requires a sample of *384* randomly selected participants. That is, with 384 randomly selected participants there will be *no more than 5 people missampled* (sampling error), and the quantitative results of the population will be *no more than 5% of what we would expect to find in the population* (no more than 5% measurement error).

SAMPLING TYPES

As noted earlier, there are two types of sampling, scientific or probability sampling and nonscientific or nonprobability sampling. There is, however, a third way to collect data that needs to be briefly discussed before turning to the two major sampling types—namely, the census.

Census

Strictly speaking, a *census* occurs when you contact every member of a population. In a census, the universe, population, sampling frame, and sample are all the same. A census has no error—you have missed no one. In reality there are very few actual censuses conducted. This is especially true when dealing with the general public as your universe and population. However, there are times when the actual population is small, such as in corporate public relations where you have access to all members of the population under study; under those conditions, a census is possible. A second instance is when you are tracking a particular set of messages and you have access to all media outlets where the messages should be reported. The question in each instance remains: Is it probable? A census means that you have contacted *all* members of the population. What occurs when someone is out on vacation? What if you do not have access to a particular media outlet (a newspaper or television or radio news log or tape of the news segment in question)?

As long as you have contacted all members of the population or have all instances where a particular message was published, then you can say with 100% confidence that your results reflect the population under study. Any inferences made are actually conclusions. However, if you missed one individual or one newspaper, then your results can only *infer* as to the population's attitude or the media placement. The problem with such inferences is that we do not know how much confidence we can place in our results. Broom and Dozier refer to this lack of confidence as *bias*: "When the missing elements are few, the potential for bias is small. As the number of missing elements increases, the potential for bias also increases."[5]

To overcome potential census problems, public relations researchers can turn to ways of sampling that take into account possible bias from the outset or allow us to estimate how much error we either have or must be willing to tolerate. We turn first to nonprobability sampling, where you know in advance what biases or errors may be. Then we turn to probability sampling, where we can estimate the amount of error we will either accept before sampling or how much error we actually obtained after sampling.

Nonprobability Sampling

Nonprobability sampling is conducted when you do not have access to every unit in a population of people or messages. When nonprobability sampling is employed you are restricted to saying, "based on what or whom we sampled, their responses were this." *You cannot generalize to the larger population, only to the sample you observed*. It's not that nonprobability samples are unrepresentative of the population—they may be—but the problem is that we will never know just *how representative* they are. There are many instances when you must resort to nonprobability sampling, for instance: when you must rely on volunteers instead of randomly selected people, when you must deal with children, when you are conducting a participant-observation, or when your access to materials is limited. Although there are many different types of nonprobability sampling techniques, five types are typically employed in public relations research: convenience (sometimes referred to as an "accidental sample"), quota, purposive, volunteer, and snowball.

As noted earlier, the nonprobability sample is often the only way to quickly and efficiently gather data. Given the restrictions placed on you by day-to-day calls for research (again, often forced by breaking events, causing you to act in a reactive rather than proactive way), a nonprobability sample is your most cost-efficient and timely option. Just remember the restrictions placed on interpretation of data gathered from nonprobability samples and the increased amount of error you will have from both sampling and measurement error when you report your results. (For a listing of nonprobability sampling techniques, see Table 9.2.)

Convenience Sampling

Convenience sampling occurs when you select participants or messages because they are available. They may not be the population of people or messages but they are accessible. As such, polling 100 people at the water fountain and asking questions concerning their morale or stopping 100 people in the bathroom line at a music concert and asking how they are enjoying the concert represent convenience sampling. Any time that you study children, you have a convenience sample—you must first get permission of the child's parents (and in a school setting the permission of the school administration) to participate in any research. Convenience sampling for interviews is also known as the "man on the street corner" method. By interviewing only those

---

TABLE 9.2. Nonprobability Sampling Techniques

- *Convenience sampling*—selecting participants or materials because they simply are available
- *Quota sampling*—selecting participants or materials because they are available, but only to the point that they meet a particular population distribution
- *Purposive sampling*—selecting participants or materials for a particular reason that is based on the researcher's knowledge of the population and the focus of the research
- *Volunteer sampling*—selecting participants based on their agreeing to be a part of a research project
- *Snowball sampling*—selecting participants based on other participants' recommendations

people at a particular location, you restrict your inferences to only those people who were at such and such location at such and such a time. Mall shopping intercept studies also fall into the category of convenience sampling.

Quota Sampling

Quota sampling occurs when you select available or accessible people or materials but weigh that sample so that certain predetermined characteristics are represented in the sample. For instance, you are conducting a mall shopping intercept study for a client who wants to know how many people have shopped at her store and what they purchased. Further, you know from secondary research that 28% of the people in previous studies looking at similar outcomes were aged 13–17. You have enough support to conduct a 1-day study of 100 people. Thus the quota for age would be 28 people aged 13–17 and you would stop sampling once you hit 28 completed surveys. Obviously, there might be other characteristics that would provide for more quotas. Once again, you are limited to responses and inferences to the people you studied: only those who were available. You have ensured, however, that important elements in the sampling frame *have not been excluded* from your sample.

Purposive Sampling

Purposive sampling occurs when you have a particular reason for only selecting certain participants or messages. You may be interested, for instance, in targeting only people who have seen a particular story in a company newsletter. Further, you have neither the time nor money to select all people who may have read the story, so you choose only those who are in the company cafeteria over a 5-day period. The sample has not been chosen to represent all the employees, only those who (1) were in the cafeteria those days and (2) only those who read the story in the company newsletter. Many focus groups participants are selected through purposive sampling. A major problem with purposive sampling comes when others confuse a random sample with a purposive sample—when you have targeted a specific subset of the population for a particular purpose.[6]

Volunteer Sampling

Volunteer sampling occurs when you select your participants based on their agreement to participate in a research project. Volunteers often only participate because they have been enticed into the research because of some payment for their time or the promise of a gift or because they have particular interest in the focus or topic of the research project. In general, volunteers are not normal people; they differ from a "normal" population both in terms of personality and motivation.[7] Even greater caution must be taken when interpreting results from volunteer samples as there are any number of biases that may account for what they may say or do.

Snowball Sampling

Finally, *snowball sampling* occurs when you have limited knowledge of the population. Snowball sampling begins by identifying a small sample of people whom you have access to and who, in turn, have access to other people. You may be interested in finding out who is purchasing a product that you will be promoting, but you do not know much about the population. One of your staff casually mentions that his daughter has several friends who have purchased the product. You begin your snowball sample by first getting a list of her daughter's friends and then contacting them for more names and contact addresses. Snowball sampling, like all forms of nonprobability sampling, cannot be generalized to the larger population.

Probability Samples

Probability samples occur when every individual or message in a particular population has an equal chance of being chosen, regardless of any particular biases held by a researcher. The key to probability sampling is found in the *random selection of potential messages or participants*. There are four different sampling strategies public relations researchers employ when they sample from a population. The strategies can be further divided into single- or multistage sampling. Although these strategies may be employed in both nonprobability and probability sampling, we find them used most in probability sampling.

Sampling from a Population over Time

Probably the most common type of sampling conducted in public relations research is simply sampling once from a population. This sampling strategy is called *cross-sectional sampling*, or "snapshot" sampling. As the name indicates, a single sample is randomly drawn from the population under study; in other words, the population is sampled once. As such, the results describe both sample and population at a particular point in time. You might be interested, for example, in finding out how many of your 10,000 employees say they will participate in the company picnic. Obviously, polling all 10,000 employees is out of the question; a random sample of employees, however, will give you an idea of how many plan to attend as of the date they were sampled. You have, in effect, taken a "snapshot" of the population. Because you randomly selected the employees, you are certain within a certain degree of error that their responses reflect how many employees in the population say they will attend. This information allows you to make your preparations or, if the number is low, to put out additional information about the picnic.

If you go back to that population again later and poll for attendance (or track messages about some event), then you are conducting longitudinal sampling. A *longitudinal sample* occurs when you sample from a population over time. There are three types of longitudinal sampling strategies (see Figure 9.1). A *trend sample* occurs when you sample different people from the population over time. Of the 10,000 employees, you randomly select 100 employees at time 1, a second 100 employees at time 2, a third 100 employees at time 3, and so forth. The trend sampling technique produces multiple cross-sectional samples, each chosen at a different time. The samples may or may not include the same people—each has an equal chance of being chosen at each sampling.

A *panel sample* occurs when you randomly select a sample from the population and then follow its members over time. Your sample becomes a panel in that you follow the sample over time. Care must be taken when analyzing and inferring from panel samples. Even though the same people have been observed over time, you cannot say for certain that a particular event or message caused any change in their attitudes, beliefs, or behaviors (that can only be established through laboratory experiments; see Chapter 11). Further, because you will lose contact with some panel members over time, you must set initial sample sizes much larger than when working with either cross-sectional or trend samples.

Cohort-trend sampling occurs when you sample different people over time, but only those people who meet certain characteristics. Age is the usual example of a cohort used in trend sampling; message length is a message example. In cohort-trend sampling you randomly sample from the population at different times but follow only those people or messages demonstrating the cohort characteristic. For instance, you are interested only in new employees, so you would randomly choose only employees who met your definition of "new," say having worked for the company less than one year. Human Resources should be able to provide you a listing of "new" employees, and you

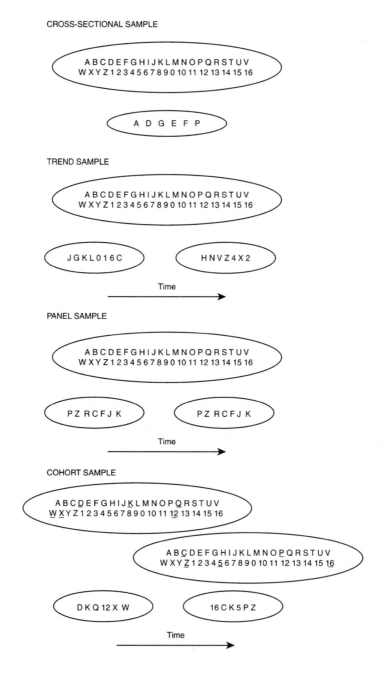

FIGURE 9.1. Sampling strategies. Underlined elements share cohort of age = 18.

annually sample them about the company's internal communications. You might be interested in how people about to reach 50 years of age feel about the AARP (formerly known as the American Association of Retired Persons). Thus, you would randomly sample 50-year-olds each year.

Probability sampling, regardless of what strategy you approach it with, allows you to generalize to the population it was drawn from within certain degrees of error. The single determiner in how much certainty you have regarding sample confidence and measurement error (accuracy) is found in *sample size*, the number of people selected who actually complete the research (message sampling generally does not examine measurement error). We turn next to the mechanics behind establishing sample size and the techniques used when drawing random samples from a population's sampling frame.

SAMPLE SIZE AND PROBABILITY SAMPLING

The amount of sampling and measurement error you are willing to tolerate or to have obtained provides both confidence in your sample's representativeness and the accuracy of the results you find when generalized to a population. The reason we can establish sampling confidence and measurement accuracy lies with an understanding of the normal curve. In this section we will look at both the normal curve and how to use its properties to determine sample size. Although you will find tables that provide sample sizes for different degrees of confidence and accuracy, it is important that you understand the underlying mechanisms and, if necessary, compute sample size for a confidence/accuracy rate. We turn first to a discussion of the normal curve.

The Normal Curve

The *normal curve* is a statistical tool that tells us what confidence we can have in our sampling and the accuracy of our measurement (in terms of the percentage of units selected at random from a larger population) based on the true population percentage. The normal curve is also called a *bell-shaped curve* because with enough samples from a population the sample's distribution is said to be "normal and equally distributed." What does this mean? As seen in Figure 9.2, if we only drew one person randomly from a population, the result would be a straight line representing the one sampling. If we drew 10 people at random, the distribution would begin to *skew* from the true population characteristic in some predictable way ("skew" means we might select

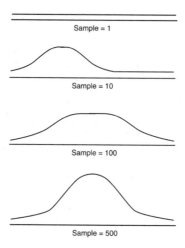

Sample = 1

Sample = 10

Sample = 100

Sample = 500

FIGURE 9.2. Sample sizes and "normal" curve shape.

closer to one side of the distribution). If we drew 100 people at random, the errors in sampling would be more equally distributed and the probability of skewing would be reduced; with 250 randomly selected people we begin to see the traditional "bell" shape of the curve; at 500 randomly selected people, the bell shape has been established.

The distribution of "samples" (people chosen randomly from a population) becomes more evenly dispersed or distributed as we make more random selections. Thus, the average for all the samplings will begin to estimate the true population characteristic. Always. It is a "statistical law." You can bet on it. We say estimate, because there will always be some error in sampling. This statistical law can be used to our advantage in determining sample size.

We know from the work of many statisticians that the area under the normal curve can be determined in terms of the sampling error that might be expected (or, turned around, how much confidence we have in our sampling). Statistical probability theory states that 68% of all samples will occur within 1 standard unit—*a standard deviation*—from the true population characteristic (see Figure 9.3). That is, we are willing to accept 32% sampling error; or for every 100 objects samples, we will have no more than 32 mis-samples. This standard unit is measurable and does not change. Obviously, you want to be more precise in your sampling. Earl Babbie suggests that we should establish 95% as our *confidence interval* for sampling.[8] Why 95%? No reason, other than

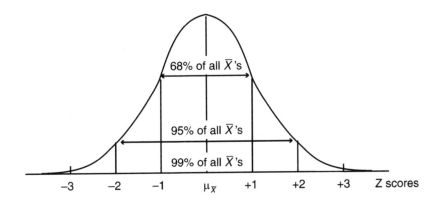

FIGURE 9.3. The hypothetical normal curve and its properties.

the social science convention of wanting to be no more than 5% wrong when inferring to a population and the fact that a 95% confidence interval just happens to be about *two standard deviations from the population characteristic* in each direction (see Figure 9.3).

Statisticians have determined standardized scores, called *Z-scores*, for the area under the normal curve. As we will see, the Z-score is used to determine sample size. Most sampling is expressed in terms of being at a 95% or 99% confidence level. Thus, two Z-scores you will want to be familiar with are *1.96* and *2.58*, the Z-scores for a 95% confidence interval and a 99% confidence interval, respectively. (Table 9.3 provides other confidence intervals and their associated Z-scores.)

Sampling Error (Confidence)

Determining the sample size that is correct for you depends on a number of factors. First, there are budgetary considerations: the larger the sample, the more it will cost to contact or obtain data. Public relations research budgets are not large and often require that you conduct the research yourself or reduce sample size due to the budget. Second, there are time constraints; in public relations you often do not have the luxury of vast amounts of time—you must get your research done on a sometimes hurried timetable or immediately after an unexpected event. Third, there are resource constraints; unlike marketing and advertising, you may not have the staffing necessary to conduct the re-

TABLE 9.3. Z-Scores and Confidence
Intervals

Confidence interval		Z-score
70.0%	. . . .	0.52
75.0%	. . . .	0.67
85.0%	. . . .	1.04
90.0%	. . . .	1.28
95.0%	. . . .	1.96
99.0%	. . . .	2.58
99.9%	. . . .	3.09

search. Fourth, prior research may provide clues as to how large the
sample size needs to be relative to acceptable measurement error. And,
finally, it may be that the precision and accuracy are determined by the
stage of research or importance to the overall campaign or program.
As noted, sampling error is typically set at a 5%, or 95% confidence,
interval. We will work at both the 95% and 99% sampling confidence
interval.

A note of interpretation needs to be interjected here. When we
say we are willing to accept or tolerate so much error in sampling,
we are saying that we expect *no more* than that amount of error.
Thus, when we set a 95% confidence interval, we are saying that *no
more than 5 units (people or messages) will be missampled*; there may be
fewer, but no more than 5 missamples. The same is true of measurement accuracy.

Measurement Error (Accuracy)

Measurement error was covered in some detail in Chapter 8. To review, measurement error represents the amount of random error
found in any measure. Measurement error may be due to failure to understand directions, failure to complete a measure, poorly written or
asked questions, and so forth. The key here, as with sampling confidence, is that we can establish how much accuracy at a minimum we
are willing to accept or, conversely, how much error we are willing to
tolerate. The nominal standard is 95% confidence in measurement, or
accepting no more than 5% random measurement error.

Measurement error is tied to sample size. Both measurement accuracy and sampling confidence are part of calculating sample size. *As you reduce each source of error, however, you increase the number of units required to be sampled from a population.*

Pragmatic Considerations

Selection of sampling confidence and error intervals will depend on how much error you are willing to tolerate. For instance, suppose you have randomly surveyed 250 employees regarding their support of a new initiative being considered. You find that 80% agree with the initiative and 20% do not. Would it make any pragmatic difference if the actual figures were 75% agreeing and 25% disagreeing? Or 85% agreeing and 15% disagreeing? As will be pointed out when we discuss inferential statistics in Chapter 13, sometimes the pragmatic is more appropriate than the scientific (what is the *real* difference if two groups are 5% apart?). However, if the results are close, say within 1% to 3% (e.g., 51% agreeing, 49% disagreeing), then choosing a 95% or 99% confidence interval may be necessary.

Calculating Sample Size

Tables 9.4 and 9.5 provide the necessary information to select a sample at given sampling confidence intervals and levels of measurement error. Table 9.4 is particularly useful because it can be used after the fact to see approximately how much measurement error actually occurred in the findings. The table is set for a 95% sampling confidence (5 errors out of 100, or a safety factor of 20 to 1). Table 9.5 shows the necessary sample sized for both 95% and 99% sampling confidence and tolerated measurement error ranging from 1% to 7%.

Before we actually look at the formula for calculating sample size, it is important to note that this sampling assumes two things. First, *we want to be extremely conservative in estimating error*; therefore, we set the probability of obtaining an erroneous outcome at 50% for a simple dichotomous response. Second, *we are looking at the entire population, not some subset of it.* That is, we are interested in all units in the population, not how, for instance, males and females differ. If that is the case, then we would need the same number of males and the same number of females drawn at random from the population as we would from the population itself. The number of units randomly drawn from populations of differing sizes with 95% sampling confidence and 95% measurement accuracy has been calculated to be:[9]

TABLE 9.4. Probable Deviation (Plus or Minus) of Results Due to Size of Sample Only

						Safety factor of 20:1					
Survey Result	1% or 99%	5% or 95%	10% or 90%	15% or 85%	20% or 80%	25% or 75%	30% or 70%	35% or 65%	40% or 60%	45% or 55%	50%
Sample of:											
25	4.0	8.7	12.0	14.3	16.0	17.3	18.3	19.1	19.6	19.8	20.0
50	2.8	6.2	8.5	10.1	11.4	12.3	13.0	13.5	13.9	14.1	14.2
75	2.3	5.0	6.9	8.2	9.2	10.0	10.5	11.0	11.3	11.4	11.5
100	2.0	4.4	6.0	7.1	8.0	8.7	9.2	9.5	9.8	9.9	10.0
150	1.6	3.6	4.9	5.9	6.6	7.1	7.5	7.8	8.0	8.1	8.2
200	1.4	3.1	4.3	5.1	5.7	6.1	6.5	6.8	7.0	7.0	7.1
250	1.2	2.7	3.8	4.5	5.0	5.5	5.8	6.0	6.2	6.2	6.3
300	1.1	2.5	3.5	4.1	4.6	5.0	5.3	5.5	5.7	5.8	5.8
400	.99	2.2	3.0	3.6	4.0	4.3	4.6	4.8	4.9	5.0	5.0
500	.89	2.0	2.7	3.2	3.6	3.9	4.1	4.3	4.4	4.5	4.5
600	.81	1.8	2.5	2.9	3.3	3.6	3.8	3.9	4.0	4.1	4.1
800	.69	1.5	2.1	2.5	2.8	3.0	3.2	3.3	3.4	3.5	3.5
1,000	.63	1.4	1.9	2.3	2.6	2.8	2.9	3.1	3.1	3.2	3.2
2,000	.44	.96	1.3	1.6	1.8	1.9	2.0	2.1	2.2	2.2	2.2
5,000	.28	.62	.85	1.0	1.1	1.2	1.3	1.4	1.4	1.4	1.4

Note: Example: When size of sample is 500 and survey result come out to 25%, you may be reasonably sure (odds 20 to 1) that this result is no more than 3.9 off, plus or minus. Doubling this margin to 1,000 reduces this margin to 2.8. From National Association of Broadcasters, *A Broadcast Research Primer* (Washington, DC: National Association of Broadcasters, 1976). Reprinted with permission from the National Association of Broadcasters.

TABLE 9.5. 95% and 99% Sample Confidence with Tolerated Error

Error	Confidence	
	95%	99%
1%	9,604	16,587
2%	2,401	4,147
3%	1,067	1,843
4%	600	1,037
5%	384	663
6%	267	461
7%	196	339

Note. From C. H. Backstrom and G. Hursch-Cesar, *Survey Research*, 2nd ed. (New York: Macmillan, 1981). Reprinted with permission from Macmillan, Inc.

Population size	Sample size
Infinity	384
500,000	384
100,000	383
50,000	381
10,000	370
5,000	357
3,000	341
2,000	322
1,000	278

Note that the "magic" number is *384*. This represents, however, the number of final observations—the total number of messages drawn from an infinite population (for example, all the stories in the major U.S. newspapers over the campaign time frame) or the number of *completed* interviews or surveys and polls (to get to this number, you will need to sample many more people, often at a 12:1 ratio or higher).

There are times, however, when 95% confidence in sampling and measurement error are *not* good enough. Would you, for instance, sample 384 registered voters for a statewide election if you wanted to be extremely certain of an election outcome and why voters might inclined to vote as they might? It may be that a 95% sampling confidence is adequate, given that you know your population quite well. Making inferences about how the voters will vote, however, may require a more conservative measurement error—perhaps 3% would be better;

thus, you would increase your sample size accordingly to 1,067. Remember, if you were interested in how both Democrats and Republicans were voting, you would need many more respondents—and not all would answer (thus, you might want to increase your sample even more). Often polling and survey firms will increase the number of people sampled to 1,500 to cover for nonresponses.

Calculation of sample size is actually quite simple and can be done with a hand calculator. While you may use the tables provided in this chapter and other books or go to a website, such as www.ucla.edu /calculators/sampsize.html, you may have to calculate the sample size necessary for a very small population or a client who wants sampling confidence and measurement accuracy set differently than the tables provide. Either way, running through two calculations provides a feel for how sample size is calculated.

$$\text{Sample size} = \frac{(Q)(p)(1 - p)}{(Q - 1)(E/C^2) + (p)(1 - p)}$$

where Q is the population size, C is the sampling confidence required, E is the measurement error allowed, and p is the expected outcome. To calculate sample size we only have to plug in the values. If our population is infinite (i.e., above 500,000), $Q = 500,000$. If we want 95% sampling confidence and no more than 5% measurement error, our values for $C = 1.96$ and $E = .05$ (1.96 is the Z-score for a 95% confidence interval; .05 represents the maximum of error allowed). Thus $C^2 = (1.96)^2$, or 3.8416, and $E^2 = (.05)^2$, or $.0025$. p is set as the most conservative outcome, or 50 (50%); thus $(p)(1 - p) = .50 \times (1 - .50)$, or .25. Thus for an infinite population, sample size (traditionally expressed as N) would be

$$N = \frac{(500,000)(.25)}{(499,999)(\frac{.05}{1.96})^2 + (.25)}$$

$$= \frac{125,000}{(499,999)(.0006508) + (.25)}$$

$$= \frac{125,000}{(325.38) + (.25)} = \frac{125,000}{325.63} = 383.87$$

For a population of 800 with a sampling confidence of 95% and measurement accuracy of 5%, we simply change Q from 500,000 to 800. Thus we find:

$$N = \frac{(800)(.25)}{(799)(\frac{.05}{1.96})^2 + (.25)}$$

$$= \frac{200}{(799)(.0006508) + (.25)}$$

$$= \frac{200}{(0.52) + (.25)} = 259.74$$

SAMPLING STRATEGIES

Now that we know the number of units—people or messages—that need to be sampled, the question of how to actually select the units remains. There are several different strategies you can use in randomly selecting a sample, but the key is that each is done so that each member of the population has an equal chance of being chosen. The strategies range from simple random selection to cluster sampling.

Simple Random Sampling

Simple random sampling is perhaps the easiest way to sample from a population. The drawback, however, is that you must have identified *all* population members. Each unit is selected by drawing it from the population pool. You might, for instance, have a listing of all employees (say, 800) of your client's company. The "bucket selection" technique would have you cutting up each employee's name from a listing of all employees, putting them into a bucket, shuffling them several times, and then selecting the first name. Each name is then recorded, *the name put back into the bucket*, and the procedure repeated again. By putting the selected employees' names back into the bucket, the chance of everyone being selected stays the same for each selection. If you were not to return each name immediately to the bucket, then the chance of someone else being chosen would increase for each name kept out. By the time you selected your 258th employee, the 259th—the last one chosen—would have had a much greater likelihood of being chosen than the first employee selected. Another way of choosing via simple random sampling is to generate a table of random numbers. After assigning each employee a number, you randomly select numbers out of the table of random numbers. Computer programs, such Microsoft Excel, will select individuals in a simple random manner.

Simple random sampling is easy and convenient. The problem is that it may not be representative. Depending on how well the population has been shaken (distributed), some of the slips of paper may be larger than others or dog-eared (a technique some use to increase the chance of their entry being chosen in a simple bucket selection process); such slips will be chosen over other slips of paper.

Systematic Random Sampling

Systematic random sampling selects units from a population based on some system. Systematic sampling may be simple or stratified. *Simple systematic sampling* draws units from the population based on access to a sampling frame. Systematic random sampling requires that you first calculate a *skip interval*. Usually a skip interval is the population size divided by the number of people to be sampled. Thus, if you have 1,000 people in the population and you want to sample 278 people, your skip interval would be 4. To conduct the sampling you would randomly select a beginning point (say, from a directory of 10 pages, each page consisting of 2 columns, each column containing 50 names). You would randomly select a number between 1 and 10, say 7. You would then randomly choose either column 1 or 2, say 2. Then you would randomly choose a number between 1 and 50, say 36. Your simple systematic random sample would begin on page 7, the second column, and the 36th person on the list. You would then count down 4 other names and choose the 5th. From the 5th name you would skip the next 4, select the 5th, and so forth until you had your 278 people. It is important that you give everyone an equal chance of being selected; thus, when you calculate your skip interval, you should always round up. Your final selection should always occur *after* your initial starting point (otherwise, those who are between the last chosen and the first would not have a chance of being chosen and your sample would no longer be a probability sample).

   Systematic stratified random sampling occurs when your population contains subunits that do not overlap. For instance, you are interested in who will vote for your client in a mayoral election. Voting is done in precincts, of which you may only be a member of one. Rather than getting a listing of all registered voters for your city, you might be better served to get the voting lists for each precinct. If you were going to sample 400 of 18,000 people, you would weight each precinct sample by the number of people registered to vote. For instance, in precinct 1 there are 4,000 voters; in precinct 2, 8,000 voters; in precinct 3, 6,000 voters. Precinct 1 represents approximately 22% of the sample, precinct 2 represents approximately 44% of the voters, and precinct 3 represents approximately 33% of the voters. Thus, you would randomly choose 88 voters from precinct 1, 176 voters from precinct 2, and 132 voters from precinct 3. In each precinct you would use the voting lists, calculate a skip interval (e.g., 45.45, rounded *up* to 46 for each precinct) and then randomly select a starting point.

Systematic random sampling requires a complete listing of all members of the population from which you will be sampling. This is not always easy to get, nor is it always complete. The advantage is that it is easy to conduct and is representative of the sampling frame.

Cluster Sampling

Cluster sampling is used when you do not have a complete sampling frame but you know that your population consists of relatively easily identifiable subgroups, or clusters. In cluster sampling you sample in two waves. First, you randomly sample a number of clusters from the population, then you sample some or all of the units within each cluster. Because you do not have a sampling frame, you cannot conduct systematic sampling; instead, you rely on random sampling from the population. To make things even more confusing, there are times when you may be faced with several sampling frames within a sample, but without a complete listing of units for each sampling frame. Given this, you would conduct a *multistage cluster sample*. This is what faces the U.S. Census Bureau when it attempts to conduct a representative count of all Americans. The Census Bureau knows that it cannot count all the people. Therefore it breaks the population down into clusters that may include cities, towns, and villages, blocks, specific locations (houses or apartments), and finally specific individual characteristic (such as oldest working female), to name but a few.

What if you had a large multinational corporation with many plants and corporate divisions—how would you approach the cluster sample logically? First, you might want to cluster based on plant location or plant type (those in English-speaking nations, those in Spanish-speaking nations, and so forth; those that produced certain products, in the latter case). Second, you might want to cluster on different divisions across plants or locations. Finally, you might consider a combination of both. What would drive your choice of clusters, of course, are your research objectives and research questions.

SUMMARY

This chapter has introduced you to the concepts associated with selecting units (people or messages) for observation or measurement. In selecting units for research from some pool of units, the population, you have two basic options: select all the units (conduct a census) or only a few (sample from that population). After a quick discussion of the pros and cons of conducting a census, two types of sampling were examined: nonscientific, or nonprobability, sampling and scientific, or probability, sampling. The distinction between the two is one of generalizability. Nonprobability samples simply describe the units observed; probability samples allow you to generalize to the larger population within certain degrees of confidence and accuracy. We then explored how to determine and calculate the number of units to be sampled based on what you feel are the acceptable levels of sampling confidence and measurement accuracy for your research. We rounded out the chapter by looking at the various ways to actually select units.

We turn next to how we describe the outcomes of research. In so doing we will look at descriptive and inferential statistics. All formal research relies on numerical data and how you interpret the data is through numbers.

REVIEW QUESTIONS

1. Why should public relations practitioners sample from a larger population? If you want to know how people feel about some attitude, object, or plan to behave in a particular way, why not simply conduct a census of the target population, public, or audience?

2. What advantages do you have with probability sampling that you do not have when you use a nonprobability sample? Are probability samples always the best way to get a sample?

3. Differentiate between the three sources of sampling error. From a public relations perspective, which sources of error are most problematic? Which can be minimalized? Why?

4. Explain why sampling confidence and measurement error are important elements in sampling adequacy. Why is it that the larger the sample, the smaller the error rate for both sampling and measurement? Why is it that the more extreme the responses to questions or observed behaviors, the smaller the sample size requirements?

5. Differentiate between simple random, systematic random, and cluster sampling as part of a strategic program of research. What advantages does each have? What disadvantages does each have? How are each different from nonprobability sampling strategies?

PRACTICE PROBLEM

You have hired a polling/survey firm to conduct a random sample of customers for your company ostensibly to gather opinions about the aftermath of a crisis at your major plant. The crisis resulted in a major environmental spill that spoiled several miles of fragile ecosystem. To make matters worse, your plant is situated at the junction of three states. The total population immediately affected is more than six million, but you also are concerned with the impact of the crisis on local employees, stockholders, and local, state, and national legislators.

What will you tell the polling/survey firm about your sampling frame and parameters that you feel must be covered? What kind of sampling do you expect to be conducted—will you be able to conduct probability sampling, or will you have to consider a combination of both probability and nonprobability sampling? What sample size(s) do you expect? Are there any special-interest groups that must be sampled? How much error are you willing to accept?

NOTES

1. Glen M. Broom and David R. Dozier, *Using Research in Public Relations: Applications to Program Management* (Englewood Cliffs, NJ: Prentice Hall, 1990), p. 116.
2. Don A. Dillman, *Mail and Internet Surveys: The Tailored Design Method* (New York: Wiley, 2000), p. 204.
3. Dillman, pp. 198–201.
4. Dillman, p. 201.
5. Broom and Dozier, p. 119.
6. Broom and Dozier, quoting Walter K. Lindenmann of Ketchum Public Relations, p. 123.
7. Robert Rosenthal, "The Volunteer Subject," *Human Relations, 18* (1965), 403–404.
8. Earl Babbie, *The Practice of Social Research*, 8th ed. (Belmont, CA: Wadsworth, 2001).
9. Philip Meyer, *Precision Journalism*, 2nd ed. (Beverly Hills, CA: Sage), p. 123.

Chapter 10

Survey and Poll Methods

Probably the most commonly used research methodology in public relations today is one form or another of the survey or poll. As we will detail later, a survey differs from a poll in numerous ways, but both have a similar goal: to obtain data from a larger population from which results can be generalized to that larger population. In Chapter 9 we explored how sampling allows us to take a smaller representative group from a population of interest and generalize findings within certain degrees of confidence, both in terms of sample representativeness and in the amount of measurement error we are willing to accept. The survey or poll provides us with a cost-effective and efficient way of collecting data from larger populations.

Consider, for instance, a typical public relations campaign where you need baseline data regarding perceptions toward a company after a crisis. How do you collect the data? You could interview important members of your public(s), but that would be very expensive and, as noted in earlier chapters, cannot be generalized to the population. You could conduct focus groups, chosen at random from the population, but again, you have problems with generalizability—participants would most likely be volunteers; the number of groups you would have to run to allow you to generalize to the larger population would be very large; and the costs again would be considerable. Content analysis cannot provide you with attitudes and beliefs regarding the company, and secondary analyses only provide you with information on data already collected. You might wish to consider an experiment (see Chapter 11), but the experiment would not reflect "reality"; it might provide useful information regarding cause-and-effect relationships, but if carried out in a sterile laboratory setting it would likely provide little or no generalizability. What you are left with is a carefully constructed survey or poll administered in one of several ways to a (hopefully) randomly selected group of respondents from the population. The sample, when compared to population demographics, should reflect the population within an accepted sampling error.

This chapter explores the survey/poll method of collecting data from a population. First we examine the differences between polls and surveys and how each can be used in public relations research. We turn next to survey or poll *designs*, or how we go about deciding how to gather the data, first from the perspective of time and respondent and then based on the *type* of survey or poll. After this we examine how a survey or poll is put together—the actual creation of a questionnaire and its component parts. Finally, we examine the impact of new technologies on this method.

POLLS VERSUS SURVEYS

Many people are confused by the terms "survey" and "poll." In general, a survey is a method of *gathering relatively in-depth information about respondent attitudes and beliefs*. Surveys are fairly long and complicated attempts to gauge how the public perceives an issue or event or person, and they allow the researcher to probe in a controlled and prescribed way why respondents feel as they do. The survey is a carefully constructed *measuring instrument*. A poll, on the other hand, is more "shallow." *Polls seek to very quickly and efficiently gauge simple opinion or certify what behaviors are or are likely to be.* Thus, if we were interested in finding out whether members of a public had seen your promotion for a local auto show running over the past week, we might sample 384 respondents simply by asking them whether they had seen the promotion and, if so, whether they would be attending. Of course, you would want to include relevant demographic data, but that data would have to be easy to collect, such as respondents' age and sex. Your poll might consist of only four questions. A survey, in contrast, seeks much more detailed data about the respondents' attitudes, beliefs, and predispositions about the promotion. You would probably ask the same four questions included in the poll, but you would try to gather more in-depth information (attitudes toward auto shows, for instance) and more demographic information, such as income, number of drivers in the household, and so forth.

Thus, when we want a "quick" snapshot of a public, we might

turn to the poll. During television rating periods, for instance, polls conducted by telephone simply ask respondents (1) whether they are watching television at that time, (2) what channel they are watching, and (3) whether they have cable or satellite access. You could ascertain the respondent's sex by voice type (although you might still have to ask), you know by the telephone number the general demographic breakdown of the area, and you know what is on the various channels once you find out if they have cable or satellite access at the time of the call. Total time to conduct the poll will be less than 5 minutes.

When you need more in-depth analysis, such as whether a client's product is being perceived positively, whether a company's corporate culture has been accepted by employees, or whether a candidate's position on the issues is getting through to potential voters, you turn to the survey. Because the poll is similar to the survey in terms of the mechanics of implementation and the design, we will refer to both methods throughout this chapter as "surveys."

DESIGN CONSIDERATIONS

The first design concern is *who* will be surveyed and *how* the respondents will be selected. Once you have determined how the sample will be selected, you have to consider the most appropriate *method* to gather the survey data. The first concern addresses sampling, whether the public relations campaign requires multiple measures from the population and whether you need to "track" respondents' perceptions. The second concern deals with how you will contact respondents and gather the information. Both concerns provide you with advantages and disadvantages, primarily in terms of speed and the costs of data collection. Table 10.1 provides speed and cost information on four popular methods of gathering data by means of surveys. Note that the telephone and Internet surveys are remarkably similar in their strengths and weaknesses.

Time and Respondent Selection

As discussed in Chapter 9, there are two general survey designs employed in most research. The first, the *cross-sectional* design, simply takes a "snapshot" of the population at a given time. Cross-sectional surveys sample from the population once and provide a glimpse of how that set of respondents thinks, feels, or behaves *at that particular time*. The vast majority of surveys conducted are cross-sectional in design. The second, the *longitudinal design*, seeks to gather data at multi-

TABLE 10.1. A Comparison of Mail, Telephone, Person-to-Person, and Internet Surveys

	Mail	Telephone	Person-to-person	Internet
Cost per response	Low[a]	Medium	High	Low
Speed of initiation	Medium	High	Low	High
Speed of return	Low	High	Medium	High
Number of interviews completed	Low	High	High	Medium
Design constraints	Medium	High	Low	High
Convenience for respondent	High	Medium	Low	High
Risk of interviewer bias	Low	Medium	Medium	Medium
Interview intrusiveness	Low	High	High	Medium
Administrative bother	Low	Low	High	Medium
Survey control	Medium	High	High	Medium
Anonymity of response	High	Medium[b]	Low	Low

Note. Adapted from Singletary, *Mass Communication Research: Contemporary Methods and Applications* (New York: Longman, 1994). Adapted with permission from Allyn & Bacon.
[a]Recently mail costs have risen to such an extent that the cost difference between mail and telephone today is small.
[b]In the case of random digit dialing, responses may actually be anonymous.

ple points in time. There are three types of longitudinal surveys, the most often employed being the *trend design*. A trend survey takes *different samples* from the *same population* at *different points in time*. A trend survey can best be visualized as multiple cross-sectional surveys. The advantage to a trend survey is that you can track an issue over time. The *panel design* not only allows you to track issues within the general population but also provides you with information as to how certain individuals perceive issues or events over time. The major disadvantages to the panel design relate to initial sampling and the costs associated with keeping the panel intact. If you need 95% sampling confidence and a maximum of 5% measurement error (see Chapter 9), you will need 384 panel members *at the end of the research*. The *cohort trend design* allows you to measure multiple times from the population but provides a "constant" from which to draw inferences. A cohort is a subpopulation of interest. Cohorts could be age groups, people who have purchased certain products, or recent college graduates with degrees in public relations who have been practicing less than one year.

An important point to remember is that the longitudinal survey uses the same questionnaire each time a sample is drawn from the population. Use of different questionnaires—or changing the questions within the questionnaire—leaves you in an "apples and oranges" situation—you cannot draw valid inferences when change occurs because you are now measuring two *different* objects. Keep this in mind if you employ a longitudinal survey design, because the initial design of the questionnaire has far-reaching implications.

Survey Type

Once the decision as to survey design has been made, you must decide how you will actually gather the data. In general there are four basic ways to collect data: via telephone, mail, the Internet, or person-to-person. Each has its advantages and disadvantages (see Table 10.1). Because of advances in technology, the telephone survey's popularity has diminished somewhat, but it is still the method of choice when you need results quickly. Mail and Internet surveys are similar in that they can utilize multiple types of measurement scales and respondents respond to them at their leisure, but response rates can be problematic. The person-to-person survey, like the in-depth interview, provides rich data (and, like the in-depth interview, offers insight gained from viewing the respondent's residence or office), but access to respondents can present special problems, and associated costs are much higher than with other methods.

Telephone

The telephone survey has several advantages over other collection types. Obviously, when you collect data by telephone you have a pretty good idea of *who* is answering your questions. You know *when* the questions were answered. You know *where* the survey was conducted (residence or business, for instance), although the greatly increased use of cellular phones has complicated the picture somewhat. And, finally, you have an *exact toll* of the number of telephone calls it took to get the number of *completed* surveys. There are, however, disadvantages associated with telephone surveys. For instance, not all potential respondents have telephones; thus, sampling error is always present. Many people are now using Caller ID or call blocking to monitor who is calling, and even more people now have answering machines used not only for messages but also to screen calls. Finally, you have to write your questionnaires differently for telephone than you do for other collection types (for instance, telephone respondents have difficulty in responding to a semantic differential-type scale).

Returning to advantages, the telephone survey offers a level of control only found in the person-to-person interview, but at a much lower cost. Telephone surveys can be administered to remote areas or areas that you might not want to send an interviewer to. They also allow you to contact people at different times of the day and to set up callbacks if necessary (a callback is scheduled when the respondent cannot complete a survey at that point in time but provides a time when he or she can finish it.) Finally, telephone surveys allow a supervisor to be present to handle any problems with respondents or to answer questions about the survey. A drawback is that telephone interviewers need to be trained and practiced in administering the survey, adding time and cost to an already tight interview schedule.

The costs associated with telephone surveys are not insignificant. Although some observers indicate that the cost differences between mail and telephone surveys are narrowing,[1] telephone surveys still cost more, especially if you are conducting your first survey. Associated start-up costs begin with establishing a bank of telephones (with long-distance lines if you are conducting national or international research) located in a dedicated room (employees generally do not like their desks and telephones used for research purposes). You must then hire and train interviewers (female interviewers, by the way, are preferred to male interviewers because respondents are less likely to hang up on a female voice). You need to keep detailed records on each completed phone call, which can slow down data collection. And, finally, you might have to purchase telephone lists from which to make your calls.

A secondary problem with telephone surveys stems from marketing firms' practice of calling potential customers under the pretense of surveying them about their product, only to turn the "interview" into a sale. Added to this is the fact that more and more people are being surveyed each year, many of whom are being "interviewed" by *computer software* (respondents are told to press 1 for one response and 2 for another, and so forth). While just 20 years ago it was an event to be included in a telephone survey, nowadays it seems like everyone wants to know what you think.

A third problem with telephone surveys is gathering data to open-ended questions. When you ask such questions as "Why?" or ask respondents to provide additional data, those responses must be written *exactly as spoken* (if you record the interviews, you must include a statement to that effect in your introduction; be prepared to lose many respondents who do not want their answers recorded). Open-ended responses are difficult to write verbatim and take considerable time. We know, however, that open-ended questions provide a richness of response not otherwise possible, and the data really help us to better understand respondents' answers to closed-ended questions as well. A 10-minute survey without open-ended questions quickly becomes a 30-minute survey with them. For instance, a political survey conduced in 1980 by the present author asked respondents to come up with reasons why they liked *and* disliked candidates—a proven predictor of voter preferences and way to gather data about the likes and dislikes of about almost anything (see Figure 10.1). Interviewers were instructed to probe for as many as four reasons for liking and four reasons for disliking each candidate (there were two candidates). All other questions were closed-ended. The survey took about 45 minutes to complete. As you might imagine, although the data gathered were rich, response rates suffer when you have to ask open-ended questions (it took almost twice as long as usual to get our 384 surveys completed). Today's typical respondent would probably hang up before completing the survey.

Telephone surveys will not go away. They simply provide you with some degree of control over who is responding, thus reducing your sampling error. They also allow you to spot problems with survey administration and questionnaire design that may have slipped through the cracks, allowing you early on to revamp both the questionnaire and administration at a significantly lower cost than associated with mail or Internet surveys (in which the questionnaire cannot be recalled without embarrassment or knowledge of those already contacted). Finally, for situations where you need a quick understanding of how a particular public feels or thinks or perceives, the telephone offers the quickest and most efficient means of collecting data.

Mail

The mail survey has one significant advantage over the telephone survey: respondents completing the survey questionnaire can see, read, and think at length about the questions being asked. This enables you to measure attitudes in a variety of ways and makes it easier to include open-ended questions.

The problems associated with the mail survey are typically found in lack of control over who actually completed the survey and the inability to track who has (and who has not) returned surveys. The first problem is difficult to overcome without actually asking respondents to provide their names, something that makes anonymity impossible (and may also compromise confidentiality). One possible approach is to offer respondents the executive summary of the findings if they will include their business card with the survey, which is then removed and stored in a different file than the returned questionnaire; this provides a measure of anonymity (no link between respondent's card and questionnaire) and *indicates* who actually completed the questionnaire.

The second problem, tracking who has not returned surveys, can be attacked in several ways. First, you can include a specific identifica-

We only have a few questions left. I'd like to ask you a few questions about the two candidates for District Attorney.

20. Is there anything in particular about the Democratic candidate X that might make you want to vote *for* him? (**LIST GOOD POINTS IN THE ORDER IN WHICH THEY ARE GIVEN BY THE RESPONDENT. IF YOU ARE GIVEN FEWER THAN FOUR GOOD POINTS, PROBE: "IS THERE ANYTHING ELSE THAT MIGHT MAKE YOU VOTE FOR X?" LIST AS MANY AS FOUR GOOD POINTS.**)

_____

_____

_____

_____

21. Is there anything in particular about the Democratic candidate X that might make you want to vote *against* him? (**LIST BAD POINTS IN THE ORDER IN WHICH THEY ARE GIVEN BY THE RESPONDENT. IF YOU ARE GIVEN FEWER THAN FOUR BAD POINTS, PROBE: "IS THERE ANYTHING ELSE THAT MIGHT MAKE YOU VOTE AGAINST X?" LIST AS MANY AS FOUR BAD POINTS.**)

_____

_____

_____

_____

22. Is there anything in particular about the Republican candidate Y that might make you want to vote *for* him? (**LIST GOOD POINTS IN THE ORDER IN WHICH THEY ARE GIVEN BY THE RESPONDENT. IF YOU ARE GIVEN FEWER THAN FOUR GOOD POINTS, PROBE: "IS THERE ANYTHING ELSE THAT MIGHT MAKE YOU VOTE FOR Y?" LIST AS MANY AS FOUR GOOD POINTS.**)

_____

_____

_____

_____

23. Is there anything in particular about the Republican candidate Y that might make you want to vote *against* him? (**LIST BAD POINTS IN THE ORDER IN WHICH THEY ARE GIVEN BY THE RESPONDENT. IF YOU ARE GIVEN FEWER THAN FOUR BAD POINTS, PROBE: "IS THERE ANYTHING ELSE THAT MIGHT MAKE YOU VOTE AGAINST Y?" LIST AS MANY AS FOUR BAD POINTS.**)

_____

_____

_____

_____

FIGURE 10.1. Sample political interview page with open-ended questions.

tion number on the questionnaire; be aware, however, that this will reduce your return rate as it appears that you are matching responses to respondents. Second, you can insert an identification number on the return envelope; again, you could be seen as matching responses to respondents. A novel way of attacking the identification problem is to use the respondent ID number as the four-digit extension to your return zip code (for instance, 33186-0001 would be your return zip code and respondent 0001). Because envelopes are typically thrown away after retrieving the questionnaire, anonymity and confidentiality are not compromised. You simply strike a line through that respondent's name on your sample listing. If you assign numbers to questionnaires *as they are returned*, do not include this number on the individual questionnaire.

As noted, mail surveys have increased in cost. Part of this cost increase relates to postage, but to achieve an acceptable response rate (which may be as low as 10% in an international mailing) may necessitate multiple mailings. Dillman argues that you can get good response rates of up to 60% by following a five-stage method (this assumes, of course that your sampling/measurement error is 5% and you still need 384 *completed* surveys)[2]:

1. *Send each respondent a brief prenotice letter a few days prior to the questionnaire.* Note here that you send a *letter*, not a postcard. The letter is sent first-class mail, indicating importance. The prenotice letter asks the respondent to be on the lookout for the questionnaire and emphasizes the importance of his or her completing it. (Note that marketing surveys are also doing this now, so be careful of "hyping" your research too much.)

2. *Mail the survey packet with a detailed cover letter indicating the importance of the research.* You should also indicate where you got the respondent's name and address and assure the respondent that his or her responses will be anonymous and will remain confidential (you do this on the questionnaire also). Include in this packet a first-class postage-paid envelope; hand stamp the letter if possible, to indicate a "personal touch." (Believe it or not, this increases the response rate!)

3. *Mail a thank-you card about a week after you have mailed the questionnaire.* Tell the respondent how much you appreciate his or her time and trouble. Emphasize that, if the respondent has not yet filled out his or her questionnaire, he or she should please do so and return it as soon as possible. A thank-you letter is expensive to send, but it helps to yield a higher return rate.

4. *Send a replacement survey packet out if you have not received a questionnaire between two and four weeks after the initial mailing.* A cover letter

is necessary and should include (a) a statement that the questionnaire has not been received and (b) a reiteration of the importance of getting the respondent's input.

5. *Make a final contact with the respondent about a week after the replacement survey packet has been mailed.* Contact is best made by telephone if you have access to respondents' telephone numbers. If not, then use FedEx or UPS or Priority U.S. Mail or special delivery as the mode of delivery for your urgent appeal. This final contact initiative is expensive, but it can dramatically increase return rates.

One final comment on delivery. The fax has quickly become a delivery medium for surveys. The fax has the same problems inherent to the mail survey. Approach any fax survey as you would a mail survey.

Internet

While the mail survey will continue to be an important survey tool for gathering data, the Internet survey is quickly moving up in use. Like the mail survey, the Internet survey has advantages and disadvantages. Depending on whom you are surveying, the Internet survey may make collecting data easier. But, as Osama Ghazi Awadallah found in an Internet survey of senior vice presidents and CIOs (chief information officers) of the top 100 public relations firms identified as being at the forefront of Internet technology, the vast majority e-mailed back and asked for a mail or fax version of the survey.[3] A second concern with Internet surveys is a lack of confidentiality. Unless, like Wright and Stacks,[4] you bring in an outside firm to create your survey homepage or to take you to the survey site, there is no guarantee of anonymity or confidentiality that can be provided Internet respondents. It is fairly simple to track back Internet responses (and most MIS departments have the capability of tracing e-mails and site visitors).

The advantages to the Internet survey lie the speed in which it is returned and the fact that the data can be directly inputted into statistical or spreadsheet packages for data analysis (some firms will provide you with basic statistical analysis, but it is always best to do your own analysis of the data). An obvious disadvantage stems from the sophistication it takes to answer an Internet survey and whether people actually have access to computers. As people become more adept at the computer, however, these disadvantages will disappear.

The Internet survey should be approached in much the same way as the mail survey. Following Dillman's five steps should increase response rates, but at least you should consider sending out first-class prenotice and follow-up mailings to stimulate responses. Prior notification via e-mail might be considered the first of a six-step program to increase response rates, but the last step, the final contact, should always be by non-Internet methods.

Person-to-Person

The person-to-person interview offers you the most control over data gathering. It is also the most expensive and possibly the most dangerous collection method (in term's of interviewers' safety). Person-to-person surveying takes considerably longer to complete but usually provides more fully completed surveys than any other type (most researchers will consider a survey completed if respondents have filled out most of the responses, though not necessarily all). Since the person-to-person survey is conducted as an interview, the respondent typically answers almost all of the questions. This may be a function of the trust that typically develops between the interviewer and the interviewee.

Conducting the person-to-person interview requires the interviewer to visit the respondent, usually at work or more typically at home. This is both expensive and potentially dangerous, especially if you have to send interviewers out to "bad" areas in the community. Time and travel costs must be factored in when determining your survey time frame, and these are significant costs. The person-to-person survey is best utilized when the questionnaire requires detailed responses and open-ended responses. Further, if you are developing a product or service that needs explanation, the person-to-person survey is an excellent way to gather data about it and potential customers.

A modified five-step procedure should maximize completed surveys. A prenotice letter should be sent, but it should be followed up by a telephone call setting up a date and time for the interview. Once the interview is completed, a thank-you letter should be sent, possibly followed up by a personal phone call. In many instances interviewees will be provided some type of reward for completing the interview (in mail surveys it is common for a dollar bill to be inserted in the survey packet as a way of nominally thanking the respondent for his or her time).

One final note regarding person-to-person surveys and a word of caution: there is a form called "man on the street" or "street corner" interviewing; it is sometimes referred to as the *random intercept method*. This method involves stopping people at random on the street and asking them to participate in a survey or poll. This method, although person-to-person and used quite often, cannot provide generalization to the larger population of interest. Even though the people are chosen "at random," not all people who may visit that area have an equal chance of being included in the survey (see Chapter 9); therefore, the sample is a *nonprobability sample*. The same is true of telephone call-in surveys or polls where potential respondents are asked to call a special (800 or 900) number or visit a special website and "let their opinions be known."

QUESTIONNAIRE CONSTRUCTION

It is beyond the scope of this volume to go into meticulous detail about constructing the questionnaire. There are several excellent books that provide detailed instructions for questionnaire construction, prenotice and follow-up letters, and so forth.[5] This section provides you with the necessary information to construct a questionnaire. The types of questions asked and how they are formatted will depend greatly on what survey method you employ and what you are seeking.

Formats

There are two major formats used in creating survey or poll questionnaires. Each questionnaire, however, follows a general format. That format has an *introduction* at the beginning, a *body of questions* that follow some logical order, a section that asks for personal or *demographic information*; and a *concluding statement*.

The introduction is extremely important. It accomplishes several things. First, it provides credibility to the survey by indicating who is sponsoring it. It also provides a touch of interpersonal communication. Finally, it should provide the respondent with a chance to refuse to continue (this is controversial; many survey companies simply go from the introduction to the body without asking permission to continue, assuming that respondents who do not want to participate will terminate the interview—usually by hanging up the telephone or walking away). A sample introduction might be:

> Hello, my name is _____ (FIRST NAME ONLY). I'm with ABC Public Relations, and we are currently conducting a survey of registered voters regarding the upcoming municipal election. I'd like to ask you a few questions regarding several of the candidates and the issues they are addressing. The survey should only take about 10 minutes. Would you mind answering a few questions? (IF YES, CONTINUE; IF NO, THANK THE RESPONDENT AND HANG UP.)

Inserted in **UPPERCASE BOLDFACED** type would be the interviewer's instructions. For instance, if the respondent indicates that he or she would like to help out, but this is a bad time, the interviewer might be prompted to say: "(**I UNDERSTAND. WHAT TIME WOULD BE BETTER FOR ME TO CALL YOU BACK?**)" This information then would be put on the respondent contact card (see Figure 10.2), and recontact would be attempted at that date and time. If the respondent refused to continue, the instructions might prompt the interviewer: "(**WELL, THANK YOU FOR YOUR TIME. IF YOU HAVE ANY QUESTIONS REGARDING THIS SURVEY, PLEASE FEEL FREE TO CONTACT JANE DOE AT 555-5555.**)." The interviewer would then wait a few seconds and then hang up. (It is always best to have interviewers wait until the respondent hangs up as a courtesy and also to make sure that the respondent does not have any questions.)

The body of the questionnaire is typically divided into sections, sections that logically flow from one topic to the next. For instance, you might begin an image survey of automobile dealers by asking general questions about local automobile dealers, then move to a section that deals with your particular dealer specifically. Depending on the information you need, the number of sections will vary. As you move from one section to another, provide *transitions* and *signposts*. A transition might be: "Now, I'd like to ask you a few questions about your perceptions of the Yellow Pages and their usefulness." A signpost tells the respondent where they are in the interview: "Finally, I'd like to ask you a few questions about your feelings about purple billboards." The signpost "finally" signifies a change in topic and in this case the end of the section or body.

Within the body of the questionnaire you will include instructions for either the interviewer or the respondent, or both. These instructions will differ, depending on whether the questions are being asked and recorded (as in a telephone or person-to-person survey) or are seen and responded to (as in a mail or Internet survey). Some surveys require that you begin the body of questioning by "filtering" respondents to particular sections based on their response to the *filtering question* or simply terminating the interview based on that filtering response. For instance, if you are conducting a survey that needs registered voters, the filter question might be a yes/no response to "Are you currently registered to vote?" A "yes" response would continue the interview; a "no" response would terminate the interview with a statement of thanks, such as "Thank you, that concludes our interview. You have been very helpful."

Unless you have a filtering question, which is most often a demographic question, all demographic and psychographic questions

TELEPHONE INTERVIEW CALL RECORD

Telephone number: _____

Location: _____

Date	Time	Interviewer	Result of interview	Time length	Recall

INSTRUCTIONS:

1. Complete this form as you complete each interview or attempted call.
2. If line is busy, note under "Results of interview" and "Recall."
3. If no one answers after 6 rings: recall code = 0.
4. Try for recall the same night as initial call.
5. Total attempts at recall before eliminating number is 3.

Abbreviations
NA = No answer
NH = Not home
WR = Will return (when)
REF = Refused (why, at what point
    in interview)
IC = Interview completed
PIC = Partially completed
    interview
DISC = Number discontinued
WN = Business number,
    eliminated from sample
OO = Out of order, eliminated
    from sample

Recall code
A = Have talked to respondent; recall
    possible (when)
B = Have talked with respondent; re-
    call impossible (why)
C = Have not talked with respondent;
    recall possible (when)
D = Have not talked to respondent;
    recall impossible (why)

COMMENTS:

_____

_____

_____

_____

FIGURE 10.2. Respondent contact card.

should be placed at the end of the survey—for two reasons. First, people are hesitant to answer personal questions, especially when they have yet to develop a bond between themselves and the interviewer. Second, demographic questions, although very important in final analyses, are less important than the respondent actually answering the measurement questions found in the body (and we can almost always determine sex audibly in a telephone survey and socioeconomic status through the exchange code and address in telephone and mail surveys). The best way to transition to the demographics section is the simple statement "Finally, I'd like to ask you some questions for statistical comparison" and go to the first question, which may be their sex or marital status, or income, or educational level and so forth.

The final section of any questionnaire is the closing. Much as in closing a letter, you want to leave the respondent with a good feeling. Therefore, you might conclude by saying or writing: "Thank you for your time. I know how valuable time is and I really appreciate your taking the time to complete this survey. Do you have any questions [in a mail/Internet survey you might state it: If you have any questions, please feel free to write me at . . . or call me at . . . and I'd be glad to discuss the results with you]?" If you offered an executive summary of the results in the cover letter or introduction, repeat that offer here. In a telephone survey, get the respondent's name and address in order to send the summary. In a mail survey have respondents include their business card or fill in a 3" x 5" note card with their name and address. If you make such a promise, be sure to follow up and mail the material as soon as possible. The same is true if you promised some reward for participating.

Asking Questions

As noted earlier, the types of questions asked in a survey will depend greatly on the type of survey being used. Telephone surveys require that the questions be clear and very unambiguous. It should not come as a surprise that the Likert-type question (with verbal gradations of agreement) is used most in telephone surveys; nor should it surprise you that categorical (ordinal and nominal) responses are preferred to other types of more open-ended measuring instruments. The time allowed is very limited, and respondents will have problems answering complex questions and the interviewers transcribing complex responses. Therefore, the byword for asking questions is: *Keep it simple.* This means that you should avoid whenever possible stating a question in the negative (with the exception of Likert-type statements, of course, which necessitate your including positively and negatively worded statements; see Chapter 8). For example, avoid yes/no questions stated as a negative to actually indicate a positive response, as found on many political voting ballots (i.e., are you aware that voting yes on "X" is a vote for candidate Y).

Further, in telephone surveys, the interviewer must provide the respondent with the actual response categories for each question, up to the time that the respondent can answer them without prompting. This means the following items must be read word for word to the respondent:

1. This product is the best in the world.   SA A NA/ND D SD
   (" 'This product is the best in the world.' Do you strongly agree, agree, neither agree nor disagree, disagree or strongly disagree, with this statement?")

2. This product has no equal in cleaning power.   SA A NA/ND D SD
   (" 'This product has no equal in cleaning power.' Do you strongly agree, agree, neither agree nor disagree, disagree, or strongly disagree with this statement?")

The interviewer would then indicate on the questionnaire (most likely laid out as a mail questionnaire) the respondent's answer or place the response on an answer sheet or code it on an optical scan sheet or even put the response into a statistical package or spreadsheet program. The key points are that *the questions are asked the same way each time*, and *respondents' answers are immediately recorded*.

What happens if a respondent does not understand the question? Should the interviewer reinterpret it? No, the interviewer must simply restate the question. In locations where two or more languages are commonly spoken, the interviewer must (1) speak (and write) the second language and (2) work from a questionnaire that has been translated into that language and "back translated" into English. But, again, to avoid tarnishing the data, in cases of confusion, the question can only be restated. Additional interviewer "amplification" on an ad hoc basis would result in data that are different from the rest of the sample. This means that you must plan ahead and test out your questionnaires carefully with all subpopulations within the population. Also remember that the Likert-type responses are not always directly translatable into some languages. Thus, you may have to work with two separate samples and then try to interpret responses between the samples (see Chapter 8).

A mail survey uses a questionnaire that is laid out. Directions in the mail survey are written out and direct the respondent from section to section or question to question. For instance, "If you answered YES to question 4, go to question 5; if you answered NO, go to section IV, Demographics." The same is true with Internet surveys and you can code automatic jumps from question to question based on response. An advantage to mail surveys (and less so with Internet surveys) is the ability to use semantic differential-type measures of attitude. As noted in Chapter 8, however, be very careful how you lay out the statements; the same is true for Likert-type scales. *When asking open-ended questions, be sure to leave enough space for the answer.* Some surveys prefer to use boxes instead of lines for responses to closed-ended questions; there is no hard-and-fast rule. Generally, however, the better the layout, the easier it is to read and follow, the higher the return rate.

REPORTING SURVEY RESULTS

When you report results from any type of survey, certain things must be included. The first is the type of survey and the dates when it was conducted. Mail, Internet, person-to-person, and telephone surveys all have different characteristics, and indicating how people were contacted and when that contact took place are important secondary pieces of information. Include here who actually conducted the survey. Was it done by an outside research firm or done internally? The reader or reviewer has the right to know, and it may also lend credibility to the report and its findings. (See Figure 10.3.)

The findings of this Chicago Tribune/WGN-TV poll are based on telephone interviews with a random sample of 899 Illinois registered voters likely to vote in the Nov. 7 general election.

For samples of this size, one can say with 95 percent certainty that results will differ by no more than plus or minus 3 percentage points from results obtained if all likely voters in Illinois were questioned. The margin of potential error for sub-groups within the larger sample is greater.

Market Shares Corp. of Mt. Prospect [Illinois] conducted the poll Friday [October 20, 2000] through Monday [October 23, 2000].

FIGURE 10.3. "How the poll was conducted." From *The Chicago Tribune*, October 25, 2000, p. 2-1. Reprinted with permission from the Chicago Tribune Companies.

Second, whenever possible always include the number of attempted contacts, either as a number or a proportion. For example, you obtained 384 completed surveys, but you had to call 2,402 people to get them. Your response rate is a lowly 16%, and it indicates how hard it was to contact selected respondents at a number that meets your sampling confidence and measurement error requirements. Mail surveys, especially those drawn from smaller lists, such as membership lists, typically report their response rates. A "good" response rate is determined by a number of factors, including the length of the questionnaire (longer ones reduce response rate), whether the sample includes international respondents (which also reduces the response rate), and whether you are sampling from special populations (such as CEOs or upper management, which will reduce response rate). Babbie suggests that a 50% response rate is adequate, 60% is good, and 70% is very good.[6] This follows from an approach such as Dillman's five-step contact method. Most public relations practitioners have neither the time nor the money to follow such procedures unless they have an established research component in their research program. Even so, time constraints would probably suggest that the most effective way to conduct surveys would be by telephone, where you continue to randomly draw from the population until the sample meets the size requirement for sampling confidence and measurement error. That said, corporate public relations practitioners often use mail (and more increasingly Internet) surveys. Depending on the importance of the issues being researched, experience indicates that a response rate of about 40% is quite acceptable (although some response rates as high as 80% have been obtained).

Third, always include the error rate(s) for *each question* asked. A good survey write-up or presentation will provide these data. A national sample of 1,500 respondents will have a measurement error rate of 3% at 95% sampling confidence. It is even better to include both sampling error and measurement error, although you do run the risk of confusing people by including both (the best way would be to indicate that you randomly contacted by telephone 663 respondents, which gives you 95% confidence in your sample and a measurement error of 1%, but even this is confusing). You can always use Table 9.4 (p. 166) to figure out exactly what your measurement error is and report that by each question or scale.

Finally, the question(s) as asked should be reported and the descriptive statistics provided for each question. This tells your audience what you actually asked. When writing up the final report, always include a copy of the questionnaire as an appendix.

NEW TECHNOLOGIES

We round out our discussion of survey methodology by looking at new technologies and how they will impact survey research. Remember, however, that the technologies are only ways of getting your questionnaire out to your sample. Regardless of how good a technology you have, poorly designed and written surveys are still basically worthless. What are some of the new technologies that you may employ in the near future? Babbie suggests there are six new technologies that will impact on survey research, some of which we are already seeing in action.[7] Computer-assisted telephone interviewing (CATI) puts the questionnaire on a computer screen, and data are typed into a file that will later by analyzed; CATI now allows for both closed- and open-ended responses to be entered and analyzed. One could argue that the Internet survey is a form of CATI. Computer-assisted personal interviewing (CAPI) is an extension of CATI but is used with laptop or Personal Information Managers (PIMs) in person-to-person interviews. Computer-assisted self-interviewing (CASI), where you provide computers to the respondents and they enter their responses to your questions on the computer screen, is a sort of middle ground between CATI and Internet surveys, where the respondent uses his or her own computer. Touchtone data entry (TDE) has been around for a while now; it requires that you use your telephone touch pad to enter responses to questions. Finally, the whole area of voice recognition (VR) is showing promise, where the interviewer asks the questions, but the computer system uses a voice recognition program to enter respondent answers as data.

SUMMARY

This chapter has introduced you to a method of data gathering that has become a favorite in public relations. It provides you with fairly fast, accurate, and generalizable data on perceptions, issues, or concerns. It is important to remember that sampling your population is a first step in conducting a survey. How you choose your respondents and how often you sample them should be an early factor in any research program. Whether to survey or poll should be the next consideration; are you interested in rapidly gathered behavioral insight into a problem or potential solution, or do you need an in-depth understanding of the population of interest? With the former, a poll will do; with the latter, you need to construct the longer survey questionnaire.

Next, you must plan how to administer the survey—which type of contact do you use? Here time and cost considerations are paramount. With other than telephone surveying, you need to forewarn your respondents, follow up, and finalize the survey. Finally, you need to write the questionnaire, taking into account whether it will be read or heard. If a telephone survey is the method of choice, you must set up a phone bank and hire and train your interviewers; with person-to-person interviews, you must hire and train your interviewers and arrange to have them transported to each respondent's location.

REVIEW QUESTIONS

1. Differentiate between a poll and a survey. What does each do well? What are the limitations of each? Which is used most in public relations research? Why?

2. There are a number of different types of surveys; distinguish between each, providing each type's strengths and weaknesses.

3. Has new technology altered how you construct a poll or survey? Why or why not?

4. Don Dillman suggests a multistep approach to mail surveys. Discuss this strategy and how it might be used in Internet or fax surveys.

5. When reporting survey results, what are the minimal reporting requirements? How do these tie in with the discussion in Chapter 3 on reporting ("Ethical Concerns in Public Relations Research")?

PRACTICE PROBLEM

How does the public relations profession use research? Design a survey instrument that answers this question. What kind of cover letter would you use? What enticements might get busy senior practitioners to answer your survey? How long should the survey be? Which of the two general formats would work best in this situation? What kinds of questions are most appropriate (is there a measurement problem here?)? How would you conduct the survey?

Assuming that you are following Dillman's multistep approach to mail surveys, what sample size would be appropriate? Would you conduct a simple random, systematic random, or cluster sample? Could you (should you?) adapt Dillman's technique to an Internet survey? If so, what problems might you anticipate (e.g., in respondent identification, follow-ups, and so forth)?

NOTES

1. See, for instance, Michael Singletary, *Mass Communication Research: Contemporary Methods and Applications.* (New York: Longman, 1994).
2. Don A. Dillman, *Mail and Internet Surveys: A Tailored Design Method,* 2nd ed. (New York: Wiley, 2000).
3. Osama Ghazi Awadallah, "The Internet and Public Relations Practices: A Survey of Senior Public Relations Practitioners," master's thesis, University of Miami, August 1999.
4. Donald K. Wright and Don W. Stacks, "Listening," program presented at the annual meeting of the Arthur W. Page Society meeting, Charlestown, SC, September 2000.
5. See: Dillman; Earl Babbie, *Survey Research,* 7th ed. (Belmont, CA: Wadsworth, 1995); C. H. Backstrom and G. D. Hirsch, *Survey Research,* 2nd ed., (New York: Macmillan, 1981); and N. M. Bradburn and S. Sudman, *Improving Interview Method and Questionnaire Design* (San Francisco: Jossey-Bass, 1979).
6. Earl Babbie, *The Practice of Social Research,* 9th ed. (Belmont, CA: Wadsworth, 2001), p. 256.
7. Babbie, pp. 265–266.

Chapter 11

Experimental Method

The experiment is probably the most rigorous kind of research conducted but, at the same time, is almost never found in public relations research. This is true in terms of the academic investigation of public relations theory and in the actual practice of public relations. This chapter introduces you to a research world that is vastly different from any other looked at thus far. It is different for two reasons. First, public relations practitioners seldom have the time or the expertise in the method to conduct research to the exacting standards of experimentation. Second, a great many public relations practitioners do not see testing theory as a major element of their research agendas; instead, they rely on descriptive (survey and poll) and qualitative (focus group and interview) methods to gather and analyze data.

Experiments are truly different than other forms of research. The experimental method requires researchers to carefully control for any sort of influence outside that which is being studied. This means that experiments are by nature *artificial*. By design they do not offer glimpses of how things operate in the "real world." Instead, they look for *hypothesized relationships between variables*. It was noted in Chapter 10 that the longitudinal survey could not establish a causal relationship between a public relations program (outputs) and the final objective (objectives and goals). Only the experiment, it was noted, could do this. Why? This chapter will answer this important question and address the implications of experimental research in public relations.

Before we turn to the experiment, let's examine the argument that public relations practitioners do not need or use experimental research. First, if you accept that public relations is theory-driven (that we *can* predict outcomes based on our knowledge of such "variables" as the media, persuasion, message channels, and so forth), then the only way we can actually test whether the theory is "good" is by the most rigorous testing possible. Perhaps 20 years ago you might hear the argument that there is no theory of public relations, but you do not hear this today. Second, most public relations practitioners are directly or indirectly influenced by experimental research. Any public relations practitioner who works in the engineering, chemicals, energy, or health care industry has to interpret experimental research and report it to the pubic. Melvin Sharpe notes that the ROPE model (discussed in Chapter 2) can be seen as an experiment of some sort: the benchmark measure is the pretest, the program is the treatment, and the evaluative research is the posttest. As he notes, "Public relations, if managed strategically according to ROPE, is an experiment in action."[1] An understanding of just what an experimenter does and how he or she thinks should certainly make the job easier.

We turn first to an understanding of the philosophy of the experiment. What is the experimenter attempting to do? What does he or she mean when speaking of control, relationships, and causation? How does she go about designing an experiment that will demonstrate control, relationship, and causation? And, finally, how does the experimental method influence daily practice.

WHAT IS AN EXPERIMENT?

The experiment is the *sine qua non* of the research world. It is the only way that we can definitely test whether something actually causes a change in something else. Experiments have both independent variables and dependent variables. The *independent variable* in effect causes a change in the *dependent variable* (thus, the dependent variable is dependent for its value on the independent variable). In crisis management situations, for instance, it is suggested that crises compress time, which in turn, makes changes in the way organizations make decisions.[2] Not only does this *prediction* makes sense, but we have a number of case studies that suggest time compression does change the way people make decisions. What we lack is experimental validation that time compression (independent variable) changes the way decisions are made (dependent variable). Obviously, it would be very difficult to create a truly crisis situation. Instead, we would have to turn to simulations—experiments—in which crisis situations or scenarios are provided to people under differing amounts of time to respond.

Philosophically (and ethically) there is a difference between reporting how an organization handled a crisis situation and putting an organization into a crisis situation. This is one of the basic differences between the experimenter and researchers who use different methodologies. As an experimenter you really do *not* care about reality—it would be nice, but it's not what you are looking for. In this example, you might be testing the theory that crisis type and response time produce different decision-making outcomes. You need to establish a situation whereby the crisis ("minimal" vs. "major" crisis) and time (immediate reaction needed vs. some time for response) can be manipulated and then to observe what happens under different crisis and time conditions (see Figure 11.1). The key is to *control* the independent variables defining the crisis situation (whether minimal or major) and the response time (i.e., whether immediate response is required or a delayed response is allowed) and then measure the kind of decisions made. In doing so you are giving up reality in favor of control. It is this degree of control that makes the experiment what it is and also allows us to see if two variables (e.g., degree of crisis and amount of time) are related to an outcome (i.e., the decision making). Further, we can also test whether one or both variables cause different decision making to occur.

Three concepts are important to the experiment. First is the establishment of relationships between variables. Second the establishment of whether these relationships are causal. And third is the amount of control you can exert over factors not related to the variables of interest—including research participants, laboratory conditions, and measurement.

TESTING RELATIONSHIPS

The major goal of an experiment is to establish that two or more variables are related to one another in predictable ways. What we are actually talking about here is the testing of theoretical relationships in such

Independent variables	Minimal Crisis	Major Crisis
Immediate Response Required	DECISION?	DECISION?
Delayed Response Allowed	DECISION?	DECISION?

Dependent variable = Decision

FIGURE 11.1. Relationships independent and dependent variables.

as way as to be sure that what we expect to find is so *because the rela-tionships truly exist* and not because something else we do not know ac-tually influenced the relationships. This is very difficult to establish and requires that the research be conducted in a manner that ensures that other things do not influence the relationships.

Most public relations research seeks to establish a relationship be-tween a campaign and an outcome (see Chapter 2). What we want to be able to say is that our message strategies have truly caused a change in some public's perception or behavior. The problem is that we are never actually certain that the campaign caused whatever changes oc-curred or whether something outside of our control or even our knowledge did. If the relationships we are seeking have been re-searched in the past, we have a pretty good idea of what *might* work. But, is "might" good enough? Probably not. We need to have conducted experimental research on the variables of interest to test whether *in isolation* the expected relationships truly exist.

Looked at differently—from the perspective of a reporter of rela-tionships in which many public relations practitioners often find them-selves—how do we know that one "thing" caused another "thing" to change? Suppose you are the public relations practitioner for a newly established Internet service provider. Your organization's promotional claim is that its service is faster than its competitors' because the way it packages data bits increases transmission speed. This claim is depend-ent on the actual relationship of how the data are packaged (independ-ent variable) and transmission speed (dependent variable). The ques-tion you want to know (the question of fact) is whether the packaging actually does increase transmission speed. You have observed first-hand how fast your service is, but can you say without reservation that your service is actually faster than that of other service providers? You could interview or conduct focus groups with your engineers and find out why they think (theorize) it should be faster, but that's hardly reas-suring. You really cannot survey users, because the service is new. What you need to do is to look at the experiments carried out by the engineers and see if they adequately tested the relationship.

Three Ways to Test Relationships

There are three ways that they could have experimentally tested the re-lationship between packaging and speed.[3] First, they could have con-ducted a laboratory experiment. Second, they could have conducted a simulation. Third, they could have conducted a field experiment. The *laboratory experiment* is the most controlled and "unreal" of all experi-mental methods. In a laboratory experiment we seek to establish that two variables are related—in complete isolation to any "contagion" variables, variables that might be spurious or extraneous to the relationships under study.[4] Hence, we test packaging and speed in optimum conditions, carefully making sure that everything is equal. We might even have competing packaging systems available and tested and compared them to ours. If we found our packaging system was faster than the rest, we could make the claim that our system of packaging data was faster (*how much* faster is a matter for statistics, covered in the next two chapters).

Is this good enough to go to your public with? Will your evidence hold up under the competition's scrutiny? As a cautious practitioner, you would probably want more testing, testing with contagion variables that are known to influence speed. You know from your background research that speed is greatly impacted by how the data are transmitted—across telephone wires, copper cable, or fiber optic cable, for instance. Further, you know that different receiving devices (modems, backbone connections) will influence data transmission speeds. Thus, you might want to ask your engineers to conduct *simulations* whereby different transmission lines and receiving devices are used. This also could be done in the laboratory, where other contagions could be taken into account. If the results show that your service is faster than the competition, you would probably feel pretty good about your promotional claim. But have you tested the package in the "real world" where many other things might affect transmission speed?

We know that many factors influence relationships. Thus, we need to next test the relationship between the packaging system and speed in a more "real" environment. Hence, we would conduct a *field experiment* where we would allow other influences (such as distance and weather) into play, but we would still carefully manage the study in terms of how much data were transmitted, over what kinds of transmission lines, and with which receiving devices. If we found that our transmission was equivalent to that found in the laboratory and as obtained in the simulations, then we could safely assume the relationship between our packaging system and transmission speed was true and we could make the claim in our promotions.

ESTABLISHING CAUSATION

Note that what we have been doing when establishing that relationships between variables exist is to establish that one or more variables *causes* changes in others. If there is one major advantage to the experiment, it is that it can establish *causation*. To say that a relationship exists you must first establish that *changes in one variable cause changes in the other variable*. Second, you must *demonstrate that the effect follows the cause*, that the independent variable actually caused the effect in the dependent variable(s) in that order and no other order. Finally, you must *demonstrate that no third variable influenced the relationship* between the independent and dependent variables.[5]

Obviously, these are not easily met criteria. No other research method can meet each, although the survey comes close—it can demonstrate that change has occurred, that the variables *covary*, that change in one produces change in the other, but we're not sure that the effect actually follows the cause (even with longitudinal survey design with a randomly selected sample) or that some other third spurious or extraneous variable has not contaminated the relationships. Only a carefully conducted experiment can do this through the control offered by the experimental method.

ESTABLISHING CONTROL

Control is central to the experiment. Because the experiment is so carefully controlled, the ability to generalize its findings to larger populations is diminished, a reason why public relations experiments are seldom conducted. However, with adequate lead time a series of experiments could be conducted, like those in the computer example just cited, that could be used to establish the relationship between say a message and a public's acceptance of that message. We would begin in the laboratory, where you carefully ensure that the message is the same, that a random sample from the population of interest has been obtained (just as in surveying, true experiments randomly select their participants), that those randomly selected participants are then randomly selected to be different independent variable "conditions" (for instance, the relevant message condition, a different message condition, and a no-message condition), and that all other aspects of the experiment (i.e., the experimental setting, the day of the week, the time of day, the testing materials) have been taken into account. In other words, *we would have carefully controlled everything to ensure that the results could only be due to the independent variable*—the relevant message—*and nothing else*.

Experimental control is also a function of the *comparison* of the different experimental conditions. Thus, we would compare the results from different conditions, of which some participants would have received relevant message and some who received the "different" message. If our comparisons indicate that the three groups attitudes were equal *before* seeing the message (i.e., RM = DM = NM), and that the message condition's attitudes changed after seeing it—and the no-message and nonrelevant message groups' attitudes did not—then we could safely say that the message caused the group who heard or saw it to change. Notice that by including a no-message condition, you could test to see if *either* message changed attitudes and whether differences between the types of message exposure had any effect on attitudes.

Thus, you have satisfied not only the first causation criterion, covariation, but also the second (effect follows cause) and third (you made sure that there were no other variables through random selection of participants and then randomly assigned them to either of the message conditions or the no-message condition).

Once you have established that the message did cause attitudes to change, you might consider a field experiment. In this instance you would randomly select participants and randomly assign them to either a message or no-message condition, but you would "loosen" control over the place where the message was heard or seen. You would do this by randomly selecting participants in a variety of settings to help you "evaluate a message" by listening to, or reading, or seeing the message. You then would randomly place participants into the message condition, the nonrelevant message condition, and the no-message condition. Your control over what occurs during message exposure is lessened but is still greater than when people are exposed to it in, say, their homes, where they may be distracted by the message or even ignore it. The field experiment still controls the fact that the message condition participants are focused *primarily* on the message.

EXPERIMENTAL DESIGNS

In a seminal work Campbell and Stanley laid out three general types of experimental designs.[6] The three experimental designs differed in terms of how they controlled for things that might invalidate the study (extraneous or spurious variables), which they collapsed into two general classes: "internal sources" and "external sources" that might invalidate the finding of relationships between the variables. The first type is the *pre-experimental design*, which does not provide any control or is questionable in controlling sources of invalidity. The second is the *true experimental design*, which provides complete control over sources of invalidity. The third is labeled "*quasi-experimental design*," where the designs control for most, but not all, sources of invalidity.

Sources of Invalidity

According to Campbell and Stanley, there are eight sources of *internal experimental invalidity*. These sources are things that reduce the confidence we can place in the results of an experiment's ability to establish causation (see Table 11.1). Each may be considered a variable that influences how tightly controlled an experiment is. The first two (*history* and *maturation*) deal with the participants themselves—their prior histories and how if exposure to a pretest changes how they react to the dependent variable(s) overtime. The next two (*testing* and *instrumentation*) relate to the testing situation, that is, how the data are collected. The fifth (*selection*) deals with whether the participants were randomly selected and randomly assigned to conditions, while the sixth and seventh (*regression* and *mortality[7]*) deal with what happens during the experiment over time. Finally, there is the interaction of the various sources of invalidity.

Of less concern to the experimenter are the three sources of *external invalidity*, which serve to make generalizations from the experiment to the larger world. These deal with (1) the *effects of testing* (actually pretest-

TABLE 11.1. Sources of Internal Invalidity

According to Campbell and Stanley eight sources of invalidity internal to the study can invalidate the study's findings (these are sources of error that unless controlled yield an experiment with results that are uninterpretable):

1. *History*	The specific events occurring between the first and second measurement in addition to the experimental variable.
2. *Maturation*	Processes within the respondents operating as a function of the passage of time per se (not specific to the particular events), including growing older, growing more tired, and the like.
3. *Testing*	The effects of taking a test upon the scores of a second testing.
4. *Instrumentation*	Changes in the calibration of a measuring instrument or changes in the observers or scorers used may produce changes in the obtained measurements.
5. *Regression*	Changes operating where groups have been selected on their extreme scores (or where the extremes over time are found to move toward the mean for the group).
6. *Selection*	Biases resulting in the differential selection of participants for the comparison groups.
7. *Mortality*	Loss of participants from the study.
8. *Interaction of (1) through (7)*	Confounding problems where multiple sources of invalidity interrelate to cause problems in interpretation.

ing), (2) *selection* (selecting participants from available "subject pools" without going to the larger population[8]) with each of the other 8 sources of internal validity; the interaction of all sources of invalidity, to include selection with testing; and (3) *reactive arrangements*, which occur when participants are exposed to more than one experimental condition.

Random Selection and Assignment and Group Comparisons

How does an experiment overcome sources of internal invalidity? As we will see shortly, by ensuring that you have randomly selected your participants first and then randomly assigning them to the possible conditions, most sources of internal invalidity can be controlled or at least reduced. As noted in Chapter 9, random selection is the great equalizer. Add to that the ability to compare groups that have or have not been exposed to experimental manipulations and you have the ability to test for problems associated with testing and instrumentation.

TYPES OF EXPERIMENTAL DESIGN

As noted earlier, there are three general types of experimental designs. We will look at several specific designs in each general type; for a more detailed treatment, go to any general research methods book or obtain a copy of Campbell and Stanley's *Experimental and Quasi-Experimental Design.*

Pre-Experimental Designs

Pre-experimental designs are designs that do not employ randomization or allow for adequate control. Pre-experimental designs often take the form of nonprobability sample surveys, where an event occurs and you take a snapshot of selected participants afterward. Campbell and Stanley lay out three such designs:

1. $\underline{X \quad O}$

2. $\underline{O \quad X \quad O}$

3. $\underline{X \quad O}$
    $\quad\quad O$

where X stands for some event or manipulation, O the observation, and the underline represents time.

The "one-shot case study" design (1) represents a study in which selected participants (a convenience sample usually) are shown something or have participated in some event and then are surveyed for their
feelings or behaviors. Because there was no randomization, we have major problems with history, maturation, selection, and mortality. We do
not know about the rest because there is no group comparison.

The "one-group pretest–posttest" design (2) adds an observation
that is usually some type of pretest. In this design you observe, manip-
ulate or participate, and then observe again. Again, history, maturation, and selection are definite problems, but at least we know how
many participants did not participate after the event (mortality is thus
"controlled"). However, the pretest may have sensitized participants
to the situation, so testing and instrumentation are now problems. Regression could be a problem, but we have nothing to compare against,
so we really do not know.

The "static group comparison" design (3), in which a group that
does not receive the manipulation (a "control" group) is added, makes
it possible to check for possible problems with testing and instrumentation but does nothing to help us with the other sources of invalidity
because of a lack of randomization.

True Experimental Designs

The true experimental design has two things going for it. First, it adds
random assignment (R) to conditions. Second, it ensures that the
proper comparisons are present to test for instrumentation and testing.
Campbell and Stanley suggest three such designs, each differing by the
complexity of comparison:

1. R   O   X   O
      R   O   O

2. R   O   X   O
      R   O   O
      R   X   O
      R   O

3. R   X   O
      R   O

Each of these designs controls for all sources of invalidity through randomization (thus history, maturation, and selection are controlled) and
comparison (thus maturation, testing, instrumentation, regression, and
mortality are controlled). The first design, the "pretest–posttest control

group" design (1), uses two groups, each pretested and posttested. The second design, the "Solomon four-group" design (2), provides more control, because you can test to see whether the pretest really had any effect on the groups, but it is more costly in terms of groups (i.e., you will need significantly more participants). The third design, the "posttest-only control group" design (3), also controls for all sources of invalidity, but your ability to provide exact comparisons is limited—but it is the quickest to conduct.

Quasi-Experimental Designs

The final set of designs is called "quasi-experimental." A quasi-experimental design is one that offers control over most but not all sources of invalidity. In most instances the designs suffer from a lack of randomization and not from comparison. They typically are found outside the experimenter's laboratory and are often confused with the field experiment, where randomization and control are still exercised but within predictable varying degrees. Two quasi-experimental designs that are seen most in the field are the (1) "time series" design and (2) "nonequivalent control group" design:

1. <u>O   O   O   X   O   O   O</u>

2. <u>O   X   O</u>
   <u>O   O</u>

The time-series design controls for all sources of validity except history and possibly selection and instrumentation. Selection is questionable because of a lack of randomization and instrumentation owing to a lack of control group comparison (testing can be checked via the multiple observations both before and after the manipulation). The nonequivalent control group design actually controls for all seven internal sources of invalidity (even history, because we can at least see if the two groups are initially the same on the variables of interest), but the interaction of sources is questionable due to a lack of randomization.

The Tradeoff between Internal Validity and Generalizability

As noted earlier, the control you exercise as an experimenter will limit the findings' generalizability to other situations or populations. For the academic theorist, this tradeoff is gladly accepted, because academic public relations researchers are theorists first and practitioners second.

The artificiality of the laboratory is something they accept as part of adding to public relations' body of knowledge. Some may over time dabble in simulations and field studies, but for the most part they see their role in the field as creating, extending, and testing theoretical relationships. The analogy between the medical researcher and the family physician is apt here: the medical researcher is seeking new ways to make our health better, to conquer cancer, and so forth; the physician takes that knowledge and disperses it to his or her patients. *The same should be true with public relations academics and practitioners.*

EXPERIMENTAL METHODOLOGY AND PUBLIC RELATIONS

How does experimental methodology serve to enhance public relations? First and foremost, experimental research tests relationships that have been theorized òr hypothesized and adds that information to the field's body of knowledge. Unfortunately, this part of public relations research has been relegated almost exclusively to the academic side of the fence. As we see more doctoral programs in public relations, however, we should see increased experimental research being conducted by the practitioner under the guidance of people trained to conduct advanced experimental research in the profession. Second, practitioners should conduct experiments anytime they want to pretest some message or see if the relationship between two variables is strong enough to be used in the field. This means that the practitioner needs to have the means and availability of participants to conduct experimental research. In addition, practitioners must factor in the time it takes to conduct a controlled experiment in their campaigns. Finally, as noted at the beginning of this chapter, many practitioners work in industries where experiments are a way of life; their job is to explain those experiments to a public that quite simply neither understands nor really cares what the experimenter has done (unless, of course, the experiment was "wrong" or produced unexpected negative findings). Understanding how to conduct an experiment is an important piece of information in selling the results to the public.

SUMMARY

This chapter has examined the least understood and practiced of all public relations research methods, the experiment. It has explored the philosophy of the experimenter and looked at what advantages the experiment provides the public relations practitioner. Specific attention was given to how experiments establish relationships between variables, how to test for causation, and how the experiment controls for factors that may invalidate its findings. The control required for a good experiment was explored and extended into three different types of experimental designs—pre-experimental, true experimental, and quasi-experimental. Finally, the relationship between experimental methods and public relations was examined.

REVIEW QUESTIONS

1. Explain why experimental research is not a high priority in today's public relations. Do you think that it should receive more attention? Why or why not?

2. Is causation important in public relations? If it is, why can't surveys or polls test relationships between a cause and an effect? What does the experiment do that allows for establishing causal links between a cause and an effect?

3. What are "sources of invalidity" and how does a *good* experimental design control for each? Do any of the sources of invalidity really impact on public relations practice? Why or why not?

4. Differentiate between pre-experimental, true experimental, and quasi-experimental designs. Which is used most in public relations today? Why?

5. Is the lack of experimental research in public relations tied to poor or nonexistent theory? Can you find examples in the public relations body of knowledge where experiments have been conducted and their results used in daily practice?

PRACTICE PROBLEM

Your company has over the past 5 years been susceptible to crisis. You know that there are different ways to address crisis communications, each tied to a different strategy. You suspect that your stockholders will react better to the next crisis if you prepare your communications in a particular way, a way that was not used in previous crisis communications. Design a true experiment to test your hypothesis that open and honest communication immediately after a crisis will yield more positive stockholder responses than "stonewalling" for a period of time and then only providing information that backs the company's position. How does your design control for internal sources of invalidity? Does it control for external sources of invalidity, or are these sources of invalidity not important in public relations?

NOTES

1. Melvin Sharpe, in reviewing the first draft of this chapter, February 2001.
2. See, for example, Otto Lerbinger, *The Crisis Manager: Facing Risk and Responsibility* (Mahwah, NJ: Erlbaum, 1997).
3. See, for example, John V. Pavlik, *Public Relations: What Research Tells Us* (Beverly Hills, CA: Sage, 1987). See also Fred N. Kerlinger and Howard B. Lee, *Foundations of Behavioral Research*, 4th ed. (Fort Worth, TX: Harcourt College Publishers, 2000).
4. Don W. Stacks and John E. Hocking, *Communication Research*, 2nd ed. (New York: Longman, 1999), pp. 270–271; see also Kerlinger and Lee, 449–464.
5. Stacks and Hocking, pp. 274–275; Kerlinger and Lee, pp. 449–464.
6. Donald T. Campbell and Julian C. Stanley, *Experimental and Quasi-Experimental Designs for Research* (Chicago: Rand McNally, 1963).
7. Stacks and Hocking argue that a better term is "attrition."
8. Kerlinger and Lee, p. 477.

Chapter 12

Descriptive Statistical Reasoning and Computer Analysis

Formal research, or the scientific approach to research, relies heavily on numbers. Numbers, however, are only placeholders; they can take on any meaning. As we discussed in Chapter 8, on measurement, assigning numbers to observations allows us to conduct research with a precision not available in informal or qualitative research. Further, the use of numerical data is essential in answering questions of fact. This chapter introduces you to the world of *statistics*, the analysis of numbers. We will look at one of two kinds of statistical analysis: descriptive analyses. *Descriptive analyses simply describe how the data gathered are distributed within the sample or census observed.* In Chapter 13 we will look at inferential statistics. *Inferential statistics go one step further and provide evidence that what you observed was not due to chance.* In general, public relations practitioners work primarily with descriptive statistics and seldom see or deal with inferential analysis. As we will see, however, knowledge based on inferential analyses allows you to answer the question "How sure are you of these results?"

The focus of this chapter is on application and interpretation, not on formulas and hand computing. The personal computer has made statistical analysis easier—almost too easy, as statistical packages not only offer to "crunch" the data but also suggest which tests are most appropriate. The intelligent computer user learned long ago that the computer cannot replace the human brain in understanding a problem and then choosing the right tool to analyze it. We will not hand compute, but we will look at some formulas to better understand what the statistical tool is analyzing and, if need be, how it can be used in hand calculating (almost all descriptive tests can be easily computed by hand).

Because statistical reasoning requires an understanding of data, we will briefly re-examine the two major types of data—data that are categorical in nature and data that are continuous in nature—and their assumptions. We will then review several specialized statistical computer packages and contrast them with what is available in spreadsheet and database applications. Finally, we will look at several descriptive statistical tests important to public relations research. We turn now to a review of data.

One final caveat: *statistical analysis is secondary to the collection of data*. If the data are not collected correctly, any statistical analysis will be rife with errors. The data are only as good as the method by which they have been collected.

REVIEW OF MEASUREMENT LEVELS
AND "VARIABLES"

Chapter 8 introduced the concepts of "data" and "measurement" by noting that there are two general levels of data, categorical and continuous, each further broken into two other levels. We noted that the levels differed in how they were measured. Categorical data distinguish between classes or categories. The most basic, *nominal data,* simply distinguish between the units being counted. *Ordinal data* not only distinguish but also order the units according to some criteria, such as larger or smaller, more or less, and so forth. Categorical data make no assumptions about equivalence of data "points." The data are simply placed into classes and counted.

Continuous data are placed on a continuum and not in categories. When the data are defined as *interval* in nature, the assumption is that the individual data points or units are equidistant apart. That is, the distance between 1 and 2 is one unit and the distance between 1 and 5 is four units (we are only discussing data here, not attitude scales, which must be interval and possess an arbitrary zero point). When data are defined as *ratio* in nature, the interval assumption is extended to include an absolute zero point. Thus, as noted in Chapter 8, a measure of temperature may be a ratio (such as Kelvin, which has a true zero point—absolute lack of heat) or interval (such as Celsius or Fahrenheit, which have arbitrary zero points, 0°C and 32°F, respectively, where water freezes). It was also noted that we can move down from ratio to interval to ordinal to nominal, but we cannot move upward; data "reduction" occurs only in a top-down fashion.

In addition to level, data must be defined as being measured or manipulated for statistical analyses. Most categorical statistical analyses assume that the data are simply observed, thus the observations are simply labeled as a "variable." Continuous statistical analysis, however, looks for differences in the measured variable as defined by some other variable. The measured variable is called a *dependent variable*, while the other variable is called an *independent variable*. The dependent variable's value is determined by the level or class of the independent variable. For instance, a person's sex (independent variable) may differentiate between earned incomes (dependent variable). In most public relations research the independent variable is categorical and the dependent variable can be either categorical or continuous.

Although we will continue to use the terms categorical and continuous when describing how data are analyzed, statistical theory redefines them according to how they are *distributed*. Data distributions can be defined by either categories or a continuum. When statisticians refer to continuous data, they use the term "parametric." *Parametric data*, because they are at least interval in nature, have a tendency to group together, to have a common mean from which they individually vary. Parametric data are said to fall under the normal curve. When statisticians refer to categorical data, they use the term "nonparametric." Categorical data, because they are found in categories, become *nonparametric data*. Although the terms are used interchangeably, we will use continuous and categorical when discussing descriptive statistics and parametric and nonparametric when discussing inferential statistics.

It is important to understand that the way the data are initially defined determines whether you conduct categorical or continuous analyses. This distinction becomes even more important when we look at inferential statistics. As a preview, percentage scores (which range from 0% to 100%) are not continuous. Why? They seem continuous; they have an absolute zero point and the distance between 1% and 2% is 1%. A percentage, however, is based on categorical data—0% means that no observations were placed in that category. Thus, *it is the underlying definition of the data that should dictate the statistical analysis*, not *how they are reported*. A trivial distinction? Perhaps, but consider an economic analogy: Would you invest in a stock that traded at a unit value of 1,000 if you did not know which stock exchange and what monetary unit it was based on? After all, $1,000 is not the same as £1,000 or 1,000 lira. The same is true with statistics, and you will find that many will "bend the rules," just as you will find that people purport to measure attitudes as a dependent variable on a 4-point scale and with only one statement (see Chapter 8).

Description versus Inference

When you conduct a survey or poll or content analysis (which yields quantitative, categorical data for the most part), you will most often report what you *observed*. Such reporting is straightforward: 28% of your sample were male, 70% were female, and 2% failed to report their sex; or, alternatively, 22% of the sample strongly agreed, 26% agreed, 20% were undecided, 24% disagreed, and 10% strongly disagreed that your new product was beneficial. What you do *not* know is whether the observations occurred by chance (error due to measurement or sampling) or because they occurred naturally and truly reflect the differences in both sample and population. This is what *inferential statistics* tell you— what the probability is that what you found accurately reflects the sample you observed or whether it was due to error. In the earlier case of sex, say, the true population parameters were that males made up about 25% and females 75% of the population. Obviously, your results are fairly close to those numbers, and inferential statistics could tell you precisely how close (or far). In regard to the product benefit example above, what we do not know is whether the distributions observed could have occurred purely by chance or not. As you will see in Chapter 13, inferential statistics can provide us with this data. Most of the time you will not be asked for the inferential statistics; instead, you will be asked how confident you are of the results. As we will see, inferential statistics provide you with that degree of confidence.

USING COMPUTER PACKAGES

One of the many images some still have of data analysis is a room full of adding machines with people entering numbers and pulling the machines' handles. This certainly was better than the even earlier image of a person with pencil and paper *hand* calculating statistical analyses. Only a few years ago the image changed to someone inserting a bunch of punch cards containing data into a "card reader" and submitting the data to a mainframe computer and then waiting patiently for the statistical analyses to be run. Those images have been replaced by hand calculators or desktop, laptop, and notebook computers that today routinely accomplish complex statistical analyses.

Today's public relations researcher can analyze the data he or she gathered almost anywhere he or she wants to. Sophisticated computerized statistical analysis packages such as SPSS (also known as the Statistical Package for the Social Sciences), the Statistical Analysis System (SAS), MiniTab, and SYSTAT not only will perform the most complex statistical analyses but also will "tutor" you if you cannot decide which statistical tool is best for you. The problems with this, of course, are that (1) the statistical packages are expensive and (2) you still need to understand what the tools offered will do and how to interpret their output. Adding to the confusion is the fact that some basically nonstatistical programs—such spreadsheet programs as Lotus 123 and Microsoft Excel and such database programs such as dBase, FoxPro, and Access—all offer statistical tools as add-on features. Statistical packages, although more expensive, offer more statistical tools and the analyses are presented in a more understandable manner (and, importantly, their manuals are superior—almost statistics books in and of themselves). You can conduct the basic statistical analyses presented in this chapter with spreadsheet or database programs, but using statistical packages makes them easier to conduct and to interpret.

The Statistical Package for the Social Sciences, version 10.07,[1] is used in this chapter for several reasons. First, it is fairly inexpensive. The base and advanced units are both priced under $1,000 and a student version is available for less than $200 that has most of the tools needed but is limited to 50 variables. Second, SPSS can be run on both Windows- and Mac-based computers, that is, it is a *cross-platform* program. Third, SPSS offers multiple levels of statistical and technical help. Fourth, it is probably the easiest of the statistical packages to operate. Lastly, it includes almost any tool you need (or want to purchase) for statistical analyses.

The remainder of this chapter presents the basic analytical tools you will need to conduct basic public relations research. We begin by looking at how to input data into the computer and then turn to the task of describing and interpreting quantitative data. Some of the analyses were introduced in earlier chapters. In this chapter we will (1) establish what the analyses are, (2) what SPSS tools are used to conduct the analyses, and (3) how to interpret the SPSS output.

ENTERING DATA INTO THE COMPUTER

Anyone who has ever kept a checkbook ledger or entered figures into a spreadsheet program can enter data. The basics of data entry are quite simple but important (see Table 12.1 for a sample data set):

TABLE 12.1. Sample Data Set*

ID	No	Sample	Gp1	Gp2	Gp3	Pg4	Pg5	Pg6	Gp7	Gp8	Gp9	Gp10
1	36	1	2	3	3	4	4	2	4	2	3	3
2	384	1	2	2	4	4	4	4	5	3	3	2
3	595	2	4	4	4	5	4	4	4	4	4	5
4	527	2	2	4	4	5	4	3	4	4	3	3
5	245	1	1	2	4	4	4	2	4	3	3	2
6	1472	3	5	2	2	4	3	2	4	2	2	4
7	233	1	2	2	2	4	4	2	4	4	4	2
8	820	2	2	4	5	5	4	1	4	4	4	2
9	722	2	1	2	2	2	3	4	3	3	2	4
10	75	1	1	2	2	5	4	2	4	2	4	2
11	364	1	5	4	4	5	2	3	4	3	3	3
12	1453	3	1	1	4	5	3	1	3	5	4	2
13	848	2	3	4	5	5	3	4	4	3	3	4
14	480	1	2	4	2	5	4	3	4	4	3	3
15	39	1	2	3	2	5	4	3	4	3	3	2
16	185	1	2	2	1	5	5	4	4	2	2	3
17	148	1	2	4	4	4	3	4	4	2	2	4
18	496	1	2	3	3	.	.	2	4	4	4	4
19	813	2	2	4	5	4	3	2	4	4	3	2
20	129	1	2	2	2	4	5	2	4	3	2	3
21	483	1	2	2	2	4	4	4	4	3	2	4
22	283	1	3	3	5	5	4	2	3	4	4	2
23	436	1	1	2	1	4	4	4	4	4	4	2
24	537	2	1	1	1	1	.	.	2	2	4	.
25	626	2	2	2	2	4	2	1	3	3	2	4

Note. *Periods indicate *no data*.

1. Before you enter any data, determine what type of data you are dealing with.
2. Code the data, keeping in mind that the computer is more efficient when processing numbers than when processing alphabetical data (called a "string" variable); therefore, whenever possible use numbers for both ordinal *and* nominal data.
3. Create your variable names and whatever labels you will associate with them (e.g., if sex is a variable, you may label males as "1" and females as "2").
4. Prepare your "data set" by defining each variable. SPSS allows for only 8 alphabetical characters in a variable name. Figure 12.1 demonstrates the definitional process whereby you define a variable name, add your labels, and establish what your "missing values" will be. (It is best to keep missing values as simply blank entries until you get proficient with the program

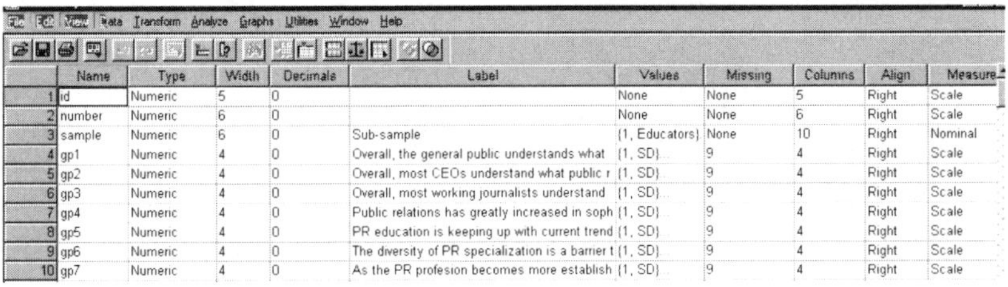

	Name	Type	Width	Decimals	Label	Values	Missing	Columns	Align	Measure
1	id	Numeric	5	0		None	None	5	Right	Scale
2	number	Numeric	6	0		None	None	6	Right	Scale
3	sample	Numeric	6	0	Sub-sample	{1, Educators}	None	10	Right	Nominal
4	gp1	Numeric	4	0	Overall, the general public understands what	{1, SD}...	9	4	Right	Scale
5	gp2	Numeric	4	0	Overall, most CEOs understand what public r	{1, SD}...	9	4	Right	Scale
6	gp3	Numeric	4	0	Overall, most working journalists understand	{1, SD}...	9	4	Right	Scale
7	gp4	Numeric	4	0	Public relations has greatly increased in soph	{1, SD}...	9	4	Right	Scale
8	gp5	Numeric	4	0	PR education is keeping up with current trend	{1, SD}...	9	4	Right	Scale
9	gp6	Numeric	4	0	The diversity of PR specialization is a barrier t	{1, SD}...	9	4	Right	Scale
10	gp7	Numeric	4	0	As the PR profesion becomes more establish	{1, SD}...	9	4	Right	Scale

FIGURE 12.1. Data definition in SPSS 10.0. SPSS for Windows version 10.07, 1999, Chicago, IL. Reprinted with permission from SPSS, Inc.

and then you can assign numbers to missing data, such as 999 for age of 0 for sex.)

5. Enter the data as spreadsheet entries where the columns represent the variables (sex, race, educational level, scores, and so forth) and the lines represent each individual's responses (see Figure 12.2).
6. Save your data set and give it a name (in SPSS the name will be followed by the file name extension .SAV; for example, Peanuts1.SAV or PR_Audit.SAV).

Data entry is not difficult, but it is repetitive. All data entries have random errors associated with them. Thus, you should carefully review the data and compare the items against the forms or questionnaires used to gather the data. Whether you code directly from the original forms or transfer your observations to a "coding sheet" is up to you. For a price you can submit your data to professionals who will code, enter, and check for errors. You also may enter your data on "bubble sheets" and have them scanned into files. The one advantage to coding the observations from the data sheets directly to the computer file is that you get a "feel" for the data and a better understanding when asked what different analyses mean. A useful trick, regardless of data entry method, is to initially run a "frequency" analysis of all variables and then inspect the results for out-of-line entries (e.g., sex is coded and entered for 200 survey respondents as male = 1 and female = 2, and your frequency analysis finds 100 entries of "1," "male," 98 entries of "2," "female," and 2 entries of "3"; any missing values would be listed as either system missing—blanks—or missing values—values you have told the computer are "missing data").

	id	number	sample	gp1	gp2	gp3	gp4	gp5	gp6	gp7	gp8	pg9	gp10
1	1	36	1	2	3	3	4	4	2	4	2	3	3
2	2	384	1	2	2	4	4	4	4	5	3	3	2
3	3	595	2	4	4	4	5	4	4	4	4	4	5
4	4	527	2	2	4	4	5	4	3	4	4	3	3
5	5	245	1	1	2	4	4	4	2	4	3	3	2
6	6	1472	3	5	2	2	4	3	2	4	2	2	4
7	7	233	1	2	2	2	4	4	2	4	4	4	2
8	8	820	2	2	4	5	5	4	1	4	4	4	2
9	9	722	2	1	2	2	2	3	4	3	3	2	4
10	10	75	1	1	2	2	5	4	2	4	2	4	2
11	11	364	1	5	4	4	5	2	3	4	3	3	3
12	12	1453	3	1	1	4	5	3	1	3	5	4	2
13	13	848	2	3	4	5	5	3	4	4	3	3	4
14	14	480	1	2	4	2	5	4	3	4	4	3	3
15	15	39	1	2	3	2	5	4	3	4	3	3	2
16	16	185	1	2	2	1	5	5	4	4	2	2	3
17	17	148	1	2	4	4	4	3	4	4	2	2	4
18	18	496	1	2	3	3			2	4	4	4	4
19	19	813	2	2	4	5	4	3	2	4	4	3	2
20	20	129	1	2	2	2	4	5	2	4	3	2	3
21	21	483	1	2	2	2	4	4	4	4	3	2	4
22	22	283	1	3	3	5	5	4	2	3	4	4	2
23	23	436	1	1	2	1	4	4	4	4	4	4	2
24	24	537	2	1	1	1	1			2	2	4	
25	25	626	2	2	2	2	4	2	1	3	3	2	4

FIGURE 12.2. SPSS data entry. SPSS for Windows version 10.07, 1999, Chicago, IL. Reprinted with permission from SPSS, Inc.

DESCRIBING QUANTITATIVE DATA

Most of the data you present will take the form of describing results. When we describe data, we are telling others what the cumulative outcomes are for specific variables. We can describe data as a simple table one variable at a time (*univariate* analyses) or in combinations of variables (*bivariate* or *multivariate* analyses). We can make these descriptions with categorical and continuous variables and in combinations of each or both.

Univariate Categorical Analyses

Categorical descriptive analyses take the form of frequency counts and percentages. A frequency table is a simple analysis of each variable (e.g., promotion rating) and its categories (1 through 5) (see Figure

12.3). Each frequency table is divided into three parts. The first part provides information about the variable: the variable name and label (promotion rating), the coding categories used (1–5), and the labels (none in this case). The second part consists of the actual counts for each category, to include missing data. The third provides three interpretations: the actual "percent," including missing data; the "valid" percent, which corrects for missing data; and the "cumulative" percent, which adds the valid percentages for each category as they increase. To conduct a frequency analysis in SPSS, you would point your mouse to "Analyze" on the program command bar and select "Descriptive Statistics." A menu opens with several options; select "Frequencies." A new window opens with your data set variables on the left and nothing on the right; highlight the variables you want to analyze by clicking on them and then click the right-arrow button (see Figure 12.4). You have several options, but for a frequency analysis do not make any other selections. Once you have moved the requisite variables to the right, click on the "OK" button and the analysis will be run.

When making presentations you will probably want to describe your data visually. To do so, you would select "Charts . . . " from the Frequencies menu (see Figure 12.5). This provides you four options:

Frequencies

Statistics

Promotion Rating (1=terrible; 5 = excellent)

N	Valid	100
	Missing	0

Promotion Rating (1=terrible; 5 = excellent)

		Frequency	Percent	Valid Percent	Cumulative Percent
Valid	1.00	8	8.0	8.0	8.0
	2.00	12	12.0	12.0	20.0
	3.00	20	20.0	20.0	40.0
	4.00	30	30.0	30.0	70.0
	5.00	30	30.0	30.0	100.0
	Total	100	100.0	100.0	

FIGURE 12.3. Output: Frequency analysis. SPSS for Windows version 10.07, 1999, Chicago, IL. Reprinted with permission from SPSS, Inc.

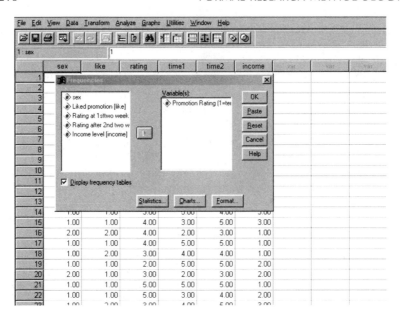

FIGURE 12.4. Univariate categorical command screen. SPSS for Windows version 10.07, 1999, Chicago, IL. Reprinted with permission from SPSS, Inc.

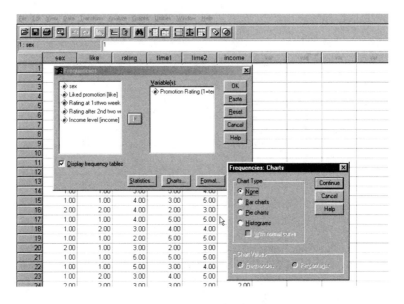

FIGURE 12.5. Univariate categorical command screen—charts. SPSS for Windows version 10.07, 1999, Chicago, IL. Reprinted with permission from SPSS, Inc.

bar charts, pie charts, and histograms (with or without a normal curve imposed, used with continuous data). The bar and pie charts provide basic information based on individual categories (see Figure 12.6). SPSS also has a powerful "Graphics" command that will provide you with a number of additional charting options, to include 3-D charts and movable axes.

Bivariate Analyses and Beyond: Cross-Tabulation

While univariate analyses are important (and are almost always used to present demographic data on the sample or population observed), bivariate analyses allow you to examine how two different variables break down. In bivariate or multivariate analyses which variable is the independent or dependent variable is really up to you. Typically the independent variable is the one you are concerned about because it

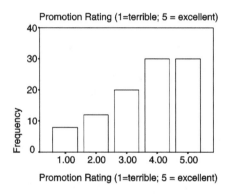

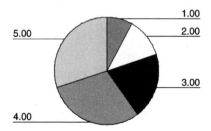

FIGURE 12.6. Output: Univariate categorical charts. SPSS for Windows version 10.07, 1999, Chicago, IL. Reprinted with permission from SPSS, Inc.

changes how you interpret the dependent variable. In categorical analysis, however, both variables are nominal or ordinal. For instance, *sex* or *gender* is a major demographic variable and *knowledge of male and female preference* (independent variable) is often important in gaining an understanding of many variables of interest, such as buying habits (dependent variables).

Perhaps you have asked a general question about awareness of an issue, using the ordinal measure of "very aware," "aware, "unaware," and "very unaware." You can run two univariate analyses for sex and awareness, and that tells you how many (or what percentage) of the sample fell into each category. This is important information, but it does not really answer the question whether sex differentiates between categories of awareness. You want to conduct a categorical bivariate analysis, or a cross-tabulation of sex by awareness.

Conducting a cross-tabulation requires that you again select "Analyze" and "Descriptive Statistics." At the bottom of the descriptive statistics menu is "Crosstabs." Selecting "Crosstabs" opens a window where you are asked to select the "row" and "column" variable (see Figure 12.7). A rule of thumb: always make the variable with the fewest categories your column variable. Thus SEX would be highlighted and moved to the column panel and AWARE highlighted and moved to the row panel. Next, you would select the "Cells" option and indicate which statistics you want (counts and what kinds of percentages: row,

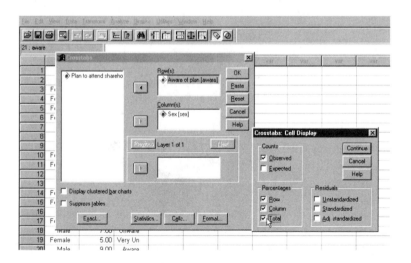

FIGURE 12.7. Crosstabs options in SPSS. SPSS for Windows version 10.07, 1999, Chicago, IL. Reprinted with permission from SPSS, Inc.

column, total). Since you do not want to make multiple runs, it is best to select all three percentages. Select "OK" and then "OK" again to run the analysis and interpret the output (see Figure 12.8).

The Crosstabs output first tells you how many valid, missing, and total cases (entries) you have. The actual Crosstabs information is found in a table where each of the two categories represents a cell. If you selected in Cells to see the observations and row, column, and total percentages, you would see within each cell four numbers: the actual number of observations per cell, the percentage that that cell is of the row it is a part of, the percentage that that cell is of the column it is a part of, and finally the percent of the total number of observations that the cell accounts for. Note that there is an additional row and column, each labeled "total." The totals for each represent the univariate statistics for each variable.

Multivariate cross-tabulation adds "layers" to the analysis. That is, with three categorical variables (say, sex, awareness, education),

Crosstabs

Case Processing Summary

	Cases					
	Valid		Missing		Total	
	N	Percent	N	Percent	N	Percent
Aware of plan * Sex	20	100.0%	0	.0%	20	100.0%

Aware of plan * Sex Crosstabulation

			Sex		Total
			Male	Female	
Aware of plan	Aware	Count	8	2	10
		% within Aware of plan	80.0%	20.0%	100.0%
		% within Sex	80.0%	20.0%	50.0%
		% of Total	40.0%	10.0%	50.0%
	Unware	Count	1	3	4
		% within Aware of plan	25.0%	75.0%	100.0%
		% within Sex	10.0%	30.0%	20.0%
		% of Total	5.0%	15.0%	20.0%
	Very Unaware	Count	1	5	6
		% within Aware of plan	16.7%	83.3%	100.0%
		% within Sex	10.0%	50.0%	30.0%
		% of Total	5.0%	25.0%	30.0%
Total		Count	10	10	20
		% within Aware of plan	50.0%	50.0%	100.0%
		% within Sex	100.0%	100.0%	100.0%
		% of Total	50.0%	50.0%	100.0%

FIGURE 12.8. Output crosstabs. SPSS for Windows version 10.07, 1999, Chicago, IL. Reprinted with permission from SPSS, Inc.

you would get a Crosstabs for sex × awareness, sex × education, and awareness × education. The inclusion of additional variables makes interpretation very difficult. To conduct a multivariate Crosstabs you would select those variables and place them in the "Layers" panel.

Most cross-tabulations are presented as two-way tables of either the actual observations or percentages (see Figure 12.9). SPSS offers a chart option that is a bar chart with the variables clustered within one of the variables, such as MALE and FEMALE within SEX and AWARE and UNAWARE within AWARE. Thus, you would have two bars for males and two for females, each indicating the number of males and females aware and unaware.

Univariate Continuous Analyses: Measures of Central Tendency

Continuous data are found along some continuum instead of being placed in categories. In Chapter 9 we discussed the normal curve and its properties. All continuous data have their own "normal distribution." If the data are perfectly distributed, then those data should be distributed as the hypothetical normal curve described in Chapter 9 (see Figure 12.10). Regardless of whether the data are perfectly distributed (an unusual case), they can be described according to the data

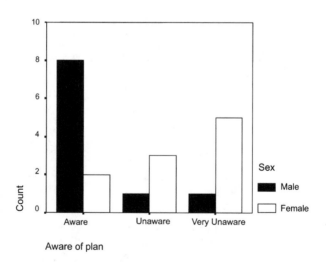

FIGURE 12.9. Output: Graphic representation of a 2 × 2 crosstabs. SPSS for Windows version 10.07, 1999, Chicago, IL. Reprinted with permission from SPSS, Inc.

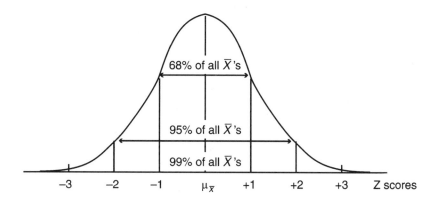

68% of all $\overline{X}$'s

95% of all $\overline{X}$'s

99% of all $\overline{X}$'s

−3   −2   −1 $\mu_{\overline{X}}$ +1   +2   +3   Z scores

FIGURE 12.10. The hypothetical normal curve and its properties.

set's mean, median, mode, range, and variance. Each of these describes the data set's *central tendency*, or how the data are distributed around the mean. Further, we know that within this distribution 68% of the data will be within one standard deviation from the mean in either direction and 95.5% will be within two standard deviations from the mean. This knowledge is very instructive; it allows you to observe not only what the "average" (i.e., mean) response is but also how the people observed vary in terms of that average. For instance, if you found that the average attitude of 10 people toward a particular client service on a 7-point scale was 5.8 (7 = strongly like), you know that the 10 people sampled liked the service considerably. But, if you looked at the distribution of all scores and how they varied from 5.8, you could make a better interpretation. Suppose that 1 of the 10 people you sampled scored a 7 and the rest were clustered around 4.8. This tells you that the majority of your sample was closer to being neutral than actively liking the service (means, as we will see, are highly sensitive to extreme scores). On the other hand, if your scores were clustered between 5.5 and 6.0, then you know that the sample mean was a good indicator of the whole sample's feelings about the service.

There are many univariate continuous statistics. We will focus on the five most important to a basic understanding of continuous data: means, medians, modes, variance, and standard deviations. The mean is often called the average response. The *mean* is obtained by taking the scores (data), summing them, and then dividing them by the number of valid observations. The sum of the following five scores—1, 3, 5, 7, 9—is 25; the mean is the sum divided by the number of observations:

$(1 + 3 + 5 + 7 + 9) \div 5 = 5$. As noted earlier, however, the mean is sensitive to extreme scores. What if the data were 1, 2, 1, 3, 10? The mean would be $17 \div 5$, or 3.4, which is clearly not representative of the data. In this case the *median*, the score that represents the midpoint or the 50th percentile of the data set when listed along the continuum—1, 1, 2, 3, 10—better describes the central tendency of the data set. The median would be 2. What if there were an even number of data points? The median then would be the average of the two scores that fall around the midpoint. For instance, 1, 1, 2, 3, 5, 10 would have a median of $(2 + 3) \div 2$, or 2.5. Finally, the *mode* is the most frequently occurring value. In the data we just described the mode would be 1; it occurred twice in the data set. There may be more than one mode; thus you may have bimodal (two equally occurring values), trimodal (three values), or more (see Figure 12.11).

The *variance* defines how the data are distributed around the mean. The variance represents the amount of dispersion around the mean and is obtained by first calculating the *difference* between each score and the mean by subtracting each score from the mean, squaring the result, summing all the squared amounts, and then dividing that result by the number of observations:

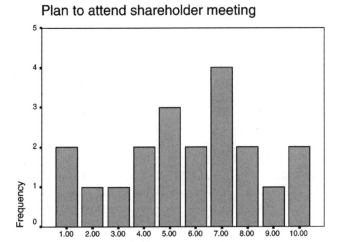

Plan to attend shareholder meeting

Plan to attend shareholder meeting

FIGURE 12.11. Output: Five mode values (1, 4, 6, 8, 10). SPSS for Windows version 10.07, 1999, Chicago, IL. Reprinted with permission from SPSS, Inc.

$$\text{Variance} = \frac{\Sigma(\text{score} - \text{mean})^2}{N}$$

where $\Sigma(\text{score} - \text{mean})^2$ is each score subtracted from the mean of all scores, squared and then summed, and N is the total number of scores observed. Table 12.2 shows the variance for 10 observations of an interval measure that ranges from 1 to 11, or *6.899*.

Finally, the standard deviation tells us the range of scores that we would normally expect a certain percentage of the scores to fall within the continuum, *based on a normal curve*. We already know that 34% of all scores on any continuum will fall normally within 1 standard deviation above and 1 standard deviation below the mean of all scores. Calculation of the standard deviation is easy; you simply take the square root of the variance ($\sqrt{6.899}$, or 2.63). Based on the data in Table 12.2, the standard deviation would be ±2.63 units from the mean of 6.10, or between 3.47 and 8.73. Sixty-eight percent of all scores would be expected to be found between 3.47 and 8.73.

To run a continuous univariate analysis with SPSS is quite simple. You click first on "Analyze" then "Descriptive Statistics" and then on "Frequencies." Once the Frequencies window opens, deselect "Display frequency tables" (unless you want to look at data from both categorical and continuous levels). Click on "Statistics" and choose the central tendency statistics you want (almost always mean, median, and mode) and choose the measures of dispersion you want (usually range, standard deviation, and variance). (See Figure 12.12.) Your output will be

TABLE 12.2. Calculating the Variance of 10 Scores

Observation	Score	Mean	Score – Mean	(Score – Mean)^2
1	3	6.1	–3.1	9.61
2	6	6.1	–0.1	0.01
3	9	6.1	2.9	8.41
4	7	6.1	0.9	0.81
5	11	6.1	4.9	24.01
6	5	6.1	–1.1	1.21
7	8	6.1	1.9	3.61
8	2	6.1	–4.1	16.81
9	4	6.1	–2.1	4.41
10	6	6.1	–0.1	0.01
Σ(sum)	61		0.0	68.99

Variance = 68.99 ÷ 10 = 6.889
Standard deviation = $\sqrt{6.889}$ = 2.63

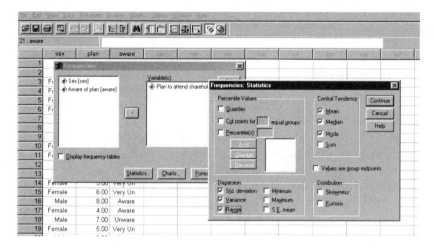

FIGURE 12.12. Continuous command screens for measures of dispersion. SPSS for Windows version 10.07, 1999, Chicago, IL. Reprinted with permission from SPSS, Inc.

displayed as a table with the variable name and label, the number of observations, the number of missing observations, and the statistics asked for. In the case of multiple modes, a note will accompany the table (see Figure 12.13). Graphically, you can have a histogram printed with or without the normal curve for that data set superimposed on it (see Figure 12.14).

Frequencies

Statistics

Aware of plan

N	Valid	20
	Missing	0
Mean		1.8000
Median		1.5000
Mode		1.00
Std. Deviation		.8944
Variance		.8000
Range		2.00

FIGURE 12.13. Output: Measures of dispersion. SPSS for Windows version 10.07, 1999, Chicago, IL. Reprinted with permission from SPSS, Inc.

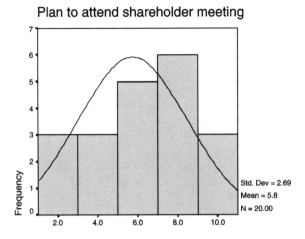

Plan to attend shareholder meeting

FIGURE 12.14. Output: Graphic display of mean and standard deviation with normal curve. SPSS for Windows version 10.07, 1999, Chicago, IL. Reprinted with permission from SPSS, Inc.

Bivariate Continuous Analyses

Just as with categorical descriptive analysis, it is sometimes more informative to analyze how two variables interact with each other. With continuous data we can analyze how a categorical independent variable changes the mean responses of its subcategories. For example, you have been asked to see how much interest there is in attendance at the annual shareholders' meeting by company midlevel management. You conduct a quick survey, asking 20 randomly selected managers if, on a scale of 0 (definitely disinterested) to 10 (definitely interested), they would be interested in attending. Further, because senior management has been concerned by the lack of participation by female managers in the past, you need to report back interest in attending by sex of manager. The appropriate analysis is found under "Analyze," "Compare Means," and "means." A window opens which asks that you select the dependent and independent variables (see Figure 12.15). In this case, your independent variable is "sex"; your dependent variable is "plan." The results of this analysis are shown in Figure 12.16. Interpretation might be as follows:

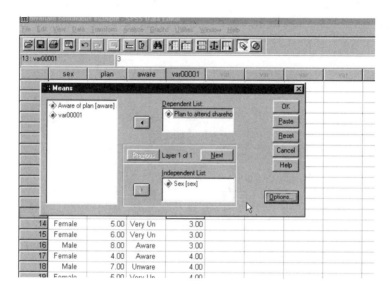

FIGURE 12.15. Command screens for bivariate continuous analysis. SPSS for Windows version 10.07, 1999, Chicago, IL. Reprinted with permission from SPSS, Inc.

Means

Case Processing Summary

| | Cases | | | | | |
| | Included | | Excluded | | Total | |
	N	Percent	N	Percent	N	Percent
Plan to attend shareholder meeting * Sex	20	100.0%	0	.0%	20	100.0%

Report

Plan to attend shareholder meeting

Sex	Mean	N	Std. Deviation	Variance
Male	7.2000	10	2.6583	7.067
Female	4.3000	10	1.8886	3.567
Total	5.7500	20	2.6926	7.250

FIGURE 12.16. Output: Bivariate continuous analysis. SPSS for Windows version 10.07, 1999, Chicago, IL. Reprinted with permission from SPSS, Inc.

Interest in attending this year's shareholders' meeting by midlevel management is equivocal. The average response for the 20 managers randomly selected was 5.75 on a 10-point scale (10 = definitely interested). However, it appears that interest is higher for males (mean of 7.2) than females (4.3).

You could not say that the mean difference between male and female managers was actually different (this would require an inferential analysis, as covered in Chapter 13) but simply that males and females do report different degrees of interest. Examination of the variance and standard deviation for each suggests that females' expression of interest has less error and is more concentrated around the mean response of 4.3 (variance = 3.57, standard deviation = 1.89) than for males (variance = 7.07, standard deviation = 2.66).

Of course, you could have simply asked whether the 20 managers were "planning to attend," coded responses as "yes" (1) or "no" (0), and conducted a cross-tabulation of sex by attendance. You would not, however, have been able to provide the same depth of analysis with the categorical analyses that you did with the continuous analyses, also perhaps more accurately previewing managers' level of interest.

Correlation

A special bivariate case is the *correlation,* or a measure of the relationship between two variables. A correlation expresses two things. First, it tells you how two (and only two) variables are related in a linear fashion. Second, it tells you both how much one variable influences the other variable—and how much the two variables account for, or "explain," the variance in the relationship (as well as how much the two fail to explain). Although a correlation is usually thought of as a number of data points scattered throughout an area, you also can think of it as two circles (mathematical Venn diagrams), each showing the relationship to the other by how much one explains the other by overlap (see Figure 12.17).

Correlations may be calculated between categorical variables, continuous variables, or categorical and continuous variables. Most correlations are found between continuous variables and are analyzed via the Pearson product–moment, or *r,* correlation. Continuous variable correlations are expressed in terms of a continuum from +1.00 through 0.00 to –1.00. A +1.00 or –1.00 correlation would produce ven diagrams of *total* overlap, whereas a correlation of 0.00 would produce two circles with *no* overlap. In the case of a positive correlation, an increase in one variable, time on the job, produces a positive increase in the other

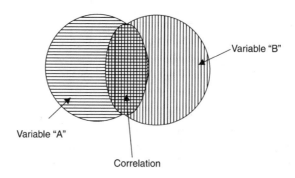

FIGURE 12.17. Visualizing a correlation.

variable, salary. The longer we are on the job, the higher our salary should be. Not all, however, have their salaries increased over time; thus, we would not expect a perfect (+1.00) correlation. Instead, we would expect the relationship to be weaker, say around +.50. The correlation could have been negative: as time on the job *increased*, salary *decreased*.

What is a "good" correlation? Stacks and Hocking suggest that correlations below ±.30 are "weak," between ±.40 and ±.70 "moderate," between ±.70 and ±.90 "high," and above ±90 "very high."[2] Correlation coefficients express how much one variable explains the other. We can also find out how much their relationship does not explain, something very important when we look at measurement reliability. To do this we simply square the correlation coefficient and subtract it from 1: $1.00 - r^2$ = unexplained variance or random error. Thus, a reliability coefficient of .70, while "moderate" by one standard, is low by another ($.70^2 - 1.00 = .49 - 1.00 = .51$, or accounting for 51% of systematic variance in a measure while 49% of the variance is random error). Even a .90 correlation still produces 19% random error!

When you report a number of correlations, you use a *correlation matrix* and demonstrate the correlation graphically with a *scatter diagram*. A correlation matrix can be produced by most statistical computer programs. To conduct a correlational analysis you select "Analyze," "Correlate," and "Bivariate" from the SPSS command bar. This opens and you choose among three types of correlations (see below). The SPSS output shown in Figure 12.18 examines the relationships between an automobile's weight, engine displacement in cubic inches, horsepower, and gasoline mileage. Note that the coefficients above and below the diagonal (1.00—a variable correlated with itself is "perfect") are mirrored; that is, they are produced twice. You would only

Correlations

		Vehicle Weight (lbs.)	Engine Displacement (cu. inches)	Horsepower	Miles per Gallon
Vehicle Weight (lbs.)	Pearson Correlation	1.000	.933	.859	-.807
	Sig. (2-tailed)	.	.000	.000	.000
	N	406	406	400	398
Engine Displacement (cu. inches)	Pearson Correlation	.933	1.000	.897	-.789
	Sig. (2-tailed)	.000	.	.000	.000
	N	406	406	400	398
Horsepower	Pearson Correlation	.859	.897	1.000	-.771
	Sig. (2-tailed)	.000	.000	.	.000
	N	400	400	400	392
Miles per Gallon	Pearson Correlation	-.807	-.789	-.771	1.000
	Sig. (2-tailed)	.000	.000	.000	.
	N	398	398	392	398

FIGURE 12.18. Output: Correlation analysis. SPSS for Windows version 10.07, 1999, Chicago, IL. Reprinted with permission from SPSS, Inc.

report the coefficients above the diagonal. Scatter diagrams show the actual data as they are dispersed between the two variables, in this case all negatively correlated—that is, a line drawn through the data points would run from high to low (see Figure 12.19). The less dispersed the data are, the higher the correlation coefficient; the more dispersed, the lower the correlation coefficient. The scatter diagram also allows you to see if the relationship is truly linear (the line between two variables must be a straight line); if the dispersion seems to look curvilinear, then there may be something else that is influencing the relationship; the problem is, you do not know what the missing variable is without much more sophisticated statistical analysis.[3]

Correlations that are conducted with categorical data cannot be expressed on the +1.00 to −1.00 continuum. Because the categorical variable is not continuous, it has a correlational range to 0.00 to +1.00. This greatly reduces the interpretability of the correlation, as it cannot be determined whether there is a negative relationship. Instead, it is expressed in terms of the variables' *strength of association*. When computing categorical correlations with ordered or ranked data, Spearman's *rho rank* correlation is used; when computing ordinal by nominal, or ordinal or nominal by interval correlations, Kendall's *tau-b* correlation is used. Both are restricted to a 0.00 to +1.00 range.

Advanced Descriptive Statistics

Before we leave descriptive statistics we need to briefly discuss two descriptive statistical tools used in measurement. The first is the reli-

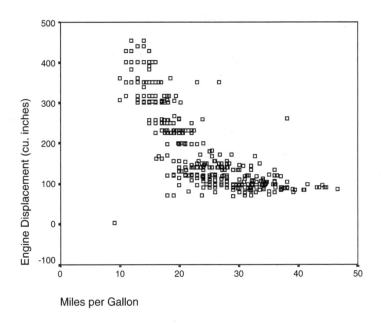

FIGURE 12.19. Output: Scatter diagram. SPSS for Windows version 10.07, 1999, Chicago, IL. Reprinted with permission from SPSS, Inc.

ability statistic, the second is factor analysis. Both are beyond complete description, but a good source for further reading would be Frederick Williams's *Reasoning with Statistics*. Since SPSS provides both tools, we will briefly demonstrate how to conduct each and look at sample output.

A Measurement Case: Reliability Statistics

Reliability statistics can be computed for categorical and continuous data. Continuous measures (e.g., Likert-type and semantic differential-type) are usually reported via Cronbach's coefficient alpha.[4] Categorical measures are usually reported via the KR-20 coefficient.[5] To conduct a reliability analysis, you would select "Analyze," "Scale," and then "Reliability Analysis." A panel will open, and you will select those variables (scale items) you want to run your analysis on (see Figure 12.20). Before you run the analysis, however, you need to click on "Statistics" and select the "Descriptives for" and select all three options (Item, Scale, and Scale if item deleted). Figure 12.21 provides a coefficient alpha for this measurement scale. The reliability coefficient

File   Edit   View   Data   Transform   Analyze   Graphs   Utilities   Window   Help

1 : id   1

	id	number	sample	gp1	gp2	gp3	gp4	gp5	gp6	gp7	gp8	pg9	gp10
1	1										2	3	3
2	2										3	3	2
3	3										4	4	5
4	4										4	3	3
5	5										3	3	2
6	6										2	2	4
7	7										4	4	2
8	8										4	4	2
9	9										3	2	4
10	10										2	4	2
11	11										3	3	3
12	12										5	4	2
13	13	848		2	3	4	5	5	3	4	4	3	3	4
14	14	480		1	2	4	2	5	4	3	4	4	3	3
15	15	39		1	2	3	2	5	4	3	4	3	3	2
16	16	185		1	2	2	1	5	5	4	4	2	2	3
17	17	148		1	2	4	4	4	3	4	4	2	2	4
18	18	496		1	2	3	3			2	4	4	4	4

Reliability Analysis

id
number
Sub-sample [sample]
Public relations has gr
PR education is keepi
The diversity of PR sp
As the PR profesion b
Most PR practitioners
Most PR practitioners
Most PR practitioners

Items:
Overall, the general publi
Overall, most CEOs unde
Overall, most working jou

OK   Paste   Reset   Cancel   Help

Model: Alpha

List item labels   Statistics...

FIGURE 12.20. Command screen: Reliability Analysis (Coefficient Alpha). SPSS for Windows version 10.07, 1999, Chicago, IL. Reprinted with permission from SPSS, Inc.

for the 3 items is only .64, indicating the scale is not very reliable. Note that if you deleted any item, your reliability would go down.

The KR-20 statistic is automatically run if the scale data are dichotomous. This is established in part when you create your data set and tell SPSS what level of data your variable is. Ordinal scales are also analyzed by the coefficient alpha.

Factor Analysis

As tempting as it is to use reliability analysis for validity analysis by taking items from the scale based on their "Scale if item deleted" value, a factor analysis should be run on the scale items first. *Factor analysis is a statistical tool that establishes the dimensionality of the measure and tests for subdimensions. All measures should be submitted to factor analysis.* Why? First, although we assume that a measure is unidimensional, or that certain subdimensions are present, we really do not know until we test for them. Second, different populations and samples perceive things differently. And, third, perceptions toward attitudes change over time. Thus, to be certain that we are actually measuring what we

Reliability

****** Method 1 (space saver) will be used for this analysis ******

                    R E L I A B I L I T Y A N A L Y S I S - S C A L E (A L P H A)

		Mean	Std Dev	Cases
1.	GP1	2.0000	.8421	252.0
2.	GP2	2.7937	.9885	252.0
3.	GP3	3.0516	1.1011	252.0

	Mean	Variance	Std Dev	N of Variables
Statistics for SCALE	7.8452	5.1114	2.2608	3

Item-total Statistics

	Scale Mean if Item Deleted	Scale Variance if Item Deleted	Corrected Item-Total Correlation	Alpha if Item Deleted
GP1	5.8452	3.2389	.3838	.6479
GP2	5.0516	2.4475	.5453	.4297
GP3	4.7937	2.3238	.4692	.5486

Reliability Coefficients

N of Cases = 252.0   N of Items = 3

Alpha = .6493

FIGURE 12.21. Output: Measurement Reliability Analysis—Coefficient Alpha. SPSS for Windows version 10.07, 1999, Chicago, IL. Reprinted with permission from SPSS, Inc.

think we are measuring, a factor analysis provides a test for the measure's construct validity with the sample you are working with.

Conducting a factor analysis is much like running reliability analyses. Before we go through the steps, a word of caution should be sounded. To be certain that the underlying dimensionality has been adequately tested, you should try to have at least a 10:1 ratio of respondents to items. This means that for a 10-item measure you should have at least 100 respondents. Many factor analyses are run on fewer, but it is best to never drop below a 6:1 respondent-to-item ratio. To run a factor analysis, select "Analyze," "Data Reduction," and "Factor" from the command bar. A panel opens and you are asked to move the items you want tested; select and move them to the "Variables" window (see Figure 12.22). The only change you will need to make is on the button "Rotation." Select "Varimax" as the rotation (varimax rotation forces the factors as far "apart" as possible, thus ensuring there is minimal overlap between the factors.)

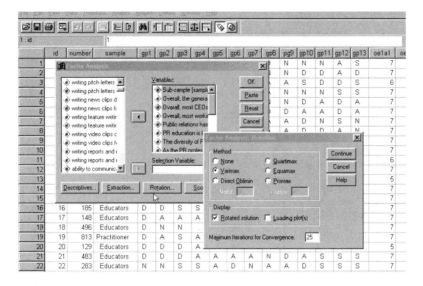

FIGURE 12.22. Command screen for factor analysis. SPSS for Windows version 10.07, 1999, Chicago, IL. Reprinted with permission from SPSS, Inc.

A factor analysis will provide an output that is at first confusing and difficult to interpret. What you are interested in, however, is the "Rotated Component Matrix." The rest of the output provides initial descriptive information about the factor structure, such as the number of underlying factors and the initial way the items were tested. Figure 12.23 provides the rotated factor matrix for 13 questions used in a study of public relations education measuring "perceptions of public relations."[6] The analysis produced five initial factors, labeled "components," which consist of "sub-sample" items. In Chapter 8 we noted that a measurement dimension should have a minimum of two items, each loading or being found on one factor greater than ±.60 and not greater than ±.40 on any other factor. (If the item was stated negatively, we would expect that it would result in a matrix entry on the negative side.) Analysis finds that only three factors met this requirement. Factor one obtained three items, each dealing with attitude and respect (.766, .754, and –.713). Factor two obtained three items dealing with understanding (.739, .819, .692). Factor three obtained three items dealing with trends (.732, .603, –.721). Labeling the factors is subjective, but you might call the first "Public Relations Respect," the second "Knowledge of Pubic Relations Function," and the third "Public Relations Trends."

Rotated Component Matrix

	Component				
	1	2	3	4	5
Sub-sample	2.082E-03	-1.04E-02	-3.49E-02	-3.53E-02	.928
Overall, the general public understands what public relations is.	-8.32E-02	.739	-.103	-.104	-6.12E-02
Overall, most CEOs understand what public relations is.	7.536E-02	.819	.112	8.214E-02	-7.12E-02
Overall, most working journalists understand what public relations is.	.244	.692	-3.82E-02	.152	.273
Public relations has greatly increased in sophistication (last 5-10 years)	-.106	6.229E-03	.732	-.390	5.019E-02
PR education is keeping up with current trends in the profession.	.369	-2.48E-02	.603	8.728E-02	7.651E-02
The diversity of PR specialization is a barrier to a "standard" set of skills for PR career success.	-.305	.171	.196	.525	.360
As the PR profesion becomes more established and appreciated, PR education will also.	.158	-1.54E-02	.721	.288	-.134
Most PR practitioners have very positive attitudes toward PR college graduates.	.766	.117	9.410E-02	4.016E-03	6.326E-02
Most PR practitioners respect college professors who teach PR.	.754	9.211E-02	7.596E-03	5.241E-02	-1.84E-02
Most PR practitioners think college PR programs are too easy.	-.713	4.996E-02	-.181	6.734E-02	8.153E-02
I think that PR programs should be in schools or departments of journalism.	6.606E-02	-1.40E-03	-1.66E-02	.819	-8.51E-02

Extraction Method: Principal Component Analysis.
Rotation Method: Varimax with Kaiser Normalization.
a. Rotation converged in 7 iterations.

FIGURE 12.23. Output: Factor analysis. SPSS for Windows version 10.07, 1999, Chicago, IL. Reprinted with permission from SPSS, Inc.

Had you used all 13 items as one large measure, you would not have a valid measure of perceptions about public relations. The testing for underlying dimensions provided you with a more valid measure of how the respondents perceived public relations and increased the subdimensional measures' reliability.

SUMMARY

This chapter introduced you to the world of statistical analysis. Statistics are computed on quantitative data and provide us with a way to describe those data. We began with a review of what constituted data, explored the use of the computer in data analysis, and then looked at basic categorical and continuous descriptive statistical tools. In so doing we looked at how to run descriptive analyses using the Statistical Package for the Social Sciences computer package and interpret its output. Finally, we looked at two advanced descriptive tools that public relations researchers should be familiar with, namely, reliability analysis and factor analysis. We turn next to going beyond a simple description of the data gathered from a sample to making inferences as to how confident we are that whatever differences we obtain are due to the relationship between the variables under study rather than random error.

REVIEW QUESTIONS

1. It has been said that "descriptive statistics describe." What does this mean?

2. What makes categorical statistics different from continuous statistics? Does one provide more information than the other? If so, what information does one provide that the other does not?

3. People often infer that descriptive statistics can be extended to larger groups. Explain why this is not possible (or, if it were possible, what kind of sampling would have been conducted to make it possible).

4. What is a measure of central tendency? How does it differ from frequency statistics? Is a percentage a categorical or a continuous statistic? Why?

5. Why are factor analyses and reliability statistics descriptive statistics?

PRACTICE PROBLEM

You have just completed a content analysis of media coverage for your client.
You present the following table; interpret what it means:

Coverage/Media	N	%	Cumulative %
Positive	120	80.0	80
Newspaper	80	66.6	
Television	25	20.8	
Radio	15	12.5	
Negative	30	20.0	100
Newspaper	20	66.6	
Television	8	26.6	
Radio	2	6.6	
	150	100.0	

Average reader/listener age: 38.6 years
Average educational level (years): 11.6 years
Salary: average = $38,400; median = $32,000

NOTES

1. *Statistical Package for the Social Sciences,* version 10.07 (Chicago: SPSS, 2000).
2. Don W. Stacks and John E. Hocking, *Communication Research,* 2nd ed. (New York: Longman, 1999), p. 349.
3. For more on "partial" and "point biserial" correlations, see Frederick Williams, *Reasoning with Statistics: How to Read Quantitative Research,* 4th ed. (New York: Harcourt Brace Jovanovich, 1992), Chs. 11–13. This is a highly "readable" statistics book.
4. L. J. Cronbach, "Coefficient Alpha and the Internal Structure of Tests," *Psychometrika, 16* (1957), 15–41.
5. J. Cohen, "A Coefficient for Nominal Scales," *Educational and Psychological Measurement, 20* (1960), 37–46.
6. Don W. Stacks, Carl Botan, and Judy VanSlyke Turk. "Perceptions of Public Relations Education," *Public Relations Review, 25* (1999), 9–28.

Chapter 13

Inferential Statistical Reasoning and Computer Analysis

Consider the following situation: The research presentation was going along just fine. The numbers made sense to you, and your interpretation seemed to be right on target, based on what you knew of the topic from research. The client, however, was not as satisfied with the numbers. They seemed, he said, "too simple." "How confident are you that the numbers truly represent what we are seeing in the market?" he or she asks. Your response could make or break the contract you have been working so hard on.

You respond. "Based on what I've found, I'm very certain that the numbers truly reflect the market—especially, the differences between major demographics." The client persists: "How sure are you?" Based on the extra computer analyses you ran, you answer, "Better than 95% sure."

In Chapter 12 we examined how to describe data gathered from a population or sample. In this chapter we go one step beyond simply describing the data and examine *relationships* between the variables of interest. In public relations such relationships are assumed when we present our data; it is important, however, to test just how much *confidence* you can place in what you describe. This chapter explains how to statistically test for observed differences between variables and at the same time estimate how much confidence we have in drawing conclusions regarding any observed differences among the variables we have described.

MAKING QUANTITATIVE INFERENCES AND TESTING RELATIONSHIPS

As noted, seldom will a public relations practitioner be asked advanced statistical questions. Should you be asked, however, it is best to at least understand the logic and theory behind such questions. Most of the time advanced statistical tests are used in academic research, where researchers actively test the relationships proposed by public relations theory. They use both descriptive and inferential statistics (1) to indicate what differences (or similarities) were obtained in their research and (2) to test whether the relationships obtained represent true differences in the population as reflected by the sample's results or whether they were the result of some form of error (e.g., sampling or measurement error).

The key to inferential statistics is understanding that *your goal is to establish within a certain degree of confidence that your results represent true differences as found in the population under study and were not the result of other things nor were they randomly found in the population from which you sampled.*

This chapter walks you through both the logic and tests we make to ensure that our findings represent the population from which they come. In several instances formulas will be provided but only so that you get a better understanding of what the computer is doing when it "tests" your data. Over the past decade the computing power of computers—especially desktops and laptops—has increased dramatically. What used to take hours or days to code, enter, and compute now takes only a few minutes to analyze. Further, advanced statistical packages such as SPSS (used here) offer "statistics tutors" as part of their packaging. However, be forewarned: simply accepting what a computer package suggests may not be your best option; indeed, it may lead to false findings, things that could cause you embarrassment and set your campaign or program off in the wrong direction. Understanding what the appropriate statistics are for your research is the first step in truly understanding research; knowing when and how to use and analyze them is the second step.

Understanding Statistical Reasoning

Most researchers who employ inferential statistics do so because they believe that there is a difference in some dependent variable (outcome) that can be accounted for by some independent variable (output). When testing from theory you hypothesize (predict) that a specific independent variable will make changes in the dependent variable—this is referred to as the *research hypothesis*. Your *statistical test*, however, is that the independent variable did *not* result in change—this is referred to as the *null hypothesis*. That is, the two variables are *not* related. To complicate matters further, there are two types of research hypotheses: those that specify only differences in the relationship (*nondirectional*) and those that specify the direction of those differences (*directional*).

Thus, one of the major things that inferential statistics allow you to do is to establish whether a relationship truly exists and whether there was some type of causation. (We must be very careful here; as we saw in Chapter 11, only the true experiment can actually determine whether a cause-and-effect relationship actually exists; we cannot do so with survey methodology.)

Do public relations researchers formulate hypotheses when they are working on a campaign or program? Of course they do, and they probably have a theoretical reason for making such predictions, especially if they have done their homework. However, most practitioners are not cognizant of actually formalizing their research through the statement of hypothesis. To them it is only how they go about their daily activities. Therefore, there is a tendency to stop after describing the results of their research. They also realize that most clients have no background in statistics or statistical reasoning (even those with MBA degrees) and that presenting inferential tests would only confuse them.

So, why learn about inferential statistics? Because, instead of looking at the relationships as they existed when the data was collected, you are responsible for interpreting whether such relationships actually existed when the data were collected or whether they were in fact due to spurious relationships or error of some sort. That is, you are saying that you are *X*% confident that the relationships observed in your data exist in the larger population.

Probability of Error Occurrence

When we state that we are confident that the outcome of a research project is truly reflected in the population—that we have adequately sampled the population and the findings are accurate within so many units of measurement—we have established confidence in the findings. In inferential statistics we do the same. Basically, we state that we are "comfortable" if the chance of error is equal to or less than 5%; that is, we are 95% confident that the outcome was due to the relationship between variables and no more than 5% of any relationship cannot be explained. Why 95%? It happens that a 95% confidence interval is about two standard deviations from the true population mean. Thus, we are stating that we will accept the probability of error existing, but only if it is so far from the true population mean as to be insignificant.

Ninety-five percent may seem awfully confident, but would you bet your job or your contract with a major client on 5% error? If not, you might choose a 99% confidence interval, or about three standard deviations from the true population mean. Now you will only accept 1% error; you are being very conservative. We choose 95% as a sort of "minimal" confidence because we seldom run our research more than once. Medical science, for instance, often accepts a more liberal error rate—typically 20% (80% confidence interval)—because the variables are tested and retested many times. As you know, public relations research seldom has the luxury or time for retesting, as our research is often conducted on a 24-hour contingency basis. Thus, like the social scientist we have to be more conservative about the amount of error we are willing to accept.

Inferential statistics adds one more parameter to the question of error. As noted earlier, there are two kinds of hypotheses, namely, directional and nondirectional. Further, there are times that you do not actually hypothesize, instead asking "Are these variables related?" or asking a *research question*. When using inferential statistics, you are rewarded when you specify direction in that your error is only found on one side of the normal curve and your test is *one-tailed*. When you fail to predict either direction or differences, you must cover both sides of the curve (see Figures 13.1 and 13.2)—your 5% error now must be split in two, and you are now looking at actually working with 2.5% error in a *two-tailed* test. As you might imagine, finding significant differences with a two-tailed test is much more difficult. Frederick Williams goes so far as to say:

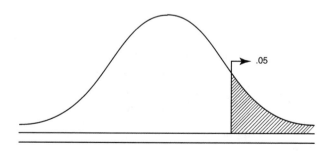

FIGURE 13.1. Rejection curve—one-tailed ($\alpha = .05$).

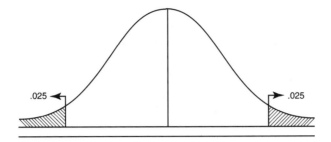

FIGURE 13.2. Rejection curve—two-tailed ($\alpha = .05$).

A one-tailed test is never used (or should never be used) unless there is a very good reason to make a directional prediction . . . mainly based on the confidence that the outcome in the opposite direction will not be obtained. If a one-tailed test is made in the absence of such confidence, the researcher [assumes] the hazard of never really testing statistically an outcome that would be opposite to the predicted direction.[1]

Why all this discussion? Because the computer program makes certain assumptions about whether you want a one-tailed or two-tailed test. If it asks you whether you want a one- or a two-tailed test, you need to know how to respond. In most instances, follow Williams's reasoning: employ the two-tailed test and you will seldom be wrong. Why? The main reason is that we are more concerned about admitting a "false positive" to our body of knowledge than rejecting true differences; we almost always opt for the most conservative outcome possible. The reason for this will become apparent as you read on.

Statistical "Significance"

We have already alluded to statistical "significance" when we talked about hypotheses in the preceding section. Statistical significance is the amount of confidence you place on ensuring that your findings truly represent those in the larger population. Looked at differently, the significance level represents the maximum amount of error—random, measurement, or sampling—that you are willing to accept for a statistical test. And some tests are more "powerful" than others, that is, they are better at discriminating whether relationships truly exist (more on this later).

When we say that we are 95% confident that our results are true—that differences found in the sample are also found in the population—we are actually saying that there may be a 1 in 20 chance that we are wrong. The higher the confidence interval or level, the lesser the chance of making a mistake and declaring that a relationship exists when, in fact, it does not. Looked at from the perspective of error, we are stating our *alpha error level* (represented as α) is set at 5% ($\alpha = .05$) or the acceptable confidence interval minus 1 ($1.00 - .95 = .05$).

For instance, you have found that males agree more with your candidate's position on a major issue than do females, but you are concerned that females will vote in larger numbers than will males. You find that male agreement with the position is 55% and female agreement is 45%. Is 55% actually larger than 45%? In Chapter 9 we looked at measurement error, where a sample of 384 randomly selected recipients would be no more than 5 percentage points from the true population parameters. The inferential test goes one step further and tells us whether our findings are due to chance or reflect the population. Stated differently, are you sure that your sample's division on the issue is the same as the population's? (To find out how the population actually thought about the position, you would have to conduct a census; since most of us have neither the time nor the money to conduct a census, we sample.) Here we must accept a basic assumption: *there will always be some differences in a sample that do not correspond to the population.*[2] Why? Because there will always be some error in every research project, whether that error be unknown or known. Thus, when we set our alpha at .05 (95% confidence in the findings being the same in the population as in the sample), we have decided that we will allow up to 5% error, regardless of error type.

What statistical significance does is to allow us to state with "reasonable" or "great" confidence that what we found in the sample regarding relationships between dependent and independent variables actually will exist in the population. Being able to make such statements as "I'm extremely confident that what we found in the people sampled occurs in the population" is what inferential statistics is all about.

Before we move on to the next topic, an important point needs to be made. In many instances not finding differences between variables is important. When you conduct a research project where you have sampled from the population, you always want to test whether the null hypothesis for demographics is supported. In other words, you want to find about the same number of males and females, the same income distribution, the same proportion of married couples, the same educational levels, and so forth in your sample as in your population. Thus, you can compare the demographics to the known population demographics. Here you would try to support the null hypothesis of no difference. How much faith (confidence) you place in findings of no difference is the same as for differences—you may make some error, but, all things being equal, you are 95% confident that the sample and population are the same regarding demographic variables and thus you have adequately sampled the population.

Statistical "Power"

Establishing your alpha level or confidence level is the first step in preparing to conduct inferential analyses. What alpha represents is the rejection of bringing "false positives" into the knowledge base. This is an important consideration; once information enters into a field's body of knowledge, it becomes accepted and tends to become permanent, and we build upon it in later studies. Obviously, we can make a mistake and accidentally accept as true a result that is false for the population (and remember, most samples will appear to have differences that may not hold true for the population—whether the differences are due to sampling or measurement error makes no difference; they are errors nonetheless).

Researchers discuss this as the relation between two types of error, namely, type I and type II errors.[3] Figure 13.3 depicts the definition of these error types and based on the truth or falsity of the relationships between variables. Note that the type I error is the *false rejection* of a true population relationship, where as the type II error is the *false acceptance* of a relationship when in fact that relationship does not exist in the population. Social scientists and public relations researchers prefer to err on the side of type I error, as do many managerial scientists; that is, we would rather dismiss a true relationship than add a false positive to our body of knowledge.

		Relationships are really:	
		TRUE	FALSE
You find the relationships:	TRUE	No problem	Type II error
	FALSE	Type I error	No problem

FIGURE 13.3. Type I and type II error relationships.

A good reason for such conservatism is when a product is tested. If there is any doubt that the product is safe, it is better to pull the product than put it on the market where certain liabilities will crop up and litigation will almost become a certainty. Closer to public relations (although product liability is something a good public relations practitioner should worry about), how do you know if the sample you have drawn is truly representative of the population (i.e., the sample has a one-to-one relationship with the population)? Random sampling *should* produce a representative sample, but we know that there is error in any sample. We also know that the larger the sample, the better the chance that the demographic relationships between sample and population will be true. Thus, by setting a very stringent alpha level, we have reduced the chance that spurious relationships will surface as putatively real ones.

We have, however, also increased the chance of a type II error—falsely rejecting a true population relationship. Thus, we need to consider in our decision-making process both type I and type II errors. This is referred to as *statistical power*. Statistical power is defined as the "ability to detect differences that are truly different, [and] is a function of the sample size."[4] Thus, the statistical power of a test is determined by the number of participants in the research. As a general rule, you want your power to be sufficient to detect true population differences at least 80% of the time (often reported as "effect size" of 20%, where power is calculated as $1 - beta [\beta]$; beta is the confidence we want to place in the sample's ability to detect true population differences; thus our effect size is $1 - .80$, or .20). Herman Cohen, a renowned statistician, recommends that we always select our samples so that a statistical power of .80 (effect size of .20) is obtained.[5] As a rule of thumb, Cohen's recommendation is well meant, but it may require that your sample be extremely large. The actual calculation of power is beyond the scope of this book, but there are add-on programs to most statistical packages (SPSS will provide power analyses for parametric (but not nonparametric) tests as part of its basic package; an add-on power analysis package may be purchased). In setting up your research you should figure in your power needs before you sample because *the power of the test and the set alpha level interact to provide sample size.* For the most part, a simple difference (males versus females on a dependent variable, for instance) requires at least 384 respondents. As you increase the complexity of the test—add more levels to the independent variable—you need a larger sample. Broom and Dozier present a fairly readable way to estimate sample size as determined by alpha and statistical power.[6]

INFERENTIAL TESTS

As discussed in Chapters 8 and 12, there are two levels of data or variables that we work with when conducting social research. A categorical variable is composed of either nominal- or ordinal-level data. A continuous variable is composed of interval- or ratio-level data. In Chapter 12 we noted that categorical variables are tested with nonparametric statistics and continuous variables with parametric statistics.

Nonparametric Analysis

Nonparametric inferential statistics work with data that are either nominal or ordinal. The underlying character of the data is based on the way it is operationalized and collected. Therefore, a major violation often found in nonparametric analysis is the treatment of percentages and proportions as continuous data—they are not continuous, since the data are collected as frequencies based on the category in which they were placed, not on some continuum. Therefore, be very careful when reading reports that are presented as cross-tabulations or frequency tables and have not been reported as nonparametric analyses.

There are a number of nonparametric statistical tests. The one found most often, however, is the Chi-Square (X^2) statistic. There are other tests for ordered variables (see Figure 13.4), but the Chi-Square statistic is found most often in public relations. For a readable discussion on other nonparametric statistics, see Frederick Williams's *Reasoning With Statistics* or Derek Rowntree's *Statistics without Tears*.[7]

Chi-Square Tests on One or More Variables

The Chi-Square statistic is quite simple to calculate, but that simplicity makes it often difficult to interpret. A Chi-Square test can be run on one or more variables. It is best, however, if there are no more than two variables in any test because results become difficult to interpret. The Chi-Square output looks exactly like the cross-tabulation discussed in Chapter 12. In a simple, one variable with two levels (i.e., sex) test you will have two rows (male and female) and one column (sex). Each cell will have whatever descriptive statistics you requested. In addition, you should now request that the "expected values" be computed. The expected values are what either the computer assigns or are provided by you based on either theory or an understanding of the population parameters.

The Chi-Square statistic is easy to compute. It consists of the *actual*

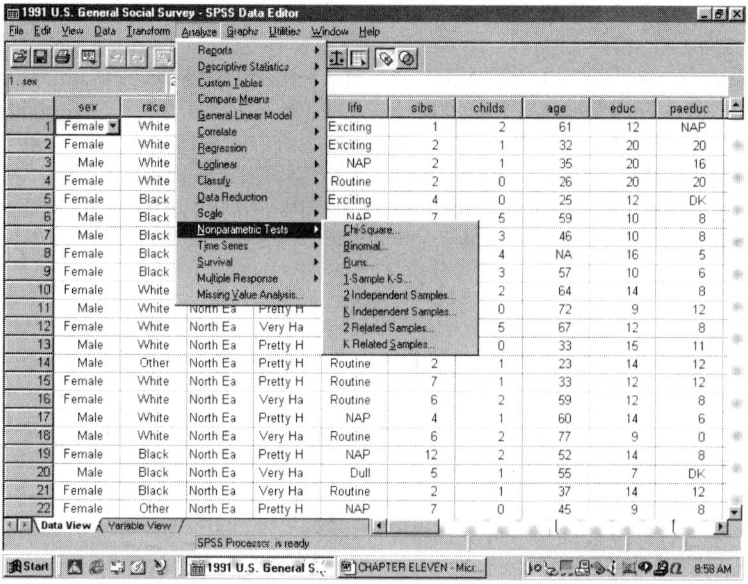

FIGURE 13.4. Command screen: Nonparametric options. SPSS for Windows version 10.07, 1999, Chicago, IL. Reprinted with permission from SPSS, Inc.

frequencies (observed, or *O*) found in each cell and the *expected frequencies* (expected, or *E*) provided or calculated. For instance, suppose you are concerned that there are significantly more females in your sample than you expected (you checked the latest census data and found that the actual proportion of males to females to be about 1:1; you obtained 75 females and 25 males in your sample of 100). The computer assigns the expected values as the total observations divided by the number of cells (it is much more complex with two or more variables, but follows the same basic approach). Thus, the computer expects that there will be 50 males and 50 females in the true population, the same you expected. The Chi-Square statistic computed by the computer takes each cell and first subtracts observed from expected, squares the result, and then divides that result by the expected. Each cell is then added and the obtained Chi-Square statistic is found:

$$\text{Chi-Square} = \frac{(O - E)^2}{E} + \frac{(O - E)^2}{E}$$

In this case you would get $(75 - 50)^2/50 + (25 - 50)^2/50 = 625/50 + 625/50 = 12.5 + 12.5 = 25.0$. The Chi-Square value obtained would be 25.

To determine the significance you must take into account the number of cells. This is done by calculating the *degrees of freedom*. A degree of freedom holds one cell constant while predicting the other. All inferential statistics have degrees of freedom; the Chi-Square degrees of freedom is calculated by taking the number of rows (R) and subtracting one and then multiplying that by the number of columns (C) minus 1 ($[R - 1] \times [C - 1]$). In our case $R = 2$ (there is only one column, and we must have at least 1 degree of freedom); thus, we get $2 - 1 = 1$. The computer then goes to stored probability tables and tells you the actual amount of error you have (or by subtracting the error from 1.00 [no error], you get your confidence interval or level). Figures 13.5a and b demonstrate how to select the Chi-Square statistic for one variable (choose Analyze, Nonparametric tests, and Chi-Square; once the Chi-Square window opens, select your variable—note that you can accept the default for equal expected frequencies or enter your own). The output is found in Figure 13.5c. The computer has calculated the same

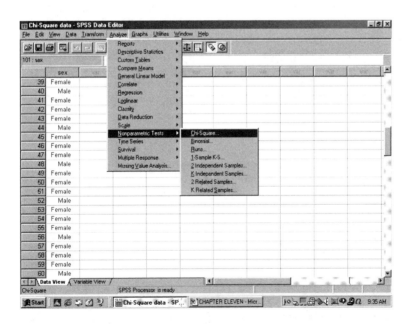

FIGURE 13.5a. Command screen: Chi-Square. SPSS for Windows version 10.07, 1999, Chicago, IL. Reprinted with permission from SPSS, Inc.

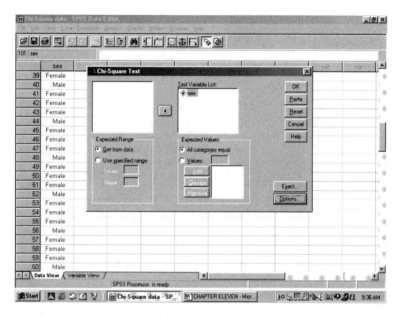

FIGURE 13.5b. Command screen: Chi-Square. SPSS for Windows version 10.07, 1999, Chicago, IL. Reprinted with permission from SPSS, Inc.

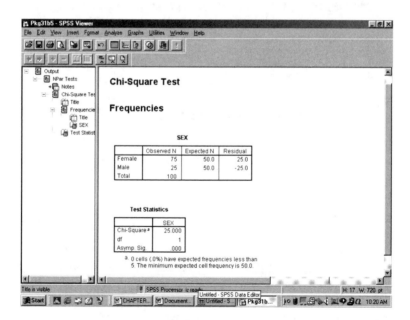

FIGURE 13.5c. Output: Chi-Square. SPSS for Windows version 10.07, 1999, Chicago, IL. Reprinted with permission from SPSS, Inc.

X^2 value (25.0) and degrees of freedom (1; this tells you that there were 2 groups) and has reported the probability of error as ".000," which would be interpreted as follows: your confidence that the number of females is larger than you expected in the population is 99.999%. There are significantly more females than you expected; thus, your conclusion based on sex must be very carefully qualified.

In most cases you will be concerned with the relationships between two variables. Suppose that we are interested in the relationship between the sex of the respondent and whether he or she likes a current promotion that you are working on. You randomly surveyed people from the area where the promotion is showing and are only analyzing those 100 who reported actually encountering the promotion. You asked them a simple question: did they like or dislike the promotion? Figures 13.6a–c demonstrate the SPSS commands necessary to conduct the Chi-Square analysis. Note that because we have two variables (sex and like), we must go back to the Descriptive Statistics option from the Analyze command and then choose Crosstabs (see Figure 13.6b). The only difference is that you chose from the options tab (Figure 13.6c), "Statistics." Choose Chi-Square and the computer produces the output found in Figure 13.6d. Note that the expected frequencies are different in each cell. This is because of the way you calculate them for more than one variable. Note, too, that the Chi-Square value obtained is 1.614 with 1 degree of freedom ($C = 2$; $R = 2$; degrees of freedom = $[2 - 1] \times [2 - 1] = 1$). The probability of error is .204 (ignore the other outcomes), a 20.4% chance of error (or our confidence is only 79.6%). Thus, we conclude that no relationship exists between the sex of the respondent and favorability toward the promotion (i.e., our null hypothesis was supported, and our research hypothesis was rejected).

Whenever you have two or more variables, the first Chi-Square analysis is done through SPSS's Descriptive Statistics. If you obtain a significant difference for the entire table, you must next run Nonparametric tests for each row or column (as we did for sex earlier). The problem comes when we want to look at a cell that is not in the same row or column as the other. In such cases we must interpolate the results based on the expected results for the two cells or re-enter the data for only those cells (SPSS allows you to transform the data, but it may be easier to simply calculate by hand and then track down a Chi-Square table to find the probability of error).

Before we leave the Chi-Square statistic we need to look at one more option. Although we know that the relationships obtained are representative or not representative of the population, the Chi-Square does not tell us how strong that relationship is. Normally we could

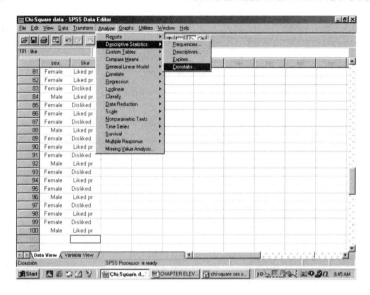

FIGURE 13.6a. Command screen: 2 x 2 Chi-Square. SPSS for Windows version 10.07, 1999, Chicago, IL. Reprinted with permission from SPSS, Inc.

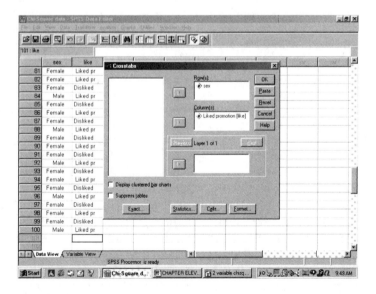

FIGURE 13.6b. Command screen: 2 x 2 Chi-Square. SPSS for Windows version 10.07, 1999, Chicago, IL. Reprinted with permission from SPSS, Inc.

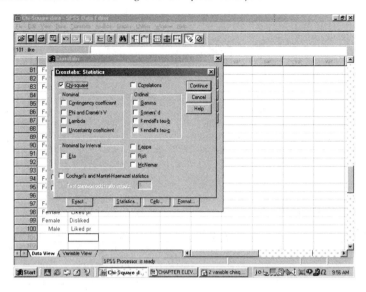

FIGURE 13.6c. Command screen: 2 x 2 Chi-Square. SPSS for Windows version 10.07, 1999, Chicago, IL. Reprinted with permission from SPSS, Inc.

Case Processing Summary

	Cases					
	Valid		Missing		Total	
	N	Percent	N	Percent	N	Percent
Liked promotion * SEX	100	100.0%	0	.0%	100	100.0%

Liked promotion * SEX Crosstabulation

			SEX		Total
			Female	Male	
Liked promotion	Disliked promotion	Count	41	10	51
		Expected Count	38.3	12.8	51.0
	Liked promotion	Count	34	15	49
		Expected Count	36.8	12.3	49.0
Total		Count	75	25	100
		Expected Count	75.0	25.0	100.0

Chi-Square Tests

	Value	df	Asymp. Sig. (2-sided)	Exact Sig. (2-sided)	Exact Sig. (1-sided)
Pearson Chi-Square	1.614[b]	1	.204		
Continuity Correction[a]	1.080	1	.299		
Likelihood Ratio	1.621	1	.203		
Fisher's Exact Test				.251	.149
Linear-by-Linear Association	1.598	1	.206		
N of Valid Cases	100				

a. Computed only for a 2x2 table

b. 0 cells (.0%) have expected count less than 5. The minimum expected count is 12.25.

FIGURE 13.6d. Output: Chi-Square. SPSS for Windows version 10.07, 1999, Chicago, IL. Reprinted with permission from SPSS, Inc.

look at strength of relationship with a Kendall's Tau or Pearson's r correlation. However, the Chi-Square procedure gives you a way of assessing the magnitude of the relationship but not its direction. To do so, simply select the Coefficient of Contingency (see Figure 13.7a). This adds an extra element to your output (see Figure 13.7b). Generally, when you obtain any Coefficient of Contingency less than .30 (a "medium" relationship in terms of magnitude), you should approach the claim that differences were obtained with caution. In this case, our Coefficient of Contingency was only .126 and not significant (.204), the same as our probability of error.

Parametric Analysis

As discussed in Chapter 12, parametric statistics offer more information than do nonparametric statistics. Based on the notion of the normal curve, the interpretations made from continuous—interval and ratio—data can be quite complex and provide in-depth understanding of sample and population relationships. We will explore in depth two

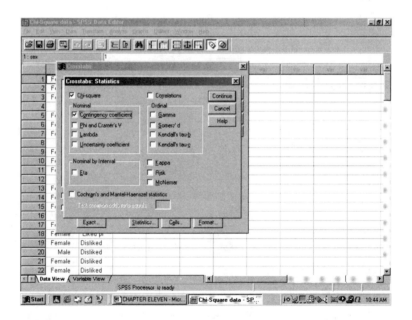

FIGURE 13.7a. Command screen: Chi-Square/Contingency Coefficient. SPSS for Windows version 10.07, 1999, Chicago, IL. Reprinted with permission from SPSS, Inc.

Crosstabs

SEX * Liked promotion Crosstabulation

			Liked promotion		
			Disliked promotion	Liked promotion	Total
SEX	Female	Count	41	34	75
		% within SEX	54.7%	45.3%	100.0%
		% within Liked promotion	80.4%	69.4%	75.0%
		% of Total	41.0%	34.0%	75.0%
	Male	Count	10	15	25
		% within SEX	40.0%	60.0%	100.0%
		% within Liked promotion	19.6%	30.6%	25.0%
		% of Total	10.0%	15.0%	25.0%
Total		Count	51	49	100
		% within SEX	51.0%	49.0%	100.0%
		% within Liked promotion	100.0%	100.0%	100.0%
		% of Total	51.0%	49.0%	100.0%

Chi-Square Tests

	Value	df	Asymp. Sig. (2-sided)	Exact Sig. (2-sided)	Exact Sig. (1-sided)
Pearson Chi-Square	1.614[b]	1	.204		
Continuity Correction[a]	1.080	1	.299		
Likelihood Ratio	1.621	1	.203		
Fisher's Exact Test				.251	.149
Linear-by-Linear Association	1.598	1	.206		
N of Valid Cases	100				

a. Computed only for a 2x2 table

b. 0 cells (.0%) have expected count less than 5. The minimum expected count is 12.25.

Symmetric Measures

		Value	Approx. Sig.
Nominal by Nominal	Contingency Coefficient	.126	.204
N of Valid Cases		100	

a. Not assuming the null hypothesis.

b. Using the asymptotic standard error assuming the null hypothesis.

FIGURE 13.7b. Output: 2 x 2 Chi-Square. SPSS for Windows version 10.07, 1999, Chicago, IL. Reprinted with permission from SPSS, Inc.

parametric tests—the *t-test* and *Analysis of Variance* (ANOVA)—often used in public relations research. At the end of our discussion we will briefly discuss some more advanced parametric inferential statistics and provide a source for further reading.

While nonparametric statistics examine the relationships between variables whose data are found in categories that are simple or ordered, parametric data looks at data that are obtained on some continuum, such as a measurement scale, actual age in years, or income by actual income (not categorized). Thus, inferential statistics look at the sample mean as an approximation of the true population mean. By comparing the differences between a grouping variable (e.g., sex, occupation) for a continuous independent variable, we are able to parcel out the variance associated with the groups (called "between"-group variance) and the variance associated with the individuals across all groups (called "error" variance). Thus, our basic parametric inferential test looks for the ratio between variance "accounted for" (understood to belong to the groups) and the random variance associated with individuals *across* all groups:

$$\text{Statistical test} = \frac{\text{Group variance}_{\text{(between)}}}{\text{Individual variance}_{\text{(error)}}}$$

When the accounted-for group (between) variance is larger than the combined individual (error) variance, we *may* have detected a relationship based on grouping. Like the single variable nonparametric test with only two levels or cells, when we have only two levels of a variable (e.g., sex = female or male), then the finding of significant differences can be directly interpreted. When you have more than two levels (e.g., income = high, middle, or low), then there may be some systematic accounting for grouped variance, but we do not know which groups differ from each other. We must conduct further analyses. When we have more than one variable, we must first see if there is any systematic variance accounted for by the combination of any of the variables (e.g., $\text{sex}_{\text{male or female}}$ and $\text{income}_{\text{high or low}}$) before we can test for each variable by itself.

Sound complicated? Actually it is quite simple, but the complexity allows us to make very complex interpretations of the relationships found in the sample and extrapolated to the population. Unlike the Chi-Square, the continuous inferential statistic is very powerful.

This power can also be a problem. For instance, you have surveyed 800 employees on their attitudes toward the event you are planning in conjunction with the company's 50th anniversary. You are concerned that both blue-and-white collar employees attend and have created an attitude scale that focuses on what employees think they would like to do at the anniversary event. Suppose you find a significant ($\alpha = .05$, effect size of .20 reported as the "p" value in the output) difference between blue-and-white collar employees' attitudes toward having a "swing" band representative of the late 1940s and 1950s. Blue-collar employees rate the band as 2.97 and white-collar employees rate it at 3.03, a difference of .06 units on a 1 to 5 scale (with 3 being the midpoint). Is the finding actually *practically different*? *No*, and the variance accounted for by each level of the group was probably very small. Thus, each group's normal curve would look like that found in Figure 13.8.

Stacks, for example, found many such significant differences in a survey he conducted for the Commission on Public Relations Education, where respondents were asked to indicate the importance of a variety of skills required for contemporary public relations practice.[8] Not surprisingly, public relations professors and public relations practitioners were significantly different from each other on most of the skills, but the differences were often less than 0.5 of a point on a 5-point Likert-type scale. Of more importance was the practical interpretation Stacks offered: although the differences were statistically significant, in practical terms the differences were so minor as to be meaningless. Further, as observed, professors and practitioners all rated the enumerated skills as important (mean responses were 4.0 or higher on most skills). The conclusion? The perception that educators and practitioners value different skills was unfounded. All were marching to the same beat.

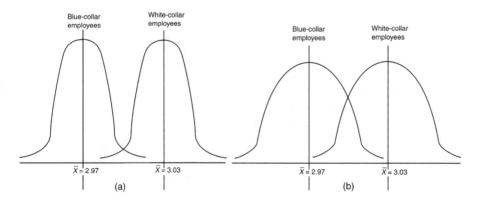

FIGURE 13.8. Significant (a) and nonsignificant (b) curves.

We turn now to four inferential tests. The first, the *t*-test statistic, should be used with small samples and only when there are two groups per independent variable. The second, the ONEWAY ANOVA (Analysis of Variance) statistic, is used when there are more than three groups per independent variable. The third inferential test is used when there are two or more independent variables—ANOVA statistic. Finally, we will look at the correlation as an inferential statistic. We begin with the *t*-test, the most used and abused parametric inferential test.

The "t-Test"

The *t-test* is probably the most used and at the same time most abused parametric statistical test. It is most used because it, like the single variable Chi-Square, is easy to calculate and at the same time easy to interpret. The *t*-test, however, comes with some severe restrictions, and it is the restrictions that are typically abused. To run a *t*-test you need to meet the following criteria:

1. The *independent variable must be dichotomous* (i.e., it contains only two groups).
2. The *dependent variable must be continuous* (i.e., interval or ratio data).
3. The *maximum number of observations is 100* (i.e., 50 males and 50 females or 42 high-income and 58 low-income respondents).

Where we find the *t*-test misused the most is in situations where the total number of observations are more than 100. Why 100? The *t*-test is based on the standard error of the mean, a fairly specific statistic and sensitive when used with small samples. When the sample size gets beyond 100, then the ability to detect differences is reduced and the ANOVA's *F*-test is better suited to identify variance accounted for. The actual formula for computing the standard error of the mean is quite cumbersome. However, all descriptive statistics typically include it, as does the frequency statistic. Computation of the *t*-test is straightforward: you simply subtract one mean from the other and then divide that result by the combined standard error of the means (which can be *approximated* if you are without your computer as each mean's standard error added together and then divided by 2):

$$t = \frac{\text{Mean}_1 - \text{Mean}_2}{\text{Standard Error}}$$

It does not matter which mean is entered first, since *t*-values may be either positive or negative. The degrees of freedom are the number of observations minus 2, or, in the case of 100 observations, 98.

There are three different *t*-tests that you can employ. The most common looks at two *independent samples* (independent means that you can only be in one group—e.g., with sex, you are either male or female). Figures 13.9a–c walk you through the independent *t*-test by first selecting Analyze on the SPSS command bar, then Compare Means, and then Independent Samples (see Figure 13.9a). Next, you select the independent and dependent variables and provide the computer with the coding for the independent variable (sex: female = 1; male = 2). Your output looks like that in Figure 13.9c.

Figures 13.9a–c represent further analysis on the promotion campaign we were interested in with the Chi-Square statistic. In the independent samples analysis we find that the females' mean overall rating of the promotion was 4.13 on the 5-point scale while that for males was 2.08. The standard error for each mean is also reported (.10 for females and .17 for males, indicating that both curves are very peaked and that scores for both sexes varied little from the mean score). The actual *t*-

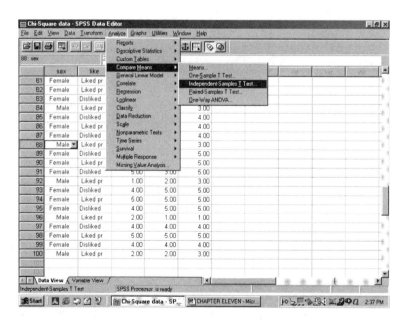

FIGURE 13.9a. Command screen: Independent *t*-test. SPSS for Windows version 10.07, 1999, Chicago, IL. Reprinted with permission from SPSS, Inc.

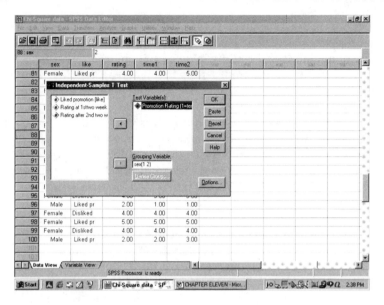

FIGURE 13.9b. Command screen: Independent sample *t*-test. SPSS for Windows version 10.07, 1999, Chicago, IL. Reprinted with permission from SPSS, Inc.

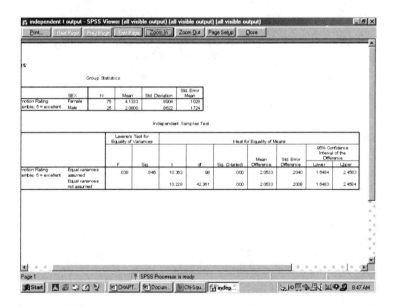

FIGURE 13.9c. Output: Independent sample *t*-test. SPSS for Windows version 10.07, 1999, Chicago, IL. Reprinted with permission from SPSS, Inc.

test information is provided, as well. The *t*-value is reported as 10.06 with 98 degrees of freedom. The probability of error is reported as .000, meaning that we are 99.999% confident that the two means are truly different (ignore the lower figure, which represents an advanced statistic, the Levene test).

Suppose we were interested in finding out how the sample perceived the promotion during the first 2 weeks and during the final 2 weeks. In this case we would run the *paired-samples t*-test. The initial commands are the same as for the independent samples *t*-test. When selected, however, you are asked to provide the two elements of the pair to be tested (this means that you must enter each element as a *separate* variable, such as Time1 and Time2; see Figure 13.10a). The output is shown in Figure 13.10b. Note that the means at Time1 are lower than at Time2, that the two variables are highly correlated (we would expect that since we measured the same people twice), and that the *t*-value obtained is –5.395, with 99 degrees of freedom (100 observations with 2-1 groups), and that the probability that the outcome was due to error (*p*) is again less than .0001, or we can be 99.999% confident that the Time2 difference is significantly greater than the Time1 difference, in both the sample and the population.

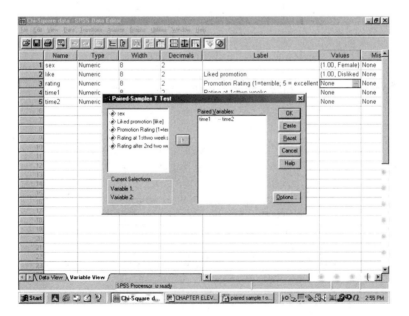

FIGURE 13.10a. Command screen: Paired sample *t*-test. SPSS for Windows version 10.07, 1999, Chicago, IL. Reprinted with permission from SPSS, Inc.

Paired Samples Statistics

		Mean	N	Std. Deviation	Std. Error Mean
Pair 1	Rating at 1st two weeks	3.5600	100	1.3433	.1343
	Rating after 2nd two weeks	4.1300	100	.9812	9.812E-02

Paired Samples Correlations

		N	Correlation	Sig.
Pair 1	Rating at 1st two weeks & Rating after 2nd two weeks	100	.626	.000

Paired Samples Test

		Paired Differences					t
				Std. Error Mean	95% Confidence Interval of the Difference		
		Mean	Std. Deviation		Lower	Upper	
Pair 1	Rating at 1st two weeks - Rating after 2nd two weeks	-.5700	1.0565	.1057	-.7796	-.3604	-5.395

Paired Samples Test

		df	Sig. (2-tailed)
Pair 1	Rating at 1st two weeks - Rating after 2nd two weeks	99	.000

FIGURE 13.10b. Output: Paired sample *t*-test. SPSS for Windows version 10.07, 1999, Chicago, IL. Reprinted with permission from SPSS, Inc.

Finally, there are times when we know how other research has reported the same or similar findings. Suppose that the promotion was first run several months prior to your campaign, that you used the same attitude measures as used earlier, and that the first research found that the mean response was 3.50 for the earlier sample. You start the *single-sample* *t*-test the same way as before. The only difference will be that the window which opens asks you for the mean you wish to test your sample against (3.50; see Figure 13.11a). The results, as shown in Figure 13.11b, indicate that your sample was no different than the previous sample ($t = 0.957$; $df = 99$; $p = .341$, your confidence that the two means are different is only 65.9%)—important information if you are going to follow the previous campaign. If the results for your sample were significantly different, you might want to reconsider how you plan to run your campaign.

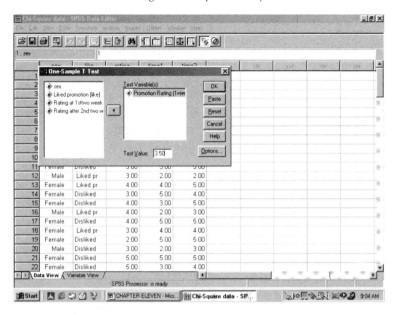

FIGURE 13.11a. Command screen: One-sample *t*-test. SPSS for Windows version 10.07, 1999, Chicago, IL. Reprinted with permission from SPSS, Inc.

T-Test

One-Sample Statistics

	N	Mean	Std. Deviation	Std. Error Mean
Promotion Rating (1=terrible; 5 = excellent	100	3.6200	1.2535	.1254

One-Sample Test

	Test Value = 3.5					
					95% Confidence Interval of the Difference	
	t	df	Sig. (2-tailed)	Mean Difference	Lower	Upper
Promotion Rating (1=terrible; 5 = excellent	.957	99	.341	.1200	-.1287	.3687

FIGURE 13.11b. Output: One-sample *t*-test. SPSS for Windows version 10.07, 1999, Chicago, IL. Reprinted with permission from SPSS, Inc.

The "F-Test" or Analysis of Variance

While the *t*-test is the appropriate statistic when testing two groups when the sample size is 100 or less, the *F*-test is appropriate when there are more than two groups or the number of respondents in the groups under study is greater than 100. As in the *t*-test, the dependent variable must be continuous (interval or ratio data). Looking back at the Independent Samples *t*-test you will see that the *F*-statistic was also provided. Notice that this statistic failed to reject the null hypothesis that the two groups were indeed different. This is due to the statistic's relative insensitivity for small data sets. We also use a special *F*-statistic when we have more than two groups regardless of the sample size, namely, the ONEWAY ANOVA.

ONEWAY ANOVA. The ONEWAY ANOVA is a natural progression from the *t*-test. With the *t*-test you know any differences must be due to the relationship between the two groups; once you add a third (or fourth or more) group, the relationships are harder to identify. Indeed, which groups differ significantly from the others? With three groups, say income (high, middle, low), do all three groups differ, or does one differ from the other two and, if so, which? The ONEWAY tells us that. For instance, consider the income example. You could have any of the following significant differences (signified by an asterisk):

	H	M	L		H	M	L
High							
Moderate	*			or			
Low	*	*			*	*	

In the first case high, moderate, and low income all differ significantly from each other; in the second case, only low differs from high and moderate income; moderate and high income are not different.

Running the ONEWAY requires two steps. First you run the overall *F*-test, which is where you partition your variance due to individuals (error) and groups (between). In most instances, if the F-statistic is not significant (probability < .05, stated as $p < .05$, or the probability is less than .05, our 95% confidence interval or level). Making it a little more confusing, there are now two degrees of freedom (*df*). The first is for groups (between) and is calculated much like the Chi-Square, only this time it is the number of groups minus 1. For three groups, the *between df* = 2. The degrees of freedom for error is the number of observations (people in most public relations cases) minus the group degrees of freedom. The total degrees of freedom will always be one less than the total sample size.

Figures 13.12a–c walk you through the ONEWAY procedure. Because you are comparing means that are levels of the same variable, the initial step is to select Analyze, then Compare Means, and then ONEWAY ANOVA. Once you choose this, you are asked for the factor variable, the one categorical variable (income in this case) and the list of dependent variables (you can process many dependent variables at once; we could do each of the three interval variables we created for the *t*-tests if we wanted to save time). Finally, you must choose which *post hoc* statistical tests (post hoc means "after the fact"; a *planned t*-test between two groups is called an *a priori* test) you will use to test for differences between groups. Notice that you have quite a large selection. Table 13.1 presents the tests in order of their rigor, with the S-N-K and Duncan (Student–Neuman–Keuls) the most liberal and the Scheffe the most conservative.

A liberal *post hoc* test "finds" differences more readily between groups than does a conservative test. Further, the more conservative

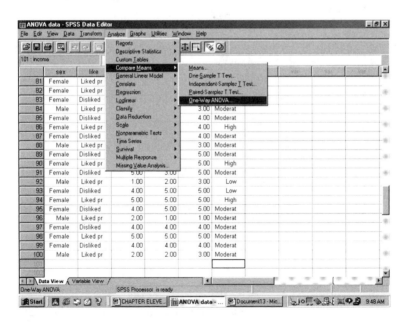

FIGURE 13.12a. Command screen: ONEWAY ANOVA. SPSS for Windows version 10.07, 1999, Chicago, IL. Reprinted with permission from SPSS, Inc.

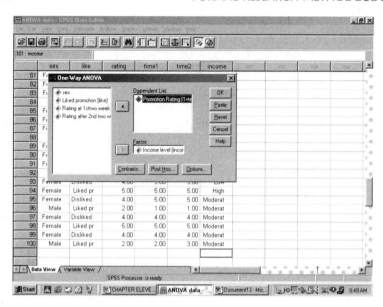

FIGURE 13.12b. Command screen: ONEWAY ANOVA. SPSS for Windows version 10.07, 1999, Chicago, IL. Reprinted with permission from SPSS, Inc.

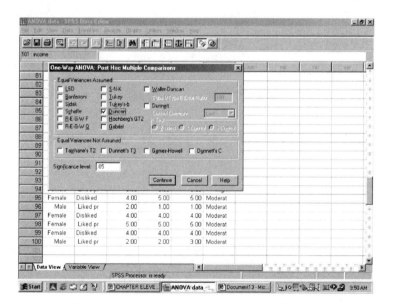

FIGURE 13.12c. Command screen: ONEWAY ANOVA. SPSS for Windows version 10.07, 1999, Chicago, IL. Reprinted with permission from SPSS, Inc.

TABLE 13.1. *Post Hoc Tests*

Test	Rigor	Requires significant *F*?
S-N-K	Liberal	No
Duncan	Liberal	No
LSD	Moderate	Yes
Bonferroni	Moderate	Yes
Tukey HSD	Moderate	Yes
Tukey-b	Moderate	Yes
Scheffe	Conservative	Yes
Etc.		

tests require that the initial ANOVA *F*-statistic be significant. The liberal tests do not require significant between-group differences. The rule of thumb is to use a test at least as conservative as the Tukey-b, and preferably the Scheffe, the most conservative test (and the one to be used when testing a theory or in a situation where true differences are extremely important). The rule of practice is that most people look for any differences they can find; therefore, they use the Duncan and S-N-K most of the time. The difference is in Type I error: Duncan and S-N-K are more likely to suffer Type I error than the more rigorous tests.

Figures 13.12d and 13.12e demonstrate the output when the groups no not differ and differ. Note that the requested *post hoc* test is completed regardless of whether the overall ANOVA is significant or not. Since it is not, then we should expect the means to be in one set, as they are. In Figure 13.12e, the overall *F*-statistic is significant (formally reported as: $F = 7.906$, $df = 2/97$; $p = .001$), and we are 99.999% confident that low-income respondents perceived the promotion significantly more negatively than did the moderate- and high-income respondents, who did not differ in their perceptions.

Multiple-Factor Analysis of Variance (ANOVA). Many relationships are not as simple as a single variable. In fact, much like the cross-tabulation table, most relationships are complex. The multiple-factor ANOVA is used when testing whether two or more *variables* differ from each other. Thus, we might expect income and sex of the respondent *both* to influence perceptions of a promotion. But even more so, we might expect that income would interact with sex to produce different results. For instance, we might expect that high-income males might be more responsive to the promotion than low-income males, and that middle-income females might be somewhere in between high- and low-income males but perceive the promotion similarly to middle-income males. Confusing? You bet, but it is what we come to expect when we test for relationships.

Oneway

ANOVA

Promotion Rating (1=terrible; 5 = excellent

	Sum of Squares	df	Mean Square	F	Sig.
Between Groups	3.069	2	1.534	.976	.380
Within Groups	152.491	97	1.572		
Total	155.560	99			

Post Hoc Tests
Homogeneous Subsets

Promotion Rating (1=terrible; 5 = excellent

Duncan[a,b]

Income level	N	Subset for alpha = .05 1
Moderate	48	3.4792
High	24	3.5833
Low	28	3.8929
Sig.		.228

Means for groups in homogeneous subsets are displayed.

a. Uses Harmonic Mean Sample Size = 30.545.

b. The group sizes are unequal. The harmonic mean of the group sizes is used. Type I error levels are not guaranteed.

FIGURE 13.12d. Output: NSD ONEWAY ANOVA. SPSS for Windows version 10.07, 1999, Chicago, IL. Reprinted with permission from SPSS, Inc.

ANOVA is not run from the Analyze—Compare Means command. To run the ANOVA statistic you go from Analyze to General Linear Model and then to Univariate (see Figure 13.13a). Next you must choose your dependent and independent variables (see Figure 13.13b). Notice that while you can have only one dependent variable you can have multiple independent variables. Next you must "build" your model. If you expect that individual variables will interact, just accept what you have. Otherwise, you must tell the program which "main effects" (the individual variables) will interact with each other (in our case our model will be: sex, income, and the interaction between sex and income [sex * income]; see Figure 13.13c). Finally, before you hit "OK," you must select your *post hoc* comparisons (Figure 13.13d). Again you are presented with a list from which you choose based on the same liberal to conservative rationale as the ONEWAY.

Oneway

ANOVA

Promotion Rating (1=terrible; 5 = excellent

	Sum of Squares	df	Mean Square	F	Sig.
Between Groups	25.509	2	12.754	7.906	.001
Within Groups	156.491	97	1.613		
Total	182.000	99			

Post Hoc Tests
Homogeneous Subsets

Promotion Rating (1=terrible; 5 = excellent

Duncan[a,b]

		Subset for alpha = .05	
Income level	N	1	2
Low	28	2.3929	
Moderate	48		3.4792
High	24		3.5833
Sig.		1.000	.749

Means for groups in homogeneous subsets are displayed.

a. Uses Harmonic Mean Sample Size = 30.545.

b. The group sizes are unequal. The harmonic mean of the group sizes is used. Type I error levels are not guaranteed.

FIGURE 13.12e. Output: Significant ONEWAY ANOVA. SPSS for Windows version 10.07, 1999, Chicago, IL. Reprinted with permission from SPSS, Inc.

The output (Figure 13.13e) will give you the overall model and component results (model is the model you chose, the df = 2 + 3 +1). Your main effects are sex (df = 1 [2 – 1 = 1]), and income (df = 2 [3 – 1 = 2]), and the interaction of sex*income (df = 2 [df = 1 * df = 2]). Interpreting the output, we find that the interaction was not significant (F = 2.94, df = 2/94, p =.058, which is greater than .05). Always check for the interaction first (as a matter of fact, any time you have more than one variable, always check for higher-"order" interaction first, as they may make any interpretations of main effects of lower-"order" interactions impossible). Since the interaction was not significant, we can look at the model, which is significant (F = 182.55, df = 6/94, p = .000), which we would expect if the main effects or the interaction were significant. Sex was significant (F = 43.56, df = 1/94, p = .000), as was income (F = 6.27, df = 2/94, p = .003).

The *post hoc* Duncan test could not be conducted on sex, because

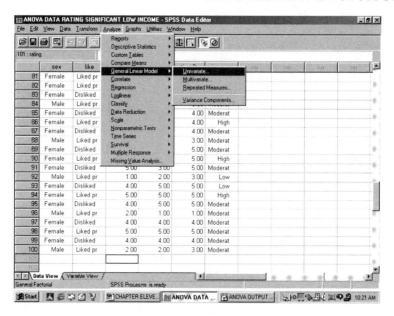

FIGURE 13.13a. Command screen: ANOVA. SPSS for Windows version 10.07, 1999, Chicago, IL. Reprinted with permission from SPSS, Inc.

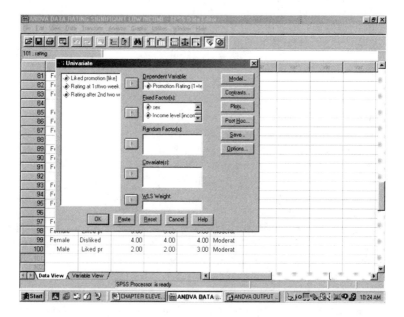

FIGURE 13.13b. Command screen: ANOVA. SPSS for Windows version 10.07, 1999, Chicago, IL. Reprinted with permission from SPSS, Inc.

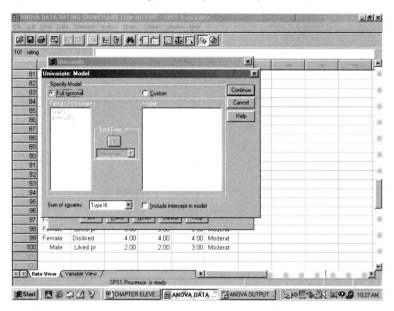

FIGURE 13.13c. Command screen: ANOVA. SPSS for Windows version 10.07, 1999, Chicago, IL. Reprinted with permission from SPSS, Inc.

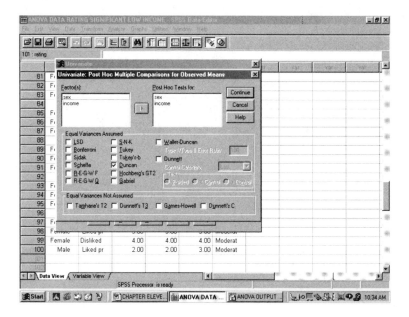

FIGURE 13.13d. Command screen: ANOVA. SPSS for Windows version 10.07, 1999, Chicago, IL. Reprinted with permission from SPSS, Inc.

Univariate Analysis of Variance

Between-Subjects Factors

		Value Label	N
SEX	1.00	Female	75
	2.00	Male	25
Income	1.00	Low	28
level	2.00	Moderate	48
	3.00	High	24

Tests of Between-Subjects Effects

Dependent Variable: Promotion Rating (1=terrible; 5 = excellent

Source	Type III Sum of Squares	df	Mean Square	F	Sig.
Model	1110.682[a]	6	185.114	182.555	.000
SEX	44.174	1	44.174	43.563	.000
INCOME	12.711	2	6.356	6.268	.003
SEX * INCOME	5.965	2	2.983	2.941	.058
Error	95.318	94	1.014		
Total	1206.000	100			

a. R Squared = .921 (Adjusted R Squared = .916)

Post Hoc Tests
Income level
Homogeneous Subsets

Promotion Rating (1=terrible; 5 = excellent

Duncan[a,b,c]

		Subset	
Income level	N	1	2
Low	28	2.3929	
Moderate	48		3.4792
High	24		3.5833
Sig.		1.000	.687

Means for groups in homogeneous subsets are displayed.
Based on Type III Sum of Squares
The error term is Mean Square(Error) = 1.014.

a. Uses Harmonic Mean Sample Size = 30.545.

b. The group sizes are unequal. The harmonic mean of the group sizes is used. Type I error levels are not guaranteed.

c. Alpha = .05.

FIGURE 13.13e. Output: ANOVA. SPSS for Windows version 10.07, 1999, Chicago, IL. Reprinted with permission from SPSS, Inc.

there are only two groups to compare. Therefore, we know that the two groups do differ significantly. Since the interaction of sex * income was not significant, ANOVA did not conduct the tests. (*Note*: This is different from the ONEWAY, which would go ahead and run the Duncan anyway). Finally, we get the same results that we did for the ONEWAY for income. Had the interaction term been significant, we would have had to recode our data into a new variable, "interaction," and then run a ONEWAY on it. We could do this while entering the data by noting that if sex = 1 and income = 1, I (interaction) = 1; if sex = 1 and income = 2, I = 2; if sex = 1 and income = 3, I = 3; if sex = 2 and income = 1, I = 4; if sex = x and income = 2, I = 5; if sex = 1 and income = 3, I = 6. We could also use SPSS's Data command to compute new variable, "I."

Finally, there are times when you will have a group that serves as a control against which to test other groups. There is a special statistical test for control group comparisons, namely, the *Dunnett's t-test*. This test takes into account that the control group is different from the other groups (it was not manipulated), and this test is much more conservative than most *post hoc* tests. Often, however, you will find Duncan or S-N-K tests run, tests that violate those statistical tests' assumptions (this is akin to running a *t*-test on a sample over 100). SPSS provides you the option of specifying which group serves as a control group and then running the Dunnett's *t*-test.

Correlations

Although we covered the correlation in the previous chapter, there are inferential interpretations we can make about the Pearson *r* and nonparametric correlations. When you get correlation matrix output you typically get three things: the correlation, the number of observations that were used to correlate the two variables, and a probability of error (see Figure 13.14a for setup—notice that you can choose between 1- and 2-tailed significance tests and the type of correlation—and Figure 13.14b). The probability of error is no different than in any other inferential test. It tells us how confident we can be that the relationships being measured are truly representative of the population. You must interpret the correlations with care; *a very low correlation also can be very significant*. As a rule of thumb, always look at the size of the correlation before making inferential judgments; if a correlation is 0.12 and its associated $p = .000$, then it is significant, but the relationship does not account for much ($.12^2 = .014$, or the relationship between the two variables accounts for only 1.5% of the explained variance—98.5% is explained by something else).

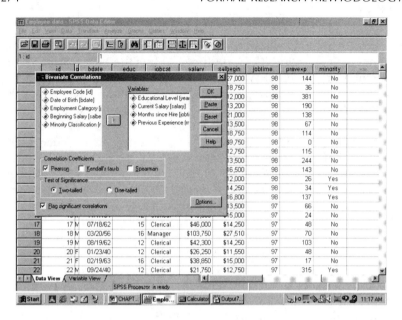

FIGURE 13.14a. Command screen: Correlations. SPSS for Windows version 10.07, 1999, Chicago, IL. Reprinted with permission from SPSS, Inc.

Correlations

Correlations

		Educational Level (years)	Current Salary	Months since Hire	Previous Experience (months)
Educational Level (years)	Pearson Correlation	1.000	.661**	.047	-.252**
	Sig. (2-tailed)	.	.000	.303	.000
	N	474	474	474	474
Current Salary	Pearson Correlation	.661**	1.000	.084	-.097*
	Sig. (2-tailed)	.000	.	.067	.034
	N	474	474	474	474
Months since Hire	Pearson Correlation	.047	.084	1.000	.003
	Sig. (2-tailed)	.303	.067	.	.948
	N	474	474	474	474
Previous Experience (months)	Pearson Correlation	-.252**	-.097*	.003	1.000
	Sig. (2-tailed)	.000	.034	.948	.
	N	474	474	474	474

** Correlation is significant at the 0.01 level (2-tailed).
* Correlation is significant at the 0.05 level (2-tailed).

FIGURE 13.14b. Output: Correlations. SPSS for Windows version 10.07, 1999, Chicago, IL. Reprinted with permission from SPSS, Inc.

ADVANCED STATISTICAL TESTING

Although it is beyond scope of this volume, there are many advanced statistical tests available to the public relations researcher. You will see and possibly work with such statistics as regression, multivariate ANOVA, log-linear, cluster analysis, and discriminate analyses, to name but a few. Obviously, to actually use these statistics requires advanced study of statistics; however, to understand what they do and how they are computed is important. An excellent general guide that is well written and aimed at communication researchers is Frederick Williams's *Reasoning with Statistics*, which was cited earlier. It is strongly recommended that you include it in your personal library. If you purchase an advanced statistical package such as SPSS, the documentation provides guidance into the whys and hows of running different statistical tests. The major difference is that Williams's book is written for communication researchers and provides communication examples.

SUMMARY

This chapter introduced you to the world of probability and making inferences from samples to populations. In reviewing the material, keep in mind that seldom will you be asked for the advanced statistical information that inferential statistics provides. Instead, approach these statistics as tools that allow you to say with X% confidence whether the relationships you observed in the data collected are actually found in the population from which your sample was drawn (if you conduct a census, remember, there is no need for inferential statistics).

A second factor guiding this chapter was the knowledge that in most instances public relations practitioners hire outside research firms to conduct their research. These contractors do understand and know statistics, but they may not approach them in a manner that is suited to public relations. Therefore, examine their findings very closely to ensure that they have run the appropriate tests and that their tests meet the assumptions laid out not only in this chapter but throughout this volume.

Understanding what statistics to use and when to use them is very powerful information. It behooves you to learn as much about the tools that analyze data as the markets from which those data are derived.

REVIEW QUESTIONS

1. Why should public relations researchers be concerned with inferential statistics? What do they provide that descriptive statistics do not?

2. An important aspect of inferential statistics is the "power" of the test. Which parametric and nonparametric tests are powerful? Which are less powerful? What does knowledge about statistical power provide you when you report your findings to clients?

3. Explain the chi-square statistic and how it should be used in public relations research.

4. Why would you want to use a *t*-test? What are the theoretical limitations on its use? Have you ever seen a *t*-test used inappropriately? If so, when and why do you think the researchers misused the statistic?

5. Like a cross-tabulation chi-square, the multiple-factor ANOVA can compare groups. What advantages does the ANOVA have over the chi-square? Can you assess magnitude of effect or shared variance from the ANOVA? Why would you want to?

PRACTICE PROBLEM

You have conducted a simple survey that has asked 100 people (1) who have either attended an event (*n* = 25) you promoted in the past and those who have not (*n* = 25) and (2) those who have contributed to the event in the past (*n* = 25) and those who have not contributed (*n* = 25) what they think about the event. You have asked a number of Likert-type questions that you have shown to be a measure of *event liking* (scores range from 3 to 21) and *event support* (scores range from 3 to 21). What inferential statistical tests are appropriate to answer your research question as to whether past participation and support will make a difference in event liking and event support? Would *t*-tests or chi-square tests for differences be appropriate? Why or why not?

NOTES

1. Frederick Williams, *Reasoning with Statistics: How to Read Quantitative Research*, 4th ed. (Forth Worth, TX: Harcourt Brace Jovanovich, 1992), p. 72.
2. Glen M. Broom & David M. Dozier, *Using Public Relations Research: Applications To Program Management* (Englewood Cliffs, NJ: Prentice Hall, 1990).
3. Fred N. Kerlinger, *Foundations of Behavioral Research*, 3rd ed. (New York: Holt, Rinehart & Winston, 1986).
4. Don W. Stacks & John E. Hocking, *Communication Research*, 2nd ed. (New York: Longman, 1999), p. 363.
5. Herman Cohen, *Statistical Power Analysis for the Behavioral Sciences*, 2nd ed. (Hillsdale, NJ: Erlbaum, 1988).
6. Broom and Dozier, see especially Appendix E.
7. Williams; Derek Rountree, *Statistics without Tears* (New York: Macmillan, 1982).
8. Don W. Stacks, "Report to the Commission on Public Relations Education/NCA Summer Conference on Public Relations: Perceptions of Public Relations Education," Washington, DC, July 1998; Don W. Stacks, Carl Botan, and Judy VanSlyke, "Perceptions of Public Relations Education," *Public Relations Review*, 25 (1999), pp. 9–28.

PART IV

Obtaining and Reporting Public Relations Research

How do you go about asking others to conduct research for you? In Chapter 14 we look briefly at the research before data are collected—the hows and whys of a request for research proposals (RFP). Many companies and public relations firms will put their research needs "out for bid," so to speak. It is important that you understand the basics of a good RFP before undertaking to propose one (and to compete for work once an RFP has been issued, if you are a research consultant or work for a research firm). Chapter 14 presents what is often the beginning point for research projects deemed too large to be carried out by a corporation or firm in-house.

Chapter 15 rounds out this primer of public relations research by examining the end product of research. Conducting research normally requires that one report the final findings in written form and often present them orally. The final write-up of a research project is examined in Chapter 15, both in terms of the executive summary and the longer final report. Finally, tips on how to present the research project orally are offered.

When you reach the end of Part IV, you should have a base from which to conduct, analyze, and interpret research. This base, however, is only that—a basic understanding of the complexities of an ever expanding and growing arm of public relations practice. As with any area, continued reading and practice will be required of all practitioners who seek to make it easier to conduct and understand research in the future.

Chapter 14

Writing and Evaluating the Request for Research Proposal

There are times when a research project is either too large to be handled internally or the public relations firm or corporate department does not have the ability to conduct the required research. In such cases public relations practitioners do what many business people do, namely, they contract with an outside researcher or research firm to conduct the research. This chapter's focus is on writing research solicitation requests and evaluating the resulting responses.

How do you go about requesting outside help in conducting research? In some instances you might turn to someone you know, you trust, and who has a reputation for conducting research in the area(s) you need. However, you often want the option of choosing the *best* from among several researchers or researcher firms. Further, by soliciting competitive research bids, you may save money and be exposed to newly devised research tools. Thus, you will write and distribute a *request for research proposal* (RFP). The RFP seeks to first advertise your research needs and then to invite interested parties—researchers (both academic and professional) or research firms—to bid on your research project(s).

Writing the RFP is not as simple as just sitting down at the computer and writing an advertisement or releasing the request as a press release, although both methods are found. The RFP, like any public document, requires careful thinking; the more time you put into what you need and when results are needed (as well as projected costs), the better the RFP will be. Quite simply, better-written RFPs receive more attention and more responses than poorly written ones.

Basically there are four steps in attracting and selecting the best researchers or firms. First, you must identify what you need. This requires that you carefully consider the four types of questions originally introduced in Chapter 1, that is, questions of definition, fact, value, and policy. Second, you must identify a host of potential researchers and firms. Although you may simply publish your RFP in the trade papers or large national or metropolitan newspapers, the best results come when your RFP is transmitted directly via the mail or Internet to proven researchers or firms or groups you know conduct research in the area(s) of need. Third, you must actually write and transmit the RFP. And, finally, you must evaluate the proposals received.

ADDRESSING WHAT YOU NEED

Before writing your RFP you must determine exactly what it is that you need. RFPs that address specific concerns or problems receive better proposals. To determine what you need, you must return to the four questions that dictate all approaches to research: questions of definition, fact, value, and policy. How you answer these questions will determine in large part the focus of your RFP. As with any research project—one you will be conducting yourself or requesting bids for—you must first do your homework. What is it you need? Is the research basic and extending previous research or is it something that is new, perhaps cutting edge? Either way, you must first define what it is that you need. Hence, the question of definition is the first question answered. *What is it that you are asking for?* In answering this question you must carefully define the concepts of interest. For instance, are you looking for attitude assessment of a product or client? Are you looking at some behavioral index of return on pubic relations activity? Or, do you need to better understand the communication climate or culture of your organization? Carefully determining what you are looking for makes it easier for others to decide (1) whether they can be of help and (2) what methodology you are expecting to be employed.

Second, you must *decide whether you simply need factual information.* It may be that you have several questions of fact that need answering. It may also be that you need to *assess the value of something intrinsic or extrinsic to your research project.* Some researchers and firms focus on answering factual questions, while others are more adept at answering questions of value. Still yet, there are others who have the backgrounds and staffs to do both (obviously, combining both fact and value data takes more time and costs more but yields very rich insights for interpretation).

Finally, *you might require information that allows you to answer questions of policy.* This question is often addressed when a public relations campaign or program is in the planning stages. There are times, however, when postcampaign results require an outside, disinterested party to evaluate the findings as secondary research. Policy questions require an in-depth understanding not only of the data gathered, but also extending the data gathering to focus groups and in-depth interviews with those who may be affected. It may be that your RFP requires—much as in engineering or other hard sciences— that several different researchers or firms work together to produce the final product. In such a case you may be looking for a large research firm or, if time allows, a university department to conduct the research.

What you are doing at this stage is problem solving. There are a number of problem-solving techniques that can be used, but John Dewey's problem-solving technique[1] offers both the depth and breadth often required at this stage of research (see Table 14.1). Dewey's problem-solving technique involves five steps. First, and most difficult, is the *identifying the actual problem.* Often the problem identified is not the actual problem but instead is the *result* of the problem. For example, parking problems may be perceived as causing both a morale problem and potentially a labor problem (Stacks addressed this problem at a large southern hospital[2]). The real problem might not be parking—there may be plenty of parking, albeit not all conveniently located—but rather the widespread perception that there *is* a problem. The two problems are not the same, and they require different types of data to be gathered when researched.

Second, you must *analyze the problem.* What aspects of the problem do you wish to attack first? When? How? Although you may not know the details of what you need, based on this analysis you should have some idea of the priorities and some framework from which to work. At this stage you might be stating overall program or campaign goals. Third, you need to *think of possible solutions to the problem.* Here you are asking yourself what kind of objectives (informational, motivational, behavioral) you will be seeking. Fourth, based on your knowledge of the problem area, *select what you believe to be the best suggested solutions*

TABLE 14.1.Dewey's Problem-Solving Technique as Applied to Public
Relations Research

1. Identify the problem
    1.1 What is the real problem?
        1.11 Definitional?
        1.12 Factual?
        1.13 Value-oriented?
        1.14 Policy?
    1.2 What are the problem's characteristics?
        1.21 Definitional?
        1.22 Factual?
        1.23 Value?
        1.24 Policy?

2. Analyze the problem
    2.1 How is the problem actually stated?
        2.11 Is the problem simple or complex?
        2.11 Is the problem compartmentalized, or does it affect other things?
    2.2 Is there a cause–effect sequence that can be identified?
        2.21 What does previous research tell you?
        2.22 What are the suspected variables?
        2.23 How does causation affect goals?

3. Possible solutions
    3.1 List all possible solutions
        3.11 Examine each separately
        3.12 Examine each as it relates to other solutions
    3.2 Set each solution into its potential objective
        3.21 Informational objectives
        3.22 Motivational objectives
        3.23 Behavioral objectives

4. Select the best possible solution(s)
    4.1 Match to program's or campaign's overall goal(s)
    4.2 Match to program's or campaign's specific objectives

5. Put solution into effect
    5.1 How do you want the solutions presented?
    5.2 What is the final evaluation of the research component?
    5.3 How has the final product impacted on the campaign or program?

to the problem. Here you begin to state the specifics that will become
part of the RFP.

Finally—and this stage can be viewed as both pre-RFP and as
part of the proposal selection process—you want to *put the solution(s)
into effect.* In terms of the pre-RFP process, you will be stating how
you want the final results reported and presented; at the selection

point, you will be making a judgment regarding which of your "bidders" is offering the best solutions (data, analysis, and reports) to your problem.

IDENTIFYING POTENTIAL RESEARCHERS AND FIRMS

Once you have decided exactly what you need, determining who might compete for the research project may help you to write a better RFP. Although this may seem out of sequence, consider that you must write for an audience. The better you know the audience, the better your RFP will be written and received by those you *expect* to be interested in bidding for the work.

According to the Council of Public Relations Firms, hiring a public relations firm most efficiently begins with the creation of a short list of three to five potential winning firms.[3] The same is true when considering research firms or researchers. The Council points out that what you are attempting to form is a partnership between you and your selected researcher or firm, so you need to conduct as much research as possible early on in the process. What should be considered when looking at potential researchers or firms? First, of course, is their *credibility*; here you need to know their history, who they have worked with in the past, and what their specific strengths or weaknesses are. Thus, you might ask:

- *Who are they?* Specifically, who are the principals and how large are their staffs? How long have they been in business?
- *What have they done and for whom?* Specifically, whom have they worked for? What kind of research projects have they been involved with? Do they specialize in particular kinds of research, or are they generalists?
- *What are their strengths and weaknesses?* Based on their credentials and background, what are they really known for? What kinds of research projects do they report *not* working on? Based on the foregoing questions, what can you pinpoint as specific advantages or disadvantages to hiring them?
- *Whom are others in the industry using?* Often word of mouth will provide you with a good list of researchers or firms, people who have done good work for others.

Broom and Dozier make five suggestions that are in line with the foregoing recommended approach[4]:

1. *Know your budget and deadlines.*
2. *Decide the role you want your researcher or research firm to play:* (a) the researcher takes the task of telling you what to do and how it should be done (as you should be aware, this is not a great idea); (b) the researcher is solely a problem-solving process facilitator, working with you to collect and analyze data; or (c) the researcher provides specific services for the research program you have designed.
3. *Know your researcher's special capabilities.*
4. *Research your research consultants.*
5. *Tell the researcher how you will use the research and how you see various research methods working within your research program.* Let the researcher know what you already know and how you plan to use the data.

Once you have these considerations in mind, you need to zero in on specific researchers or firms. Dozier and Repper offer excellent guidance in choosing the right firm.[5] Along lines similar to Broom and Dozier, they suggest that, once you have selected the top firms to do your research, you check out the firms' sampling procedures, their response rates if you require surveys, their means for obtaining and coding data, and how they will report the results. Dozier and Repper also suggest that you should not overlook the services of academic researchers and academic research services. Often you can save money by working with academic researchers, but the tradeoff is often in the length of time it takes for an academic to conduct, analyze, and report findings. Lower overhead costs keep academic bids low, but the time constraints found in much public relations research often result in academicians not even bidding (these time constrains are even greater if you choose to engage an academic department, which will have to go through the university's institutional research board for review and certification to the government that the plan does not harm any potential participant in any way).

Where do you look for research services? Most telephone books will have research firms listed in the Yellow Pages. Larger cities will have more listings than smaller cities, but through the Internet you should be able to find more firms than you could ever possibly consider. There are also useful directories to consult, such as the *Research Service Directory* and the *Directory of U.S. & Canadian Marketing Surveys & Services*. It pays to do your homework when selecting research firms. Anyone can start a research firm, so review firms for what they can and cannot do and which firms and whom they have worked for in the past. Over time you will probably learn to rely on several different researchers (academic and professional) and firms.

THE REQUEST FOR PROPOSAL

There is no definite format for the RFP. However, the more detailedly that you can specify what is needed, what the budget is, and the dates by which you will need results reported back, the better your RFP will be. Some organizations will begin with a notification phase, such as found in Figures 14.1. The notification in Figure 14.1 tells potential researchers and firms (1) what you want, (2) the projected budget(s), and (3) a little something about the organization itself. It then directs interested parties to a website for more details (it also provides a mailing address for the same thing). Newspaper or magazine notification is more widespread and is found in most newspapers and trade newsletters and magazines. It accomplishes the same basic goals—indicating what is needed and the budget.

A general outline of what might be considered a good RFP (see Table 14.2) would be to begin with a short introduction of the research. Here the *rationale* for the research and the *expected outcomes* are presented (whether financial or related to recognition or reputation, or both). This is followed by the *types of research* you are considering:

1. Which methods are needed (qualitative or quantitative or both)?
2. The relevancy to the client (you, and what you plan on doing with it).
3. The language in which the final report is to be written in (a good RFP will also tell the researchers where the data are expected to be collected; collecting data in several languages will dramatically increase costs).

Next you should cover your *research preferences*. Here you can state your research questions if you so desire. This may limit the number of proposals, but it also tells the potential researcher or firm just what it is you are looking for. It is also important to indicate *whom you expect to submit proposals*. Here you might include or exclude certain researchers (academic, for instance) or focus on researchers and firms with expertise in certain areas (organizational culture, media relations, political image, forecasting, and so on).

Once this has been completed, you must tell the prospective researcher or firm how you want the proposal to be written. Try to keep the requirements as simple—yet, as complete—as possible. For instance, indicate which forms you need completed (such as contact information, references, and the like) and then standardize them for all proposals. Doing this makes it much easier to compare responses later.

RESEARCH FOUNDATION

October 3, 2000

Dear Communication Expert:

The IABC Research Foundation is pleased to invite you to respond to three new Request for Proposals (RFP). Summary descriptions of the RFPs are included with this letter and the full RFP descriptions are accessible on our website, www.iabc.com/fdtnweb/research_projects.html.

Below are summary descriptions of the RFP topics and grant award amounts:

Intangible Assets U.S. $20,000
This study will assess the relationship between intangible assets — ideas, relationships, knowledge, people, networks, patents, common goals, goodwill — and communication. The final report will offer analysis and a diagnostic tool on applying this knowledge to organizational communication.

Virtual Work Force U.S. $10,000
This literature review and assessment will explore the virtual work force and its affect on organizational communication. It will examine which communication processes and methods are most effective in a virtual work force.

Communication Research Primer U.S. $10,000
A primer on how to perform communication research, this report will include best practice examples, techniques, tools and analysis; practical, easy-to-follow models of research; and skill-related guidance on integrating research as a critical part of a communication project.

The IABC Research Foundation is a not-for-profit organization associated with the International Association of Business Communicators (IABC). We are dedicated to the advancement of organizational communication through research, education, and professional development. With the partnership of communication experts worldwide, research produced by the IABC Research Foundation is enhancing the practice and perception of communication. The Foundation pursues research that will help to bridge the theory and practice of organizational communication.

We look forward to receiving your proposal.

Sincerely,

Natasha Spring
IABC Research Foundation Director

OUR RESEARCH, YOUR DEVELOPMENT
INTERNATIONAL ASSOCIATION OF BUSINESS COMMUNICATORS
One Hallidie Plaza, Suite 600, San Francisco, California 94102 USA
(415) 333-5300 • Fax (415) 362-8762
http://www.iabc.com

FIGURE 14.1. RFP advance notification letter. Reprinted with permission from the International Association of Business Communicators and the IABC Research Foundation.

TABLE 14.2. Request for Proposal General Outline

  I. Introduction

 II. Types of research to be considered
    A. Quantitative methods
    B. Qualitative methods
    C. Relevancy to client
    D. Report language(s)

III. Research preferences
    A. Questions to be answered
    B. Hypotheses to be tested

IV. Eligibility requirements
    A. Who is included or excluded
    B. Expertise areas required

 V. Proposal requirements
    A. Forms required and how to transmit them
      1. Contact information
      2. Short abstract of proposal (in understandable English)
      3. Resumés of all principals
    B. Specific proposal requirements
      1. Literature review requirements
      2. Overview of data collection and research methods to be employed
      3. Interim report requirements
      4. Final report requirements
    C. Budget
      1. Total budget
      2. Broken into major research areas
      3. If necessary, specifics (e.g., how much to draw a sample, telephone costs, and so forth)
    D. Timetable

 VI. Short history of your organization and how to get more information about the organization (i.e., website or addresses)

VII. Review process and important dates

VIII. How and where to submit proposals
    A. Internet
    B. Mail

Next, how long do you want the proposal to be? In what format will it be accepted (typed, but single- or double-spaced copy)? Most proposals are limited to about 2,500 words or less (about 10 typewritten double-spaced pages) and usually contain an analysis of the problem, the major questions to be addressed, a literature review, methods to be employed, how the reports will be handled, the sample and sampling techniques, a timeline (including specific delivery dates), a budget breakdown, and a synopsis of the researcher or firm's qualifications. Next, you will want the resumés of all researchers to be involved in the project (many RFPs limit this to five single-spaced 8½" x 11" pages).

It is important to include how the proposals will be reviewed and the dates that the researcher or firm can expect to be notified of decisions. Basically you start with the date you formally announce the RFP, when preliminary proposals (if asked for) are due, when finalists are announced, when comprehensive proposals are due from finalists (if necessary or asked for), when the final decision for awarding the proposal will be announced, and when the project is expected to begin.

Finally, as specifically as possible, you need to let potential researchers and firms know how to send their proposals to you. Traditionally this is done by mail (often via certified/return receipt letter), but more and more the proposals and attachments can be sent via e-mail. If the latter is allowed, be certain to let submitters know what formats you can handle and what you expect the formatting to be.

Once this is done, you may want to write a cover letter explaining the RFP and use it as a way of transmitting the RFP to specific researchers or research firms that you want to submit proposals. As noted, over time you will learn who to depend on and who are the "experts" in different kinds of research. You also may have a certain type of researcher in mind who might not be aware that the RFP has been published. Finally, you could do this by e-mail, but the personal letter adds a nice touch.

EVALUATING RFPs

Once you have written, advertised, and received submissions to your RFP, the next step is to evaluate the submissions. If you requested preliminary proposals, then you would have already conducted this phase of the RFP process, winnowing down submissions to the two or three that you really feel are what you are looking for. What would your evaluation process have looked like? Most likely you would use the same evaluation criteria you would use at the final evaluation stage. Basically you will do a comparison of all proposals that are in final consideration. Table 14.3 and Figures 14.2 and 14.3 provide examples of the questions or components you might consider in evaluating the proposals. How you rate each question or component can be done via semantic differential scales after each component (or subcomponent if any) or Likert-type scales (e.g., "Component X has . . . ") or through general comments. With a large number of proposals it is common to use measurement scales to select the finalists for a more qualitative review and final decision. Typically, however, an 11-point scale (0–10) is used, and the final scores are added for comparison in such cases.

There are many criteria on which to evaluate a proposal. Table 14.3's components are representative of what criteria you might use. Most of the evaluation components are self-explanatory. You want people who know what public relations is about and have done some work in the industry. Otherwise you will have to spend extra time bringing them up to speed as to just what public relations people do and how the project relates to public relations problems. Specific expertise is what you are seeking and should be mentioned prominently in the RFP. Here you are looking for things that make this person or firm an "expert" in a given area or areas. A proposal can be too detailed, often to the point of missing exactly what you want. Generally a good proposal will supply enough detail to assure a meeting of the minds but also provides enough "wiggle room" for subsequent modifications from both the submitter and you in response to operational requirements.

The expectations component is critical: Do they promise too much for what they say it will cost or what you see the time frame as being? As for the budget, is it adequate to cover projected expenditures, including a margin for unanticipated exigencies? Comprehensiveness is tied to expectations, but do you get a good feeling for what they want to do and how well it will meet your needs? Can they bring the project in on time and meet the deadlines you've established for reporting? Consider here, too, whether they have taken into account data collection problems that you have faced in the past (especially with international research). If you plan to use the results publicly, you might want

TABLE 14.3. Common Evaluation Components or Criteria

1. Expertise in public relations	6. Comprehensiveness
2. Specific expertise	7. Timeline(s)
3. Detail of proposal	8. Brand-name firm or person
4. Expectations (realistic or not)	9. Your involvement
5. Pricing	10. Summary

Proposal submitted by: _____

Component	Score (0 = terrible; 10 = excellent)
1. Expertise in public relations	0 1 2 3 4 5 6 7 8 9 10
2. Specific expertise	0 1 2 3 4 5 6 7 8 9 10
3. Detail of proposal	0 1 2 3 4 5 6 7 8 9 10
4. Expectations (realistic or not)	0 1 2 3 4 5 6 7 8 9 10
5. Pricing	0 1 2 3 4 5 6 7 8 9 10
6. Comprehensiveness	0 1 2 3 4 5 6 7 8 9 10
7. Timeline(s)	0 1 2 3 4 5 6 7 8 9 10
8. Brand-name firm or person	0 1 2 3 4 5 6 7 8 9 10
9. Your involvement	0 1 2 3 4 5 6 7 8 9 10
10. Summary	0 1 2 3 4 5 6 7 8 9 10

TOTAL POINTS: _____

FIGURE 14.2. Measurement-type evaluation sheet. Adapted with permission from the Institute for Public Relations.

COMPONENT	Firm XYZ	Firm ABC	Firm QRS
Expertise in public relations	Very high	Moderate	Moderate
Specific expertise	Survey good	Survey lacking	Survey very good
Detail of proposal	Very detailed	Too detailed	OK
Expectations (realistic or not)	Not really	Very good	Good
Pricing	Very expensive	Expensive	Cheap
Comprehensiveness	To the extreme	Good	Lacks total concept
Timeline(s)	Explicit	Workable	Unrealistic
Brand-name firm or person	High recognition	High recognition	Lacks industry or area recognition
Your involvement	Low	Low	High
Summary	Very good	Very good	Poor

FIGURE 14.3. Qualitative evaluation sheet. Adapted with permission from the Institute for Public Relations.

to consider the brand-name value of the firm or researcher. Using a well-known firm usually costs a little more, but their reputation may add credibility to your study; using an academic researcher also may lend credibility to the findings.

Finally, your involvement must be taken into consideration. How much will you need to be involved? If you must continually oversee or meet with the researcher or research firm, you must take into account how this will affect your routine responsibilities. Sometimes you simply want the researcher or firm to do its job and get the results back to you; at other times you might want to be actively involved. How much involvement will they allow or expect?

The summary component is important because it represents your "gut feelings" about the proposal. Never underestimate the importance of such feelings. If your evaluation here is negative and yet everything else is highly positive, reread the proposal and try to find out what is troubling you. It is much better to engage in such reevaluation now than either after the contract has been let or the final report has been turned in.

SUMMARY

This chapter has explored the request for proposal (RFP). We examined the philosophy behind why you might want to advertise for research and what benefits there are in doing so. We then looked at how to prepare to write the RFP through your own research of the problem and those whom might consider for submissions or responses to your RFP. We then turned to actually writing the RFP and the component parts that should be included in a "good" request. Finally, we explored how you might evaluate the proposals and select the one that best fits your needs and budget.

REVIEW QUESTIONS

1. Why is the RFP so difficult to write and the responses to it so difficult to assess?

2. A good RFP contains several sections. What are they?

3. How would you evaluate an RFP that came from a research company or public relations firm?

4. How do you know when you get an RFP submission, or response, that the researcher or firm can do the job it says it can do?

5. What criteria should you look at in making the decision to hire a researcher or firm based on their response to an RFP?

PRACTICE PROBLEM

Write an RFP that seeks an outside research or public relations firm to conduct basic research leading up to your public relations campaign for a political campaign where your client is running for county commissioner. Be sure that you have specified costs, expertise, analysis, timelines, and how the report is to be written. Assuming that you have three potential "winners," how will you chose the firm or researcher to do your research?

NOTES

1. John Dewey, *How We Think* (Boston: Heath, 1933); adapted from William S. Smith, *Group Problem-Solving Through Discussion: A Process Essential to Democracy* (Indianapolis: Bobbs-Merrill, 1965), pp. 108–112.

2. Don W. Stacks, "Crisis Management: Toward a Multidimensional Model of Public Relations," in D. Millar (ed.), *Crisis Communication: Theory and Applications* (Mahwah, NJ: Erlbaum, in press).

3. Council of Public Relations Firms, *Hiring a Public Relations Firm: A Guide for Clients* (New York: Council of Public Relations Firms, 2000).

4. Glen M. Broom and David M. Dozier, *Using Research in Public Relations: Applications to Program Management* (Englewood Cliffs, NJ: Prentice Hall, 1990), pp. 317–318.

5. David M. Dozier and Fred C. Repper, "Research Firms and Public Relations Practices," in James E. Grunig (ed.), *Excellence in Public Relations and Communication Management* (Hillsdale, NJ: Erlbaum, 1992), pp. 184–215.

Chapter 15

Writing and Presenting the Final Research Report

Once the research has been gathered and the data analyzed, you have but two steps left in the research cycle. The first step is to write up your findings, and the second is to present them orally to the client or appropriate corporate manager. While most public relations people seldom have trouble with the first step, the second step—orally presenting your findings—is often approached with great trepidation. This chapter rounds out the research process by looking at how to prepare and write the final research report. It then looks at both informative and persuasive oral presentations. Writing and presenting to a client or superior can be a nerve-wracking experience, one usually inflicted upon senior public relations practitioners. However, as the chief researcher you may be the only individual who can truly explain what you have found. Therefore, it often falls upon you to prepare both the written and oral presentations. This chapter seeks to make that experience more "user-friendly."

WRITING THE RESEARCH REPORT

A research report may follow any of several outlines and formats. Sometimes companies and clients have specific formats and outlines to follow. Most of the time, however, you write a report that meets the needs of the client or project. This treatment assumes that you have yet to write your first research report; therefore, we will follow a general outline and format.

Most reports are typed and, depending on client or organization, are bound as either spiral-bound or plastic-covered booklets. Most research reports are divided into three general sections. The first section presents the *executive summary*, an overview of the project and findings, what you might call an extended abstract. The second section contains the *specifics of the research*, including tables and figures that illustrate the conclusions and further amplify them through recommendations (or reservations); often it also includes a bibliography of relevant readings and materials used to produce the report. The third section usually consists of *appendices* containing the materials used in conducting the research and special exhibits (such as press releases, copies of ad copy, and so forth).

All research reports should begin with a title page that specifies the project title and relevant data, such as date of presentation, and research team members (including outside firms or researchers, if consulted). Additionally, front matter such as a table of contents, preface, foreword, and copyright or use notices should be inserted between the title page and the executive summary.[1]

Executive Summary

The executive summary is a brief summary of the research in its most straightforward and readable form. A good executive summary begins with a paragraph describing the reason for the study and/or a description of the problem(s) being researched. It then presents a very short and tight literature review, outlining the rationale for the study and any research questions or hypotheses being answered or tested. A brief description of the research method(s) employed is presented next, which should include the following:

1. How the data were collected (the methods used).
2. When the data were collected, or the study's time frame.
3. For surveys, the population characteristics and how the sample was selected, along with the sampling confidence and measurement error levels used.
4. For focus groups, how the groups were selected, any payments or incentives for participating, how sessions were conducted, and the location of each focus group.
5. For in-depth interviews, how the interviewees were selected, why they were selected, and where they were interviewed. If

they were paid for their interviews, indicate that and usually how much they were paid.

6. For content analyses, brief descriptions of the units of analyses and the category system, as well as the intercoder reliability.
7. For experiments, a brief description of the independent and dependent variables, the experimental design, and a description of how the data were gathered.

Next, the major findings or results should be summarized. This may be done in normal text format or in a bulleted paragraph format. The findings should be presented factually and in some detail. Normally, however, no tables or figures are used in the executive summary.

The executive summary's audience is usually the senior management of the client. They will use the executive summary to make decisions or to justify allocation of funds or resources to whatever program or campaign the report relates to (as a precampaign measure, as a rationale for undertaking a campaign, or as part of the final evaluation process). For that reason, make the report as brief and readable as possible. The details are presented in the next section, which may be read by the client or passed along to people he or she feels can offer interpretation of findings or implementation of results.

Research Specifics

The research report's second section fleshes out the executive summary. Here a more detailed (and referenced) rationale for the research is presented. This is essentially an argument for why the research was needed and answers the questions of definition and fact as known prior to the research actually being conducted.

Literature Review

The research report is and will become an historical document; therefore, you will want to provide as much information as possible for those who may use it as a jumping-off point for future research. The literature review should be concise and include only the most important arguments and citations. In addition, the literature review is typically formatted according to the *Publication Manual of the American Psychological Association*,[2] which uses in-text referencing (e.g., "Stacks, 2002") with a list of "references" at the end of the report. Substantive comments, such as those found in footnotes, however, should follow the Modern Language Association's *MLA Handbook for Writers of Research Reports*,[3] which uses footnotes or endnotes. Footnoting, which places the comments at the bottom of each page, is preferable for research reports. An example is found in Figure 15.1. The literature review should conclude with a listing of the research questions asked in the research (e.g., "How is the Internet used by top corporate executives in making corporate policy decisions?") or hypothesized (e.g., "Use of standardized measures to gauge public relations effectiveness produces clearer perceptions of a public relations firm's credibility.").

The literature review, then, presents a detailed yet compressed argument for the research project. It also formally states the research questions asked or hypotheses tested in the research.

Method

The method section lays out for the reader the way in which the research was conducted and how the data were collected. Here you must be specific enough for others to (1) understand how you went about collecting the data and (2) possibly replicate the study at a later time. Remember, social scientific research is driven by procedures that when followed later should produce results similar to yours. This is where you lay out the specifics of the project, the dates run, how the data

---

The practice of crisis management is best described by Otto Lerbinger (1997) in *The Crisis Manager: Facing Risk and Responsibility.* In his description of crisis situations, Lerbinger suggests three types of crises that face public relations practitioners in today's multinational climate. He further breaks these three crisis types into seven distinctly different crisis situations. Don Stacks and Donn Tilson (1999) in their tourism article further distinguish one type of crisis—malevolent crises—as particularly damaging to areas that rely heavily on tourism dollars. This they argue forms the basis for one face of a multidimensional model of public relations whereby the *intervening* public becomes important.[1]

Today's potential for crisis in the travel industry cannot be underestimated; yet, there is very little extant information regarding how the cruise industry has prepared for the inevitable crisis. This study sought to identify both potential crisis scenarios and management perception of the risk associated with each by surveying. . . .

---

[1]Tilson and Stacks employ Stacks's (1992) multidimensional model of public relations as associated with tourism in general.

FIGURE 15.1. Sample literature review with referencing and noting.

were collected, how you created your research materials (such as interview schedules or questionnaires or attitude measures), and how you assessed validity and reliability. An example of a short method section is found in Figure 15.2.

Results

After the method section comes the results section. Here you will present the data analyses run and *short* interpretations of the findings. Unlike a formal research report in the social or natural sciences produced for academic readers, very rarely will you include inferential statistical analysis. Instead, you will describe the results in terms of differences as though they were actually different or, if in fact they were not different, as similar. (You may use footnotes to explain how you came to these conclusions, but writing for the average reader requires that you do not include such statements as "$t = 4.16$; $df = 62$; $p = .025$," which would require additional explanation.)

One of the problems many research reports have is a reliance on tables and figures. Poorly written reports direct the reader to a particular table or figure and then leave it to them to figure them out. A good

METHOD

This study consisted of a two-page Internet questionnaire mailed in November 2000 to 100 senior public relations executives and 100 chief executive and other key officers of dotcom companies then trading on the public markets. All participants in this study were either chief public relations officers (CPROs), chief executive officers (CEOs), chief information officers (CIOs), or chief financial officers (CFOs). The participants were selected from a listing of the top-100 dotcom companies published by *Fortune* Magazine and verified by the company annual report. A mailed prenotice letter informed participant's that they had been selected to participate. Each participant was then sent an e-mail explaining the study's goals and was asked to click on the link to the survey, conducted by an outside web survey design firm to guarantee anonymity and confidentiality of response. Seventy-four of the 100 CPROs and 42 of the 100 CEO/CIO/CFOs responded to the survey, representing an initial response rate of 58%. Given the seniority of the participants, the response rate was deemed acceptable. Follow-up letters then were mailed to the 116 respondents, thanking them for their time and responses.

FIGURE 15.2. Typical methods section.

research report discusses what the tables or figures present and uses them only as audiovisual aids. *Remember: tables cannot tell stories; the data contained in them are only placeholders for constructs or concepts that you have carefully crafted and tested; you should tell the story and not have to rely on some table or figure that readers might misinterpret.*

When reporting results in which questionnaires have been used, report the original question, the frequency of responses (in count or percentage, or both), and any mean score if the data were operationalized as continuous data. For the most part, readers are more comfortable with frequency and percentage interpretations than they are mean, median, mode, variance, and standard deviation interpretations. Analyze your readership and present the data in ways that most readers will understand.

Discussion or Ramifications or Recommendations

As indicated by the heading, "Discussion or Ramifications or Recommendations," the final segment of the second section is your interpretation of what you found and, at the same time, a way to discuss future research and the limitations of current research. A good research report will end with a discussion of the findings that brings you back to your original argument for what might follow from the data analysis in terms of attitudes, beliefs, and behaviors. Or, alternatively, the final section may simply outline the recommendations for the program or campaign being evaluated or the need for future research. Often you will go back to the original statements made (or goals sought) in establishing the research project, review the research questions or hypotheses, and make recommendations regarding a course of action. This is the time to bring it all together and present in a few paragraphs the implications of the research. If your report is designed to persuade your audience, this is the time and place to (1) make your claims, (2) refer back to the data gathered and analyzed as evidence, and (3) substantiate those claims.

Appendices

The final section of the research report contains important materials in the form of appendices. Each appendix should be set off, preferably by tab, in the final bound report. Here you might include a copy of the materials used in conducting your research project, the questionnaire or interview schedule, and any other data that might be of interest. For instance, if you conducted a telephone survey in a particular area by telephone prefix, you might want to include a map of the area subdivided according to prefix boundaries. Appendices of tables and figures related to data presentation are often found in research reports. Rather than taking up valuable space in the body of the report, tables and figures are often located in a particular appendix for ease in reading, with in-line notations where to find them (e.g., "see Appendix B, Tables 1–4 and Figure 6"). Finally, any other exhibits you consider important may be added as appendices.

All appendices should be listed in the report's table of contents, clearly identified by number or alphabetical identifier and content. Tables and figures that are included within the body of the report are often listed in the table of contents.

THE ORAL PRESENTATION

The oral presentation has become a regular feature of the public relations research process. It is at the oral presentation that you will focus on the major points of the research project and present a convincing rendition of the research effort. Your audience at this stage is often composed of both people who understand research very well as well as those who do not but are interested in the general findings. The key to the oral presentation is finding a middle ground between these two disparate audiences.

Presentation Tips

A well-written executive summary can often serve as the outline for your oral presentation. After all, the executive summary presents the "bare bones" of your report, and you can fill in verbally wherever you feel the necessity to do so. It is important to realize that the audience will probably have two very different objectives, both often coming together by the presentation's end: (1) a simple, straightforward presentation of the research and the data presented and (2) an analysis of the implications and ramifications of the research. Thus, your presentation will be both informative and persuasive. Whatever your presentation style, there are several things to remember in an oral presentation:

1. *Oral presentations have very short "windows,"* so the material must be made as simple as possible.
2. *The oral presentation must be made to the entire audience*, not just the senior officer present (e.g., the CEO or president).
3. *The oral presentation should be presented in a conversational mode*, not read verbatim from a manuscript or memorized. You are

the expert, and you should exhibit that through a relaxed composed discussion of the research project.

4. *Audiovisuals, while important, are not as important as your interpretations.*
5. *Audiovisuals should be kept a simple as possible.* Approach them as an advertiser would a billboard—think in terms of 7- to 10-word sentences and large type.
6. *Be prepared to stop and answer questions.* Allowing questions and answering them as they come up will enhance the audience's perception of you as composed and competent.

Let's look at each in a little more detail.

Oral Communication

Oral communication relies primarily on the auditory process where you speak and others listen and on the visual process secondarily. In a perfect world, your audience will have read your report from front to back and studied it in detail. In today's world of multitasking and multimeetings, very few people have the time to totally digest what you have prepared even if they have actually read it through more than once. Your job is to present the findings in such as way as to make a highly favorable impression on the audience. Research on listener comprehension indicates that the average individual will remember only 25% of what you presented after 24 hours,[4] so keep the message simple and repeat important elements and aspects.

Making Contact

You will relax your audience and yourself if you include all audience members in your presentation. This is done primarily through eye contact. One of the many suggestions for communication/speaking apprehension is to pick out an audience member from one side of the audience, another in the middle, and a third from the other side and look at them individually while presenting. If you make a concerted effort to make eye contact with them, they generally will return it, thus relaxing each of you (try to select people you know and who you believe understand what you are going to present). The really good presenter will look at all audience members, challenging them while presenting, thus keeping them on their feet during the presentation. Your ability to do this, however, comes only after considerable practice and experience. Be prepared for some anxiety; it's a natural response to being on the "hot seat."

Conversational Mode

Keeping your presentation conversational reduces perceptions of stiffness and defensiveness. Talk your way through the presentation as though you are intimately familiar with why the research was conducted, how the project was run, and how the data emerged. Further, a prepared manuscript sounds scripted (it is, of course) and stilted; we do not talk as we write ("we don't talk like we write"). Good speechwriters focus on writing a speech to match the phraseology of the speaker and work with the speaker to make the actual presentation less scripted and more conversational.[5] You probably do not have access to a speechwriter or speaking coach, so practice your presentation as much as time will allow and talk your way through its major points.

Audiovisuals

All presentations should be accompanied by audiovisuals. Audiovisuals can be as simple as a those presented on a chalkboard or flipchart or as complex as a multimedia presentation. For the most part, the simpler you make the audiovisual, the better the audience's retention. You want the audiovisual to add to the presentation, not distract the audience from it. If your audiovisuals have to be complex, then hand out copies for later review (and let your audience know that this is the reason for the handouts). A major problem with audiovisuals is that technology has made them *too* easy to produce. Therefore, many presenters try to impress their audiences with complex and colorful PowerPoint presentations. This merely serves to distract serious audience members. "Keep it simple" is the byword for audiovisuals. If you are presenting categorical data, then a bar chart per question is better than a table of counts or percentages. If you can project a particularly important figure, do so; but remember, you are there to explain it to your audience. In sum, keep your audiovisuals simple and at the same time make sure they are important to the presentation.

Q&A

Finally, be prepared to stop and answer questions. A good strategy is to indicate at the beginning of the presentation that you encourage people to ask questions as they occur to them, rather than deferring them until the presentation's end (when they may not be as relevant). Answer questions as truthfully and simply as possible; when the question addresses an important area that you will be touching on later in your presentation, use it as a segue to that part of the presentation or simply state that not only is it an interesting question but so much so that you will be covering it in detail in a few minutes.

Presentation Types

There are two general types of presentations you will make when you formally present research results. The first is the informative presentation where you simply are reporting the project from beginning to end. This follows a simple format of describing why the research project was conducted, what questions were addressed, the results, and your recommendations. The second is the persuasive presentation where you are making an argument from the data. This is more complex and follows a claim, data, and warrant line of logic. The claim is what you want your audience to believe. The data are what you have collected, to include the method(s) you employed, the analyses you ran, and your conclusions. The warrant ties the data to the claim. If the audience already believes the claim, then the data need not be presented in detail (but they serve to reinforce the audiences beliefs). If the audience is undecided or hostile to the claim, then you must build your warrant through the logic of the data and why the project was run. This is a much more difficult task and should probably be assigned to a senior person.

Often, however, an informative presentation becomes persuasive. It may start with a simple question, such as "How should I use this information you have provided to convince X to do Y?" and puts you in the hot seat. This is where audience analysis comes in. By this time you should understand the ramifications of the research project and should be able to predict what kinds of questions you will face. Practicing with others and asking them what kinds of questions they might ask is a good way to prepare for a presentation. It may be that others in the room can answer the question for you, but it may be that you have no answer, that your research question(s) did not address this concern. In such cases, you should indicate that you do not know (honesty, even if embarrassing, is better than trying to cover up for lack of knowledge in an area) but that the question might merit further research.

Audiovisuals

Presentation of audiovisuals should by now be a secondary concern to the presentation. They are nice but not necessary. However, if you can use them, they make the presentation seem more "professional." What constitutes a "good" audiovisual presentation? Stacks and Hocking suggest that a typical audiovisual presentation includes:[6]

- A title slide
- A slide or two outlining the major concepts being researched
- A slide containing your research questions or hypotheses
- A slide indicating your method and, if relevant, sample selection procedures
- Slides with *important* results presented in the most straightforward ways possible
- Your conclusions

Each audiovisual should present important data, data that reinforce or dramatize your presentation. *The one imperative remains: keep it simple.* (A sample audiovisual presentation is found in Figure 15.3.)

SUMMARY

This chapter rounds out our study of the public relations research process. It has presented how to write and present the final report in a no-nonsense manner, suggesting a general outline for the report and two different presentation strategies. In summary, as with most things, the more you write and the more your present, the more natural the acts

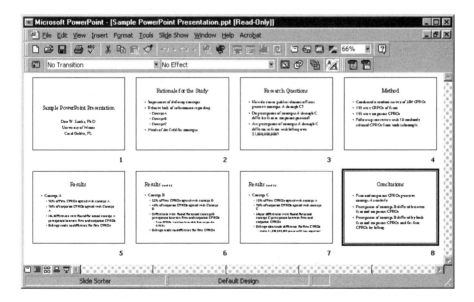

FIGURE 15.3. Sample Powerpoint presentation. Reprinted with permission from Microsoft Corporation.

become. As you begin to report others' research and then your own, you will find that it gets easier. Hopefully by now the research process found in business in general and in public relations in particular is both familiar and less intimidating than it was some 300 pages ago when we began our study of public relations research.

REVIEW QUESTIONS

1. What is the importance of the final report in public relations research?
2. Discuss briefly the different parts of the written report and how the report should be formatted.
3. How does the written report differ from the oral presentation? What suggestions would you make to someone who has never presented an oral version of a research report?
4. Should all oral presentations be done via computer, with PowerPoint slides and lots of color? Why or why not?
5. Should the oral presentation include all the findings presented in the written report, or should it simply outline the major findings? What is the role of descriptive statistics as presented graphically in the oral presentation and written report?

PRACTICE PROBLEM

Create a written and an oral report on how to conduct public relations research. Use this volume's chapters and examples as your "data" and outline. Assume that you have audiovisual support and about 15 minutes to make your presentation. The written report is to be no more than 20 pages, including tables and references.

NOTES

1. Two good examples are: Donald K. Wright, *Corporate Communications Policy Concerning the Internet: A Survey of the Nation's Senior-Level, Corporate Public Relations Officers* (Gainesville, FL: Institute for Public Relations, 1998); Don W. Stacks, *Perceptions of Public Relations Education* (Washington, DC: National Communication Association, 1998), also found at the National Communication Association's website, www.natcom.org.
2. *Publication Manual of the American Psychological Association*, 5th ed. (Washington, DC: American Psychological Association, 2001).

3. Gibaldi, J. *MLA Handbook for Writers of Research Papers*, 5th ed. (New York: Modern Language Association of America, 1999).

4. Lyman K. Steil, Larry L. Barker, and Kittie W. Watson, *Effective Listening: Key to Your Success* (Reading, MA: Addison-Wesley, 1983); research to date has not increased the percentage of information or messages remembered after 24 hours.

5. Jack Felton, former senior vice president, Communication, and speechwriter, McCormick & Co., Inc., personal communication, March 1998, College Park, MD.

6. Don W. Stacks and John E. Hocking, *Communication Research* 2nd ed. (New York: Longman, 1999), p. 414.

Index

About the Author

Don W. Stacks, PhD, is professor and director of the University of Miami School of Communication Program in Advertising and Public Relations, where he teaches primarily research methods, public relations administration and management, publication writing and design, persuasion, communication theory, and mass communication in society.The author or co-author of six books and more than 60 articles in referred journals, Dr. Stacks has presented more than 150 papers at professional societies and has served as chair of several divisions including PRSA's Educator's Academy Communication Sciences Division; AEJMC's Public Relations Division; NCA's Social Cognition and Intrapersonal Commission; and SCA's Communication Theory, Communication Education, and Applied Communication Divisions. Currently, he is directing the Educator's Academy 5th Annual Research Conference. In addition, he has served on the PRSA "Body of Knowledge" board, chaired the Commission on Public Relations Education research committee, and currently is serving his second tour as the Educator's Academy research chair. Among his awards are the University of Miami's Professor of the Year Award, the University of Miami's Provost's Award for Scholarly Activity and the Institute for Public Relations' Pathfinder Award. He recently was admitted to the Arthur W. Page Society. In addition to his academic activities, Stacks has consulted for Fortune 500 companies in media relations, crisis management, and internal corporate relations. His current research interests include tourism and hospitality management, crisis management, public relations education, integrated communications, and technology.